A History of Divorce Law

The book explores the rise of civil divorce in Victorian England, the subsequent operation of a fault system of divorce based solely on the ground of adultery, and the eventual piecemeal repeal of the Victorian-era divorce law during the Interwar years. The legal history of the Matrimonial Causes Act 1857 is at the heart of the book. The Act had a transformative impact on English law and society by introducing a secular judicial system of civil divorce. This swept aside the old system of divorce that was only obtainable from the House of Lords and inadvertently led to the creation of the modern family justice system. The book argues that only through understanding the legal doctrine in its wider cultural, political, religious, and social context is it possible to fully analyse and assess the changes brought about by the Act. The major developments included the end of any pretence of the indissolubility of marriage, the statutory enshrinement of a double standard based on gender in the grounds for divorce, and the growth of divorce across all spectrums of English society. The Act was a product of political and legal compromise between conservative forces resisting the legal introduction of civil divorce and the reformers, who demanded married women receive equal access to the grounds of divorce. Changing attitudes towards divorce that began in the Edwardian period led to a gradual rejection of Victorian moral values and the repeal of the Act after 80 years of existence in the Interwar years.

The book will be a valuable resource for academics and researchers with an interest in legal history, family law, and Victorian studies.

Henry Kha is Lecturer in Law at Macquarie University.

Routledge Research in Legal History

The Royal Prerogative and Constitutional Law
A Search for the Quintessence of Executive Power
Noel Cox

Socialism and Legal History
The Histories and Historians of Law in Socialist East Central Europe
Edited by Ville Erkkilä and Hans-Peter Haferkamp

A History of Divorce Law
Reform in England from the Victorian to Interwar Years
Henry Kha

See more at https://www.routledge.com/Routledge-Research-in-Legal-History/book-series/RRLEGHIST

A History of Divorce Law
Reform in England from the Victorian to Interwar Years

Henry Kha

LONDON AND NEW YORK

First published 2021
by Routledge
2 Park Square, Milton Park, Abingdon, Oxon OX14 4RN

and by Routledge
52 Vanderbilt Avenue, New York, NY 10017

Routledge is an imprint of the Taylor & Francis Group, an informa business

© 2021 Henry Kha

The right of Henry Kha to be identified as author of this work has been asserted by him in accordance with sections 77 and 78 of the Copyright, Designs and Patents Act 1988.

All rights reserved. No part of this book may be reprinted or reproduced or utilised in any form or by any electronic, mechanical, or other means, now known or hereafter invented, including photocopying and recording, or in any information storage or retrieval system, without permission in writing from the publishers.

Trademark notice: Product or corporate names may be trademarks or registered trademarks, and are used only for identification and explanation without intent to infringe.

British Library Cataloguing-in-Publication Data
A catalogue record for this book is available from the British Library

Library of Congress Cataloging-in-Publication Data
Names: Kha, Henry, author.
Title: A history of divorce law : reform in England from the
Victorian to Interwar years / Henry Kha.
Description: Milton Park, Abingdon, Oxon ; New York, NY : Routledge, 2021. |
Series: Routledge research in legal history |
Includes bibliographical references and index.
Identifiers: LCCN 2020031041 (print) | LCCN 2020031042 (ebook) |
ISBN 9780367420062 (hardback) | ISBN 9780367817305 (ebook)
Subjects: LCSH: Divorce–Law and legislation–England–History. |
Law reform–England–History.
Classification: LCC KD764 .K43 2021 (print) |
LCC KD764 (ebook) | DDC 346.4201/6609034–dc23
LC record available at https://lccn.loc.gov/2020031041
LC ebook record available at https://lccn.loc.gov/2020031042

ISBN: 978-0-367-42006-2 (hbk)
ISBN: 978-0-367-81730-5 (ebk)

Typeset in Galliard
by Newgen Publishing UK

Contents

Foreword vi
Acknowledgements viii

1 Introduction 1

2 The tripartite divorce system 13

3 The enactment of the Matrimonial Causes Act 1857 38

4 Divorce under the Matrimonial Causes Act 1857 75

5 The divorce courts 110

6 Divorce law reform in the early twentieth century 134

7 *Quo vadis?* The road to divorce 163

Bibliography 169
Index 186

Foreword

It is always a pleasure to be asked to write a foreword to a book, but never more so than when the book engages with an issue close to the heart. Dr Henry Kha's study in the reform of divorce law not only tells a fascinating and (I suspect) little-known story, but he draws from it an important analysis of how family law develops in an ordered society.

I write as one whose professional life as a judge was essentially engaged with the family law of England and Wales, which has itself changed remarkably even since my full-time appointment in 1992. I have been strongly aware, particularly when serving as a judge of the High Court, of how much of that development has been the result of judicial activism. A vivid example is the development in the law on surrogacy. In that, however, we have been following the work of our Victorian judicial forebears and their development of the Matrimonial Causes Act 1857. That work in no small way contributed to the subsequent pressure for new and further reform of family law.

Of course marriage and its consequences have been present since the dawn of civilisation, since most civilisations have embraced some concept of marriage and all have had to deal with the fallout from fractious human relationships. Moreover, in most societies marriage is a concept that has become deeply interwoven with religion and these religious concepts have themselves come into conflict with fractious human relationships. Although the context will vary from society to society and from age to age, the issues that underline family law are unchanging in their essence as the struggle between social stability and human fallibility.

That family law is a pressing issue can be seen from the apparent fact that after every reform the courts got busier. Again, this is no less true today than it was in the aftermath of 1857 or indeed 1937. Actually, it is perhaps more so today for in secular Western society the law now exercises a greater influence on social values because of the decline of the influence of religion and social convention in these areas.

As this book convincingly demonstrates, the reform of family law has a very complex dynamic. It is and always has been caught up in the endless swirl of religion, social convention, human realities, the need for family stability, and the security of children, mixed up with strong personal views (even expressed through novels) and the less predictable needs of the government of the time. Changes are never born of pure principle but are the product of conflict and compromise in the context of the need for peaceful human coexistence.

Dr Kha has offered us a glimpse of this complex dynamic in action in a particular place in a limited timescale. This has allowed us to see the process actually at work. It has lessons that we should not ignore. Many of us will have strong personal value systems that are not always at ease in the society in which we live. We are entitled to promote those values even at the risk of conflict. But those of us who exercise power and influence in society have to deliver a system that recognises that human hearts can be hard and we have to learn the art of compromise without sacrificing personal integrity. This book will greatly assist that process.

Sir Mark Hedley
Former Judge of the High Court of Justice in
England and Wales, Family Division

Acknowledgements

The book has required many years of hard work to take it from a nascent PhD proposal to a monograph. I would like to express my appreciation to a number of wonderful people in my life. I would like to first thank my PhD supervisors Professor Warren Swain and Dr Karen Fairweather. In particular, I extend my sincere gratitude to Warren for all the support he has given over the years. Warren has not only been the most significant influence on my academic career, but he has also been a great mentor and friend. Quoting a Chinese idiom from Luo Guanzhong's *Romance of the Three Kingdoms*, having found Warren has been as delightful as for a fish that has found water.

I am also very thankful for all the love and support of my parents and my beloved wife Yang Zhijun. My parents have always encouraged my pursuit of learning and for that I am deeply grateful. To Zhijun, thank you for all the love, patience, and kindness that you have displayed. Zhijun has given me the joy of marriage and the book is dedicated to her with love and affection.

Finally, I would like to thank the Taylor & Francis Group for supporting the book and providing permission to reuse material that was previously published: 'The Enactment of the Matrimonial Causes Act 1857: The Campbell Commission and the Parliamentary Debates' (2016) 37(3) *Journal of Legal History* 303; 'The Spectacle of Divorce Law in Evelyn Waugh's *A Handful of Dust* and A. P. Herbert's *Holy Deadlock*' (2018) 30(2) *Law & Literature* 267.

1 Introduction

The Matrimonial Causes Act 1857 introduced civil divorce[1] and the Court for Divorce and Matrimonial Causes.[2] These were important developments that led to the creation of the modern English family justice system. Before the introduction of the 1857 Act, marriage was not dissolved by a decree of the civil courts.[3] Instead, divorce was a tripartite process involving the Assizes, the Ecclesiastical Courts, and the House of Lords. This was a rather long and complicated process. The book aims to explore the motivations for the introduction and the impact of the 1857 Act by analysing its 80-year operation. It will also address the downfall of the 1857 Act during the Interwar years.

The historical background of the Matrimonial Causes Act 1857 provides an explanation for the tensions between legal change and political resistance to the introduction of civil divorce. Victorian England is often characterised as an age of reform which saw pressures for change met with some resistance.[4] K. Theodore Hoppen argues the 1857 Act was biased in favour of men because of the double standards in the grounds for divorce between husbands and wives,[5] but also maintains the 1857 Act was 'not entirely devoid of reforming content with respect to women's rights.'[6] The double standard refers to the husband only having to prove the wife's adultery in order to obtain divorce, whereas the wife had to prove not only the husband's adultery but also an aggravated enormity (i.e., incest, rape, sodomy, bestiality, cruelty, desertion).

The advances in women's rights accrued from the 1857 Act include the protection of matrimonial property for separated, deserted, and divorced wives. The

---

1 (20 & 21 Vict c 8).
2 The Court for Divorce and Matrimonial Causes was the precursor to the Probate, Divorce and Admiralty Division (now known as the Family Division) of the High Court of Justice that was established in 1875.
3 There was one notable exception during the Interregnum. The Marriage Act 1653 briefly introduced civil divorce for only seven years, but it was abolished at the Restoration in 1660.
4 Llewellyn Woodward, *The Age of Reform 1815–1870* (Oxford University Press 1938).
5 K. Theodore Hoppen, *The Mid-Victorian Generation 1846–1886* (Oxford University Press 1998) 200.
6 *Ibid.*

2 Introduction

tension between reform and continuity was characteristic of Victorian England.[7] Stephen Cretney states:

> Why then was the 1857 Act passed? Its origins certainly do not lie in any concern for abstract justice. Rather they lie in the pressing need, highlighted by the growth in personal wealth associated with industrialisation, to get rid of the ramshackle probate jurisdiction exercised by 350 or so ecclesiastical authorities and to replace it with a more efficient system of dealing with deceaseds' property.[8]

The 'pressing need' identified by Cretney refers to the public pressure from judges and politicians to abolish the Ecclesiastical Courts' jurisdiction over matrimonial causes and probate. This was based on the influence of Benthamite utilitarian law reform that persisted during the Victorian era.[9]

Only through an understanding of the legal doctrine situated within its historical, religious, social, and cultural contexts is it possible to conduct a proper assessment of the changes brought about by the 1857 Act. The book argues that the 1857 Act and its later operation was not merely a procedural change, as is so often claimed.[10] An analysis of legal doctrines reveals secularisation of the law, the abolition of ecclesiastical jurisdiction, and the expansion of women's rights as significant factors that took reform outside of the realm of merely procedural change. The establishment of the modern family justice system also dispels the myth of the 1857 Act being simply a procedural change, albeit unbeknownst to legislators at the time.

The way that the 1857 Act evolved was significantly influenced by cultural change. Law and culture are not conceptually distinct, but rather are mutually related to one another within a particular culture.[11] Legal change is inevitably bound up with cultural change. Key cultural changes include a growing acceptance of divorce, especially among the middle class.[12] In part this was built on increasing acceptance of a eudemonistic view of marriage, but also dissatisfaction with the existing law. At the same time there was a gradual cultural

---

7 During the mid-nineteenth century, there was ongoing debate over the fusion of equity and common law that culminated with compromise. The separate courts of common law and equity were unified under the High Court of Justice, but common law and equity remained separate doctrines under the Supreme Court of Judicature Act 1873 (36 & 37 Vict c 66).
8 Stephen Cretney, *Family Law in the Twentieth Century* (Oxford University Press 2003) 162.
9 William Cornish, 'Law of Persons: Family and Other Relationships' in J. Stuart Anderson, Ray Cocks, Michael Lobban, Patrick Polden, and Keith Smith (eds), *The Oxford History of the Laws of England: Volume XIII* (Oxford University Press 2010) 781–4.
10 Allen Horstman, *Victorian Divorce* (St Martin's Press 1985) 78; Sybil Wolfram, 'Divorce in England 1700–1857' (1985) 5(2) *Oxford Journal of Legal Studies* 155, 178; Margaret K. Woodhouse, 'The Marriage and Divorce Bill of 1857' (1959) 3 *American Journal of Legal History* 260, 274–5.
11 Naomi Mezey, 'Law as Culture' in Austin Sarat and Jonathan Simon (eds), *Cultural Analysis, Cultural Studies, and the Law: Moving Beyond Legal Realism* (Duke University Press 2003) 37.
12 Michael Mason, *The Making of Victorian Sexuality* (Oxford University Press 1994) 124.

rejection of marriage as solely a religiously administered sacramental institution,[13] and a greater acceptance of marriage as a civil contract which ultimately influenced the law of divorce.[14] Nevertheless, there were some who resisted the changing values on the indissolubility of marriage. William Gladstone and others resisted the introduction of the 1857 Act because of their conservative Christian beliefs on the sanctity of marriage.[15] Although they failed to stop the introduction of civil divorce, they managed to obtain some concessions that would later trouble the next few generations. These included restricting divorce based on the ground of adultery and the introduction of a double standard between the sexes in obtaining divorce. Over time these restrictions would prove to be increasingly unpopular and ultimately led to the successful campaign for comprehensive reform of divorce law and the expansion of the grounds for divorce in 1937.[16]

Legal historiography

The literature on divorce law in Victorian England can be divided into three main categories: social history, feminist history, and legal history. Social history is concerned with a historical understanding of the cultural practices and social behaviour of ordinary people in their everyday lives rather than that of monarchs and aristocrats. It is based on an eclectic mix of methodology deriving from anthropology, sociology, and statistics. The appeal of social history lies in its ambition to present an objective and scientific history. Social historians, however, are not immune to prejudice and statistics have significant limitations. G.R. Elton notes social historians of the family, such as Lawrence Stone, presented intricate details well, but were less satisfactory at arranging details in patterns.[17] Elton attributes this failure to the difficulties of applying broad themes to the actions of individuals.[18] In regards to the methodology of social history, Richard Evans states, 'When it came to the really big issues in history, it had to remain silent, because they could not be solved by quantitative methods.'[19] Statistics can be misused, misinterpreted, and misinformed. Therefore, statistics do not speak for themselves, but rather a historian must gather and interpret the data.

The scholarship of Lawrence Stone and Sybil Wolfram are predominantly concerned with the social life and customs of Victorian England. Wolfram considers

---

13 Marriage Act 1836 (6 & 7 Wm IV c 85).
14 Lawrence Stone, *Road to Divorce* (Oxford University Press 1995) 353–4.
15 Although the English Reformation changed theological perceptions on marriage, the transplantation of Lutheran and Calvinist views of marriage as a civil contract rather than a holy sacrament from the Continent to England was much slower. The indissolubility of marriage remained a popular belief among some English people. See John Witte, *From Sacrament to Contract: Marriage, Religion, and Law in the Western Tradition* (2nd edn, Westminster John Knox Press 2012) 217–8.
16 Matrimonial Causes Act 1937 (1 Ed VIII & 1 Geo VI c 57).
17 G.R. Elton, 'Two Kinds of History' in Robert William Fogel and G.R. Elton (eds), *Which Road to the Past? Two Views of History* (Yale University Press 1983) 78.
18 *Ibid*.
19 Richard Evans, *In Defence of History* (Granta Books 1997) 41.

4   *Introduction*

the expansion of divorce law as an ethnographical aspect of English kinship.[20] She argues that the growing rejection of the doctrine of coverture (i.e., the union of husband and wife as one flesh in Christianity) had a significant impact in promoting the growth of English divorce.[21] Wolfram's anthropological background provides a useful framework in understanding the interaction between English culture and the law. Wolfram argues that the 1857 Act was presented as merely procedural with its origins traced to the establishment of Lord Brougham's Law Amendment Society in 1844.[22] This account sees the reform process as a perfunctory codification of existing divorce law. Cultural factors are indeed significant, but a legal understanding based on the legislative and judicial process is just as valuable. Without it there are gaps. Wolfram does not, for example, consider the impact of the 1832 Royal Commission to inquire into the Ecclesiastical Courts and how in turn it may have influenced the introduction of the 1857 Act.

Stone was involved with the social history journal *Past and Present*, founded by British Marxist historians including Christopher Hill, Eric Hobsbawm, and E.P. Thompson.[23] Although quantification was not ubiquitously employed by all social historians, social history was significantly influenced by quantification and social science.[24] Lawrence Stone relied heavily on the use of quantitative data to explain changes in social structure and processes. In *Road to Divorce*, Stone concludes that men are not promiscuous by nature, since the 1857 Act did not lead to a surge of husbands petitioning for divorce to marry new wives;[25] Stone uses statistics to demonstrate that divorce only grew proportionately, by almost twice the rate of the general population, from 141 decrees in 1861 to 580 in 1911.[26] This argument demonstrates the limits of statistics. His claim is at best unproven and ignores the obvious point that sexually frustrated men may have turned to prostitution or extra-marital affairs while trapped in unhappy marriages.[27] Indeed, prostitution, and especially child prostitution, were matters of social concern after William Thomas Stead in *The Maiden Tribute of Modern Babylon* exposed the widespread child prostitution and human trafficking in late Victorian England.[28] Stone concludes that the introduction of the 1857 Act was a product of 'nervously defensive conservatism.'[29] However, the contemporary sources are more ambiguous. Although there was moral ambivalence about

---

20 Sybil Wolfram, *In-Laws and Outlaws; Kinship and Marriage in England* (St Martin's Press 1987) 77–106.
21 Wolfram (n 10) 180.
22 *Ibid*. 176–8.
23 J.H. Elliott, 'Lawrence Stone' (1999) 164 *Past & Present* 3.
24 Paul E. Johnson, 'Looking Back At Social History' (2011) 39(2) *Reviews in American History* 379, 379–80.
25 *Ibid*.
26 Stone (n 14) 384–5.
27 Ian Ward, *Sex, Crime and Literature in Victorian England* (Hart Publishing 2014) 121–7.
28 William Thomas Stead, 'The Maiden Tribute of Modern Babylon' in Antony E. Simpson (ed), *The Maiden Tribute of Modern Babylon: The Report of the Secret Commission* (True Bill Press 2007) 51–206.
29 Stone (n 14) 383.

introducing civil divorce, as reflected in the parliamentary debates, there was clear bipartisan support to reform the Ecclesiastical Courts. The 1857 Act was one of a series of statutes aimed at removing jurisdiction from the Ecclesiastical Courts that also encompassed Probate,[30] Admiralty,[31] and even some Church matters.[32]

Feminist histories represent a significant body of literature on divorce law in Victorian England. They include Lee Holcombe, Joan Perkin, Mary Lyndon Shanley, and Dorothy Stetson.[33] A recurring theme of feminist histories is the emphasis on female protagonists resisting the subjugation of the male patriarchy. Naturally feminist historians foreground the role of women in law reform based on the construction of gender.[34] Women activists indeed played a notable role in campaigning and influencing legal change which merits attention. However, Neil Duxbury states:

> But there is also a sense in which American feminist legal scholarship seems to have become a victim of its own success: such work is nowadays more often than not to be found in the various American journals of law and feminism, a consequence of which is that the enterprise itself has become not just less visible but more insular.[35]

This point is particularly salient as all the above-mentioned feminist scholarship is derived from North America. Feminist historians see law reform through the lens of the feminist movement and this often creates scholarship that is partial to women's interests at the expense of examining the legal concepts.[36] Shanley states, 'Once again the principle of equality, the insistence on a single standard or "moral law" for men and women, provided the feminists with their most potent weapon against public policies which rested on that assumption.'[37] Although working-class women were involved in various nineteenth-century women's movements,[38] most suffragists were educated middle-class women involved with

---

30 Court of Probate Act 1857 (20 & 21 Vict c 77).
31 High Court of Admiralty Act 1859 (22 & 23 Vict c 6).
32 Ecclesiastical Courts Jurisdiction Act 1860 (23 & 24 Vict c 32).
33 Lee Holcombe, *Wives and Property: Reform of the Married Women's Property Law in Nineteenth-Century England* (University of Toronto Press 1983); Joan Perkin, *Women and Marriage in Nineteenth-Century England* (Routledge 1989); Mary Lyndon Shanley, *Feminism, Marriage, and the Law in Victorian England, 1850–1895* (Princeton University Press 1989); Dorothy Stetson, *A Woman's Issue: the Politics of Family Law Reform in England* (Greenwood Press 1982).
34 June Carbone, 'Feminism, Gender and the Consequences of Divorce' in Michael Freeman (ed), *Divorce: Where Next?* (Dartmouth Publishing 1996) 181.
35 Neil Duxbury, 'A Century of Legal Studies' in Peter Cane and Mark Tushnet (eds), *The Oxford Handbook of Legal Studies* (Oxford University Press 2003) 963.
36 Carol Smart, *Feminism and the Power of Law* (Routledge 1989) 5.
37 Shanley (n 33) 78.
38 For example, Josephine Butler successfully led a movement to repeal the Contagious Diseases Acts in the 1880s and was supported by the activism of working-class women. See Judith Walkowitz, *Prostitution and Victorian Society: Women, Class and the State* (Cambridge University Press 1980) 99–104.

the Liberal Party.[39] This approach even in its own terms excludes most working-class women who were not involved with women's rights campaigns during the Victorian period.[40] While an understanding of the role of women in shaping the laws of Victorian England is rather important, it should not be assumed that the legal change was as a result of feminist activism.[41] Feminists had some influence but key changes such as the reform of the court structure which made divorce reform possible had completely different motivations.

Legal history is at the heart of understanding reform of divorce law in nineteenth-century England. Legal historiography is often divided between 'external' and 'internal' legal history.[42] External legal history approaches the history of law by examining legal developments in their wider context, usually in the economic, cultural, or social context. In this respect there is some overlap with social history. Internal legal history considers the history of law as an autonomous mode of discourse through an analysis of legal doctrines, documents, and processes. The book shall analyse the internal legal history with reference to external sources to provide wider context. Internal legal history provides particularly useful insights, because the introduction of civil divorce under the 1857 Act took place within the framework of a new secular judicial procedure and generated new legal doctrines in the grounds and bars to divorce. David Ibbetson argues the most valuable contribution of internal legal history is its ability to recognise changes in legal doctrine and its analysis of abstract ideas.[43] S.F.C. Milsom states:

> The life of the common law has been in the unceasing abuse of its elementary ideas. If the rules of property give what now seems an unjust answer, try obligation; and equity has proved that from materials of obligation you can counterfeit almost all the phenomena of property.[44]

He believed that the development of the common law is found within the framework of a dialogue between lawyers and judges or juries. There was nothing deterministic or dogmatic about legal development.[45] Milson wrote primarily on the legal history of English private law in the Middle Ages, thus his research focused on the history of the common law. Statutes were far more important by

---

39 Harold L. Smith, *The British Women's Suffrage Campaign, 1866–1928* (2nd edn, Longman 2007) 16–9.
40 There were, however, a few examples of working-class suffragettes, notably Annie Kenney. See Donald Read, *The Age of Urban Democracy: England 1868–1914* (Routledge 2014) 492.
41 Rebecca Probert, 'The Controversy of Equality and the Matrimonial Causes Act 1923' (1999) 11 *Child and Family Law Quarterly* 33, 40.
42 David Ibbetson, 'What is Legal History a History of?' in Andrew Lewis and Michael Lobban (eds), *Law and History* (Oxford University Press 2004) 33–5.
43 David Ibbetson, 'Historical Research in Law' in Peter Cane and Mark Tushnet (eds), *The Oxford Handbook of Legal Studies* (Oxford University Press 2003) 873–4.
44 S.F.C. Milsom, *Historical Foundations of the Common Law* (2nd edn, Butterworths 1981) 6.
45 S.F.C. Milsom, *A Natural History of the Common Law* (Columbia University Press 2003) 9.

the nineteenth century.[46] Statutes can only be understood against the backdrop of public policy and political factors. These factors play a vital part in the creation of statute. Nevertheless, Milsom's approach remains relevant in relation to the application of statute. The judiciary continued to exercise an important role in the statutory interpretation and development of legal doctrines in Victorian England. The history of law, in the words of Cretney, should be understood 'as a study of the development of legal doctrine as embodied in English statute and case law and the processes which led to change in the law.'[47]

The risk of falling into an anachronistic mindset should be avoided. Milsom states, 'Perhaps more than in any other kind of history, the historian of law is enticed into carrying concepts and even social frameworks back into periods to which they do not belong.'[48] Milsom believed that legal historians should reconstruct the legal thinking of their subject matter as if they are lawyers of the period they are studying.[49] Good legal history should trace the origins of the law[50] and understand how a fixed doctrine of the law adapted to a constantly changing environment.[51] The pitfalls of the anachronistic hermeneutic can be illustrated in Shanley's argument that the doctrine of coverture was abolished in the nineteenth century because of feminist activism.[52] In fact, many Victorian women were more concerned with the recognition of married women's property rights in common law, because of a desire to formalise pre-existing rights in equity rather than as a consequence of feminist ideology and politics.[53] Some feminist interpretations of legal history make the mistake of directly equating increased participation of women in public life with the rise of feminism.[54]

The legal historical body of scholarship on divorce law in nineteenth- and early twentieth-century England is relatively smaller than that of other periods. William Cornish provides a basic description of English family law in the nineteenth century in *The Oxford History of the Laws of England: Volume XIII*, though divorce is not the focus.[55] Stephen Waddams and Margaret Woodhouse

---

46 William Cornish, Michael Lobban and Keith Smith, 'Sources of Law' in William Cornish, J. Stuart Anderson, Ray Cocks, Michael Lobban, Patrick Polden, and Keith Smith (eds), *The Oxford History of the Laws of England: Volume XI* (Oxford University Press 2010) 42.
47 Cretney (n 8) vii.
48 Milsom (n 44) vi.
49 Milsom (n 45) xxvii.
50 Milsom (n 44) 1.
51 *Ibid*. 6.
52 Shanley (n 33) 189.
53 For example, Caroline Norton wrote a public letter to Queen Victoria in 1855 declaring, 'The natural position of woman is inferiority to man. Amen! That is a thing of God's appointing, not of man's devising. I believe it sincerely, as part of my religion. I never pretended to the wild and ridiculous doctrine of equality. I will even hold that (as one coming under the general rule that the wife must be inferior to the husband), I occupy that position. *Uxor fulget radiis Mariti*; I am Mr Norton's inferior; I am the clouded moon of that sun.' See Caroline Norton, *A Letter to the Queen on Lord Chancellor Cranworth's Marriage and Divorce Bill* (Longman, Brown, Green and Longmans 1855) 98.
54 Probert (n 41) 40.
55 Cornish (n 9) 723–843.

8 *Introduction*

have published law journal articles examining the process of introducing the 1857 Act, but without comprehensively analysing the aftermath of its enactment.[56] Allen Horstman provides a noteworthy contribution to the social and cultural aspects of divorce law reform in nineteenth-century England in *Victorian Divorce*, but there is a want of analysis of the legal doctrines and the divorce courts.[57]

The two most significant contributors to the research of divorce law in Victorian England from a legal history perspective are Rebecca Probert and Stephen Cretney. The work of both intersects with the subject of the book. Probert has published an article on the double standard of the 1857 Act,[58] and another one on the introduction of the Matrimonial Causes Act 1923.[59] Probert's method of interpreting evidence is similar to the approach taken in the book. Cretney is a scholar of modern family law and has written extensively on twentieth-century family law in England.[60] In common with the book, he argues that the 1857 Act was introduced partly as a result of the desire to replace the Ecclesiastical Courts.[61] On this issue there is a good deal more to be said. Much the same can be said of other aspects of divorce reform. A detailed analysis of the legislative process behind the 1857 Act, the legal development of the grounds and bars to divorce, and the judicial history of the divorce courts is lacking. The current book aims to fill some of these gaps.

Historical sources

The main primary sources include statutes, court cases, royal commission reports, and legal treatises. The 1857 Act and its subsequent amendments and cases are at the centre of this book. Bills, Acts of Parliament, and Hansard provide a particularly useful insight into the process behind enacting the 1857 Act. Case law by this period was a rich source for understanding the judicial development of legal doctrine and was more accurate and reliable, especially from 1865 onwards, after the foundation of the Incorporated Council of Law Reporting.[62] Not only does it provide a wealth of detail on the judicial interpretations of the 1857 Act, but just as importantly it gives insights into the lives of divorcing couples. This needs to be used with care. Lawrence Stone has noted that eighteenth-century case law can mask the true facts, because of the idiosyncratic mode of judicial communication and the theatrics of divorce litigation.[63] This is equally true of

---

56 Stephen Waddams, 'English Matrimonial Law on the Eve of Reform (1828–57)' (2000) 21(2) *Journal of Legal History* 59; Woodhouse (n 10).
57 Horstman (n 10).
58 Rebecca Probert, 'The Double Standard of Morality in the Divorce and Matrimonial Causes Act 1857' (1999) 28 *Anglo-American Law Review* 73.
59 (13 & 14 Geo V c 19); Probert (n 42).
60 Cretney (n 8).
61 *Ibid*. 162.
62 Michael Bryan, 'Early English Law Reporting' (2009) 4 *University of Melbourne Collections* 45, 50.
63 Stone (n 14) 29–32.

nineteenth- and early twentieth-century divorce cases. Nonetheless, case law still provides an important and legitimate source for appreciating the operation of divorce law in practice.

There is a great deal of useful and reliable information about the mindset of contemporaries and the process of law reform in royal commission reports, such as the Campbell Commission of 1853 and the Gorell Commission of 1912. Eighteenth-century legal treatises, such as Matthew Hales' *The History of the Pleas of the Crown* and William Blackstone's *Commentaries on the Laws of England*, provide some historical context. Hale and Blackstone provide an important understanding of commonly held legal beliefs on marital rape and the doctrine of coverture which persisted in Victorian England. Yet they are limited as sources because marriage and divorce law only form one small part of a more comprehensive text.[64] Nineteenth- and early twentieth-century legal treatises offer an insight into the minds of lawyers working within the divorce law, notably the writings of J.F. MacQueen, William Rayden and *Halsbury's Laws of England*. These sources provide detail on the most commonly used precedents on divorce law of the period and provide an overview of how the law was used in practice. These largely overlooked sources demonstrate that the courts were heavily influenced by ecclesiastical precedents when interpreting the 1857 Act. The courts were bound by statute to interpret the divorce law rather conservatively according to the principles of the Ecclesiastical Courts.[65]

Outside of the legal sources, the popular literature of Victorian England has a great deal to say about divorce. Kieran Dolin has identified that a major theme was 'the exposure of marital unhappiness, and its consequences.'[66] Victorian authors, such as Charles Dickens, Caroline Norton, and William Thackeray, wrote critically about the state of divorce law in nineteenth-century England. Evelyn Waugh and A.P. Herbert wrote unfavourably about divorce law in the early twentieth century. Probert emphasises the importance of literary sources, because they 'both reflect and influence their social context, and it is thus legitimate to draw on literary sources to *illustrate* ideas that were current at the time.'[67] At the same time fictional works may not accurately represent the law where facts are blurred and people are caricaturised.[68] Non-fiction primary sources drawn on in the book include newspapers, pamphlets, and petitions. These sources provide an account of opinions held by the media and lobby groups in Victorian England. Taken together they help to provide an understanding of the impact of the law in the wider society, as well as the influence of individuals in shaping the law. Fiction and non-fiction sources may of course both have a particular bias or agenda.

---

64 Mary Sokol, 'Blackstone and Bentham on the Law of Marriage' in Wilfrid Prest (ed), *Blackstone and His Commentaries: Biography, Law, History* (Hart Publishing 2009) 109.
65 Matrimonial Causes Act 1857, s 22.
66 Kieran Dolin, *A Critical Introduction to Law and Literature* (Cambridge University Press 2007) 140.
67 Rebecca Probert, *Marriage Law and Practice in the Long Eighteenth Century* (Cambridge University Press 2009) 15.
68 Ian Ward, *Law and Literature: Possibilities and Perspectives* (Cambridge University Press 1995) 4.

10 *Introduction*

The book is not primarily a study of popular attitudes towards law reform and legal practice in Victorian society, but external factors have a place. These are not confined to legislation. Legal historians of the family, such as Rebecca Probert, have employed the methodology of external legal history to good effect. There are unique challenges in analysing the practical effect of the law on the private lives of individuals and their families. These include the necessity to discern the differences between formal and informal marriages, separation and divorce practices, and the heavy use of demographic data.[69] The Victorian period experienced major social, economic, and political change.[70] Therefore, external sources are particularly important in providing historical context to the process of legal change, the influence of religion, society, and culture, and the practical operation of the law.

Book outline

The book is divided into seven chapters that explore the rise and fall of the Matrimonial Causes Act 1857. Chapter 2 explores the sesquicentennial-old tripartite divorce system that existed in England immediately prior to the introduction of the Matrimonial Causes Act 1857. The aim is to provide important background knowledge to the reform of divorce law in the mid-nineteenth century by explaining essential concepts of divorce that developed from early modern England. Prior to the English Reformation, marriage could not be dissolved by a divorce *a vinculo matrimonii*. A major impact of the English Reformation was the change in understandings of Christian theology, leading to the view that marriage was a civil contract rather than a sacrament. Although this led to the theological acceptance of divorce, marriage was generally held under the law to be indissoluble at least for the common man. This was perpetuated in the form of a tripartite system of divorce that was established in 1700 and allowed the petitioner to divorce in a three-stage process. This included the petitioner initiating a tortious suit for criminal conversation damages against the respondent's paramour for loss of *consortium vitae*, obtaining a divorce *a mensa et thoro* from the Ecclesiastical Courts, and finally receiving a divorce *a vinculo matrimonii* from the House of Lords in an Act of Parliament. By the early nineteenth century, the tripartite system of divorce became increasingly criticised for its excessive time and cost. At the same time, there were calls for the reform of the Ecclesiastical Courts that were inextricably linked with the pressure for divorce law reform.

Chapter 3 focuses of the enactment of the Matrimonial Causes Act 1857. The chapter begins with the campaign for divorce law reform in early Victorian England. Divorce was still largely a legal remedy reserved to a privileged few, and by exploring the high-profile *causes célèbres* of the time it is possible to see popular

---

69 Ibbetson (n 43) 876.
70 Chantal Stebbings, 'Benefits and Barriers: The Making of Victorian Legal History' in Anthony Musson and Chantal Stebbings (eds), *Making Legal History: Approaches and Methodologies* (Cambridge University Press 2012) 86–7.

expressions of discontentment towards the law that eventually led to the political clamour for reform. The criminal conversation trial of Prime Minister Lord Melbourne and the tribulations of Caroline Norton brought attention to some of the shortcomings of the divorce law. The expressions of dissatisfaction towards the divorce law from John Stuart Mill, the Law Amendment Society, and even some members of the judiciary helped foster the mood for legal change. The political manifestation of these frustrations came in the form of a royal commission on divorce (the Campbell Commission). The majority report recommended the introduction of civil divorce and a new court to hear divorce suits. The parliamentary debates on the introduction of the Matrimonial Causes Act 1857 were fiercely contested between the reformers, led by Prime Minister Viscount Palmerston, and the social conservatives, led by Opposition Leader William Gladstone. The Palmerston government ultimately prevailed, but concessions were made to ameliorate some of the detractors. These included the introduction of a double standard for the grounds of divorce based on gender and limiting divorce solely to the ground of adultery based on ecclesiastical principles and precedents.

Chapter 4 considers the legal operation of divorce under the Matrimonial Causes Act 1857. The first two judges ordinary were Cresswell Cresswell and James Wilde (Lord Penzance). They played an important role in establishing legal precedents in the grounds and bars to divorce by taking a conservative approach in applying ecclesiastical principles and precedents. The changes were not merely procedural. The legal creation of civil divorce and the operation of the family justice system profoundly changed divorce in English law and society. In order to understand the legal change, it is important to appreciate and recognise the significant cultural shifts in the mainstream social acceptance of divorce as the primary reason for change *per se*.

Chapter 5 examines the history of the Court for Divorce and Matrimonial Causes and the PDA Division of the High Court of Justice between 1875 and 1905. The transfer of the divorce division from the Court of Divorce and Matrimonial Causes to the High Court of Justice moved divorce from a fringe tribunal to a mainstream court. Divorce was increasingly becoming a widespread legal issue. The number of divorces being granted increased each successive year.[71] This reflected changing cultural norms on marriage and divorce. James Hannen (Lord Hannen), Charles Butt and Francis Jeune (Lord St Helier) were the first three presidents of the PDA Division. During this four-decade period, there was a tension between change and continuity. The PDA Division during this period generally applied the Matrimonial Causes Act 1857 rather conservatively. The grounds and bars to divorce were still largely interpreted narrowly, but there were rare moments when the Court applied the law more liberally to the facts.

Chapter 6 focuses on the campaign for divorce reform in the early twentieth century. The early attempts to introduce divorce law reform through the Hunter and Russell bills failed to gain traction and were overwhelmingly defeated in

---

71 Stone (n 14) 435.

12 Introduction

Parliament. The presidency of John Gorell Barnes (Lord Gorell) began in 1905 and marked a pivotal point for the reform campaign by giving it a sense of legitimacy. Gorell called for divorce law reform while president of the PDA Division.[72] He later led unsuccessful attempts in Parliament to extend the grounds of divorce beyond adultery and to abolish the double standard between the sexes. Gorell's political agitation led to him chairing a royal commission on divorce (the Gorell Commission), which recommended the implementation of his aforementioned policies. However, the outbreak of World War I led to the issue of divorce reform being deferred to the next generation. This chapter culminates with how the Victorian divorce law was eventually repealed. The abolition of the double standard based on gender in the grounds for divorce was achieved in the enactment of the Matrimonial Causes Act 1923. This piecemeal reform resulted in gender equality under the divorce law and chipped away at one of the central tenets of the Matrimonial Causes Act 1857. During the Interwar years, cases of fraudulent adultery, colloquially known as hotel divorces, were commonplace, as exposed by the writings of Evelyn Waugh and A.P. Herbert. This put significant pressure on the divorce law. The Matrimonial Causes Act 1937 was passed soon after the abdication of Edward VIII. The king fought for the right to marry Mrs Wallis Simpson, a twice-divorced American woman. This put the spotlight on the law of divorce. The intersection of the social and political issues created the perfect maelstrom for legal change. The passing of the 1937 Act expanded the grounds for divorce and spelled the end of the Victorian divorce law.

The book concludes by reflecting on the process of English divorce law reform from the Victorian to the Interwar years. The road to divorce reform was mired with political conservatism, double standards, and moral hypocrisy. The most glaring illustration of this can be seen in the introduction and perpetuation of the double standards in the grounds for divorce based on gender between 1858 and 1923. Divorce law reform throughout the period only succeeded with the support of the government and was driven by the efforts of mavericks at various stages of the reform process, such as Lord Lyndhurst, Lord Gorell, and A.P. Herbert. The political will of the government was often found wanting for sweeping legal change on divorce, unless popular agitation had reached a point at which it could no longer be ignored. Piecemeal reform was often more readily accepted by Parliament. Although piecemeal reform was slower in enacting significant legal change, it gradually eroded the Matrimonial Causes Act 1857 and eventually led to the demise of the Act.

---

72 *Dodd v Dodd* (1906) P 189.

2 The tripartite divorce system

The relationship between English divorce law and Christian morality is an old one and central to understanding the resistance to divorce law reform and ultimately the compromise that was reached under the Matrimonial Causes Act 1857. This connection remained important into the twentieth century. Since divorce was historically viewed as a moral issue, the predominant Christian belief of the indissolubility of marriage hindered any significant calls for the introduction of civil divorce until the early nineteenth century. It is important to appreciate the theological changes to Christian dogma during the Protestant Reformation in regards to the English Church. The outcome was the formation of a theological and legal compromise, where marriage was held to be a dissoluble civil contract, but out of reach for ordinary English citizens.

This chapter explores the formation and operation of the tripartite system of divorce that was established in 1700 and existed in early Victorian England prior to the introduction of the Matrimonial Causes Act 1857. It is argued that the English Reformation had a significant influence in permitting civil divorce in England. This then led to the creation of a tripartite system of divorce that attempted to reconcile competing views of the sanctity and secularity of the institution of marriage. However, by the mid-nineteenth century, the tripartite system proved to be expensive to access and slow to grant a divorce decree. This eventually led to a lot of pressure and calls for the introduction of civil divorce.

The influence of the English Reformation

The Roman Catholic Church permitted legal separations known as a divorce *a mensa et thoro* (from bed and board), but not divorce *a vinculo matrimonii* (from the bonds of marriage).[1] The bull of Pope Lucius III *Ad abolendam* (issued in 1184) and the letter of Pope Innocent III to the Waldensians (sent in 1208) were two of the earliest papal documents declaring matrimony as a holy sacrament.[2]

---

1 John Witte, *From Sacrament to Contract: Marriage, Religion, and Law in the Western Tradition* (2nd edn, Westminster John Knox Press 2012) 104.
2 Philip L. Reynolds, *How Marriage Became One of the Sacraments: The Sacramental Theology of Marriage from its Medieval Origins to the Council of Trent* (Cambridge University Press 2016) 556–7.

14 The tripartite divorce system

This teaching was subsequently affirmed by the Second Council of Lyon in 1274, the Council of Florence in 1439, and the Council of Trent in 1563.[3] During the Council of Trent, the Roman Catholic Church reasserted that it had jurisdiction over all Christian marriages and taught that marriage was only a valid sacrament if it was celebrated by a priest before two witnesses.[4] The indissolubility of marriage was affirmed on the grounds that the union of a man and a woman was a reflection of the covenantal love between Christ and His Church.[5] The Council of Trent offered a Counter-Reformation response to Protestant teachings. The competing theological doctrines of marriage and divorce were a source of division.

During the Protestant Reformation in the sixteenth century, Martin Luther, John Calvin, and Huldrych Zwingli rejected the Roman Catholic doctrine on the indissolubility of marriage.[6] Luther argued that a husband could receive a divorce *a vinculo matrimonii* from a secular jurist.[7] He based this on the scriptural teaching of Jesus Christ: 'I tell you that anyone who divorces his wife, except for sexual immorality, and marries another woman commits adultery.'[8] Luther used this passage to argue that if the wife committed adultery, it was permissible for the husband to be granted a divorce. Biblical teaching remained influential on English law for centuries, which explains the reason why adultery was a *condition sine qua non* as a ground for divorce.

English jurists accepted Luther's view that divorce was only available for husbands in nearly all cases. Divorce for married women was only recognised in the early nineteenth century on the grounds of the husband's incestuous adultery or bigamy.[9] Calvin adopted a more purposive biblical interpretation and regarded adultery as grounds for divorce irrespective of whether the innocent party was the husband or the wife.[10] This was not the only occasion on which Calvin's view of the biblical texts was more far-reaching. Along with Zwingli, Calvin considered abandonment as a ground for divorce and remarriage for the innocent party.[11] One impact of the Reformation on the legal systems of Protestant Europe was that the grounds for divorce became wider.[12] Scots divorce law provides a good

---

3 Gregory Klein and Robert Wolfe (eds), *Pastoral Foundations of the Sacraments: A Catholic Perspective* (Paulist Press 1998) 134–5.
4 Witte (n 1) 106–11.
5 *Ibid.* 106.
6 Max Rheinstein, *Marriage Stability, Divorce and the Law* (University of Chicago Press 1972) 22–3.
7 *Ibid.* 22.
8 Matthew 19:9.
9 Jane Addison (41 Geo III c 102), James Campbell (41 Geo III c 119); *Turton v Turton* (1830) 3 Hag Ecc 338, Louisa Turton (1 & 2 W IV c 35); Ann Battersby (3 & 4 Vict c 48); Georgina Hall (13 & 14 Vict c 25).
10 Rheinstein (n 6) 22–3.
11 This was an extension on the 'Pauline privilege,' a Christian teaching that allows a person to divorce his or her spouse if they were both unbaptised at the time of entering into the marriage. The applicant is allowed this privilege in order to preserve his or her Christian faith in circumstances where the respondent intends to abandon the marriage. See 1 Corinthians 7:15.
12 The Netherlands was one of the earliest adopters of civil divorce. See Emese von Bóné, 'The Historical Development of Grounds for Divorce in the French and Dutch Civil Codes' (2014)

example. Since the Scottish Reformation, Scots law granted civil divorce for cases of adultery or separation of the couple for at least four years. Husband and wife both had equal access to divorce.[13] This is not to suggest that there were absolutely no double standards between husbands and wives in obtaining divorce, but there were concerted attempts to promote equality between the sexes at least in comparison to the English law.[14]

The English Reformation was unique when compared to that of continental Europe. The beginning of the English Reformation was marked in 1534 when the Act of Supremacy declared the monarch as the Supreme Head of the Church of England. Although Henry VIII remained Roman Catholic in theology, the way was now open for Protestant teaching in England.[15] Richard Rex states, 'The emergence of the doctrine of the royal supremacy is inextricably bound up with the pursuit of the divorce.'[16] Although the Church of England adopted the Protestant theology on marriage, the English Reformation did not create significant changes in the legal position on divorce.

During the sixteenth century, England, in common with Roman Catholic Europe, did not permit civil divorce. But there was a beginning of a shift. Archbishop of Canterbury Thomas Cranmer led the drafting of the first edition of the *Book of Common Prayer* in 1549, wherein he outlined the doctrine of the Anglican faith in the Thirty-Nine Articles that were posthumously completed in 1571.[17] According to Article 25, matrimony is explicitly excluded from the list of sacraments, 'for that they have not any visible sign or ceremony ordained of God.' Cranmer, like Luther, viewed marriage as a human institution rather than a holy sacrament, which meant it had the characteristics of a civil contract that could be dissolved by adultery. At the same time, marriage was still seen as a sacred ordinance that promoted a Christian understanding of the earthly roles of men and women. 'The Form of Solemnization of Matrimony' in the *Book of Common Prayer* describes 'the causes for which Matrimony was ordained.'

> First, It was ordained for the procreation of children, to be brought up in the fear and nurture of the Lord, and to the praise of his holy Name. Secondly, It was ordained for a remedy against sin, and to avoid fornication; that such persons as have not the gift of continency might marry, and keep themselves undefiled members of Christ's body. Thirdly, It was ordained for the mutual

---

20(2) *Fundamina: A Journal of Legal History* 1006, 1008–9; Hugo Grotius, *The Jurisprudence of Holland* (RW Lee tr, Oxford University Press 1926) 29.

13 Charles Guthrie, 'The History of Divorce in Scotland' (1910) 8(29) *The Scottish Historical Review* 39; Ronald D. Ireland, 'Husband and Wife: Divorce, Nullity of Marriage and Separation' in G.C.H. Paton (ed), *An Introduction to Scottish Legal History* (Stair Society 1958) 95–6.

14 Leah Leneman, *Alienated Affections: The Scottish Experience of Divorce and Separation, 1684–1830* (Edinburgh University Press 1998) 2.

15 J.J. Scarisbrick, *Henry VIII* (Eyre Methuen 1968) 389–91.

16 Richard Rex, *Henry VIII and the English Reformation* (Macmillan 1993) 13.

17 Charles Hefling and Cynthia Shattuck (eds), *The Oxford Guide to The Book of Common Prayer: A Worldwide Survey* (Oxford University Press 2006) 564.

society, help, and comfort, that the one ought to have of the other, both in prosperity and adversity.[18]

The idea that the purpose of marriage was child-rearing, the prevention of sexual activity outside of marriage, and the promotion of the couple's mutual welfare would remain influential into the nineteenth century. When civil marriage became possible once more in 1836,[19] the civil definition of marriage still mirrored the one in the *Book of Common Prayer*. All marriages under this Act were required to be cognizable to marriages celebrated in the rites of the Church of England.[20]

In Victorian England marriage was still very firmly grounded in Christian dogma.[21] In *Hyde v Hyde and Woodmansee*, Sir James Wilde denied the recognition of a polygamous relationship on the following basis: 'I conceive that marriage, as understood in Christendom, may for this purpose be defined as the voluntary union for life of one man and one woman, to the exclusion of all others.'[22] At the same time, Wilde also described marriage as something that can be 'contracted,' which was a legacy of the English Reformation.[23] Once marriage began to be characterised as a secular contractual relationship rather than a sacramental union, it became more acceptable for English society to conceive that marriage could be dissolvable. Marriage as a civil contract meant that divorce was something that could be granted by a civil rather than an ecclesiastical court. Even then, divorce would be limited in order to preserve Christian moral teaching.

Despite the Reformation, the introduction of civil divorce in English law was rejected during the reign of the late Tudor monarchs. R.H. Helmholz states that the Church of England experienced 'both continuity and change' in regards to its stance on divorce, but ultimately rejected 'the reform adopted by some of the Reformed Churches on the Continent.'[24] The first attempt at reform of ecclesiastical law occurred in 1532, when Henry VIII received the Submission of the Clergy. The proposal to create a committee on reforming English ecclesiastical law took two decades to come into fruition. Following a bill to establish a law reform committee in 1550, Cranmer presented the *Reformatio Legum Ecclesiasticarum* (*Reformation of the Ecclesiastical Laws*) to the House of Lords in 1553. One consequence of the law had it been enacted would have been to empower the Ecclesiastical Courts with the legal right to grant divorce *a vinculo matrimonii* on the grounds of adultery, desertion, and moral enmity.[25] This would have made English divorce law consistent with the civil codes of other Reformed European

---

18 *The Book of Common Prayer* (Cambridge University Press 2004) 302.
19 Civil marriage existed during the Interregnum between 1653 and 1660.
20 Marriage Act 1836 (6 & 7 Wm IV c 85) s 18.
21 Rebecca Probert, '*Hyde v Hyde*: Defining or Defending Marriage?' (2007) 19 *Child and Family Law Quarterly* 322.
22 (1866) LR 1 P&D 130, 133.
23 *Hyde v Hyde and Woodmansee* (1866) LR 1 P&D 130, 130.
24 R.H. Helmholz, *Roman Canon Law in Reformation* Law (Cambridge University Press 1990) 73.
25 James Spalding, *The Reformation of the Ecclesiastical Laws of England 1552* (Sixteenth Century Journal Publishers 1992) 99–106.

states. The reform was blocked by the Duke of Northumberland, who was regent for the young Edward VI, and the Privy Council, because of fears that it would empower the Ecclesiastical Courts to use their powers against the Privy Council.[26] The death of Edward VI and the subsequent reign of Mary I prevented the enactment of the bill.

In the reign of Elizabeth I, the Church of England's *via media* identity as a Catholic and Reformed church was politically, but not theologically, settled. It was decided 'that marriage would remain indissoluble, at least for the common man.'[27] In the first Parliament of Elizabeth in 1559, a bill to revive the law reform committee was defeated in the House of Commons. In 1571, Thomas Norton, the son-in-law of Cranmer, made the final attempt to introduce the *Reformatio Legum Ecclesiasticarum*. Another bill before the House of Commons finally succeeded but no record of a committee exists.[28] Although the early attempts to reform divorce law failed, the calls for legal change would continue to persist all the way up until the introduction of the Matrimonial Causes Act 1857. James Spalding states that the failure to reform Church discipline through the *Reformatio Legum Ecclesiasticarum* under the episcopal polity of the Church of England 'created tinder in which later Puritan fire could be ignited.'[29] These events were overtaken by the English Civil War.

Divorce law in the seventeenth century

The seventeenth century was a period of popular law reform in England. Post-Reformation England was divided on religious grounds between those who sought to introduce a more radical Reformation and those who longed for the pre-Reformation Church.[30] After the execution of the Roman Catholic sympathiser Charles I in 1649, the establishment of the Puritan-dominated Commonwealth saw radical changes to marriage law. The Hale Commission of 1652, made up of lawyers, army officers, and radicals, was given the task of reforming the law.[31] Some wanted radical reform, including the abolition of the courts of common law and equity and their replacement with local courts. The radicals were in the minority and the proposal was never introduced.[32] Their ideas on the law of marriage and divorce did, however, find favour. The Hale Commission recommended the introduction of civil marriage and the transfer of

---

26 James Spalding, 'The *Reformatio Legum Ecclesiasticarum* of 1552 and the Furthering of Discipline in England' (1970) 39(2) *Church History* 162, 166.
27 Rheinstein (n 6) 24.
28 Spalding (n 25) 167.
29 *Ibid*. 171.
30 Doreen Rosman, *The Evolution of the English Churches, 1500–2000* (Cambridge University Press 2003) 73–9.
31 Mary Cotterell, 'Interregnum Law Reform: The Hale Commission of 1652' (1968) 83(329) *English Historical Review* 689.
32 G.B. Nourse, 'Law Reform under the Commonwealth and Protectorate' (1959) 75 *Law Quarterly Review* 512, 514.

18 The tripartite divorce system

jurisdiction over alimony, marriage, and guardianship of children to the Court of Common Pleas.[33]

In 1653, civil marriage was introduced in 'An Act touching Marriages and the registration thereof; and also touching Births and Burials.'[34] The legislation brought marriage law into line with the Protestant idea of marriage as a civil contract rather than as a sacrament. The Act declared that from 29 September 1653 only marriages celebrated by a Justice of the Peace would be valid.[35] All other forms of marriage were invalid. Ironically, this meant that during the Interregnum the once-legally prescribed marriage according to the Anglican rites became clandestine. A rush of church marriages occurred before the Act came into effect.

Even after the Act came into operation, some couples still chose to marry according to the Anglican rite either in addition to or instead of civil marriage.[36] In 1657, ecclesiastical marriage was legally recognised, but the option of civil marriage remained.[37] At the Restoration in 1660, Parliament passed 'An Act for confirmation of marriages.'[38] The Act confirmed the validity of civil marriages celebrated by Justices of the Peace. The granting of civil marriages ceased and ecclesiastical marriages became the standard practice once again. In *Tarry v Browne*, a judge went further and retrospectively recognised the validity of a marriage that was celebrated by a parson in sacred orders in an alehouse during the operation of the 1653 Act.[39] The marriage failed to comply with the 1653 Act, but it was held that invalidating the marriage would be contrary to God's law.[40]

The Interregnum not only affected marriage law, but also the law of divorce. The cause of reform was taken up by radical utopian writers, such as Samuel Gott, James Harrington and Gerrard Winstanley.[41] Just how far-reaching some of these views were can be illustrated by John Milton, who argued in *The Doctrine and Discipline of Divorce* that the *condition sine qua non* for divorce should only be irreconcilable difference.[42] He argued that Jesus Christ did not abrogate the Mosaic teaching on divorce[43] in the Gospels,[44] but rather Christ condemned 'the

---

33 Donald Veall, *The Popular Movement for Law Reform 1640–1660* (Oxford University Press 1970) 188.
34 The Act was also known as the Marriage Act 1653. See C.H. Firth and R.S. Rait, *Acts and Ordinances of the Interregnum* (Wyman and Sons 1911) 1139; Dorothy McLaren, 'The Marriage Act of 1653: Its Influence on the Parish Registers' (1974) 28(2) *Population Studies* 319.
35 Rebecca Probert, *Marriage Law and Practice in the Long Eighteenth Century* (Cambridge University Press 2009) 169.
36 *Ibid.* 170.
37 Keith Wrightson, 'The Nadir of English Illegitimacy in the Seventeenth Century' in Peter Laslett, Karla Oosterveen, and Richard M. Smith (eds), *Bastardy and its Comparative History* (Harvard University Press 1980) 184.
38 (12 Cha II c 33).
39 (1661) 1 Sid 64.
40 *Ibid.*
41 J.C. Davis, *Utopia and the Ideal Society: A Study of English Utopian Writing 1516–1700* (Cambridge University Press 1981) 13.
42 Scott Howard and Sara van den Berg (eds), *The Divorce Tracts of John Milton* (Duquesne University Press 2010) 44.
43 See Deuteronomy 24:1–4.
44 Howard and van den Berg (n 42) 63–4.

false glosses that depraved the law.'[45] Although some English Puritans supported this change, it was too radical for most people.[46] Three centuries would elapse before Milton's idea of no-fault divorce would be introduced.[47]

The Hale Commission's refusal to limit divorce to the grounds of adultery shows the extent to which marriage was increasingly seen as a civil contract that could be terminated.[48] The suspension of the Ecclesiastical Courts during the Interregnum led to a new method of divorce in the form of a private separation deed. This commonly accepted and legally recognised practice of divorce involved a solicitor drafting a formal deed of private separation that outlined the distribution of matrimonial property.[49] Since a wife at the time had no legal personality, she could not contract with her husband.[50] This was known as the doctrine of coverture. Sir William Blackstone explains: 'By marriage, the husband and wife are one person in law: that is, the very being or legal existence of the woman is suspended during the marriage, or at least is incorporated and consolidated into that of the husband.'[51] Consequently, a trustee was appointed to manage the deed between the husband and the wife.[52]

Private separation deeds began to appear in litigation.[53] A private separation deed was not a *de jure* divorce. Thus, such arrangements did not create a divorce *a vinculo matrimonii*. A separated person could not remarry or cohabit with whomever he or she wanted. It was even possible for the husband to sue his wife for adultery or restitution of conjugal rights even after signing the separation deed.[54] Nevertheless, the introduction of private separation deeds effectively allowed couples to initiate their own divorce *a mensa et thoro* without the need of seeking this remedy from the Ecclesiastical Courts. Private separation deeds remained popular up until the mid-nineteenth century,[55] but they were still used even as late as the early twentieth century.[56] Chancery exercised its discretion in determining what aspects of the deed it was willing to enforce, such as refusing to enforce a maintenance agreement if a wife refused to live with her husband without a sufficient reason.[57]

---

45 *Ibid*. 73.
46 Shigeo Suzuki, 'Marriage and Divorce' in Stephen Dobranski (ed), *Milton in Context* (Cambridge University Press 2010) 386–90.
47 Divorce Reform Act 1969 (UK) c 55.
48 Veall (n 33) 188.
49 Lawrence Stone, *Road to Divorce* (Oxford University Press 1995) 149.
50 This changed under the Married Women's Property Act 1882 (45 & 46 Vict c 75).
51 William Blackstone, *Commentaries on the Laws of England, Volume 1* (1753) 442.
52 Stone (n 49) 150.
53 *Whorewood v Whorewood* (1675) 1 Chan Cas 250.
54 Stone (n 49) 154.
55 *Ibid*. 181.
56 Lord Halsbury (ed), *The Laws of England: Volume XVI* (Butterworth 1911) 439.
57 *Vane v Vane* (1740) Barn C 135; Allison Anna Tait, 'The Beginning of the End of Coverture: A Reappraisal of the Married Woman's Separate Estate' (2014) 26(2) *Yale Journal of Law and Feminism* 166, 187–8.

Formal divorce took slightly longer to be recognised. The *Roos Case* (1670) was the first divorce *a vinculo matrimonii* case in English legal history and set a landmark precedent.[58] Rebecca Probert observed that the *Roos Case* 'could even be claimed as the single most important development in the history of family law.'[59] Its actual impact was limited. Divorce by this method was slow and expensive, which meant that it was largely only an option for the wealthy before the introduction of the Matrimonial Causes Act 1857. It took almost a decade from initiating proceedings until Lord Roos was granted a divorce from his wife, Lady Anne Pierrepoint. The first step was obtaining a divorce *a mensa et thoro* from the Ecclesiastical Courts. This allowed Lord Roos to legally live separately from his wife. The next step was to declare that his wife's son Ignotus was illegitimate and the offspring of Anne's adulterous partner. A private Act of Parliament was required. Lord Roos introduced a bill to this effect on 19 April 1662. Four years later, in 1666, the House of Lords unanimously passed 'An Act for the Illegitimisation of the Children of the Lady Anne Roos.'

After successfully barring Anne's children from inheriting the earldom and more importantly establishing that Anne had committed adultery, Lord Roos was able to seek a divorce *a vinculo matrimonii* through a private Act of Parliament in the House of Lords in 1670. Success would give Lord Roos the right to remarry. The bill was opposed by the Roman Catholic lords and most Church of England bishops. One notable opponent was James, the Duke of York, the younger brother of Charles II and a recent convert to Roman Catholicism. According to Rachel Weil, many supporters of the bill were more motivated by political exigencies in promoting a Protestant monarchy rather than purely out of conscience.[60] There is indeed a strong likelihood that James, as the next in line to the throne, was motivated to oppose the bill because Charles was in a childless marriage. James would not have wanted to create a precedent for the king to divorce his wife and possibly remarry and father an heir to the throne. However, by the end of the year the bill passed both Houses and established the first precedent for divorce.

The tripartite divorce system and informal divorce

The Duke of Norfolk was the first to use what became a settled process for securing a divorce.[61] After first unsuccessfully attempting to dissolve his marriage to Lady Mary Mordaunt in the House of Lords in 1692, the Duke of Norfolk succeeded in suing his wife's paramour, John Germain, in a suit for criminal conversation. However, he failed in his second attempt for a parliamentary divorce

58 Private Act of Parliament, given Royal Assent on 11 April 1670.
59 Rebecca Probert, 'The *Roos Case* (1670)' in Stephen Gilmore, Jonathan Herring, and Rebecca Probert (eds), *Landmark Cases in Family Law* (Hart Publishing 2011) 26.
60 Rachel Weil, *Political Passions: Gender, the Family and Political Argument in England 1680–1714* (Manchester University Press 1999) 131–2.
61 Sybil Wolfram, 'Divorce in England 1700–1857' (1985) 5(2) *Oxford Journal of Legal Studies* 155, 157.

in 1693. The Duke of Norfolk was finally successful in divorcing his wife in 1700 as a result of the divorce bill passing Parliament. The debate surrounding the Duke of Norfolk's divorce was polarised based on different political positions and was inextricably linked to the support for the Glorious Revolution of 1688. Whigs and Protestants supported the divorce bill as it fitted within their narrative of moral progress. After the Glorious Reformation, these groups hoped moral reform could take place in England with the greater transplantation of continental reformation ideas and values, including civil divorce.[62]

The tripartite divorce system involved both a judicial and legislative procedure. The husband would file a tortious suit of criminal conversation against his wife's adulterous partner and recover compensation in the Assizes. Criminal conversation was not available to wives.[63] The husband would then seek a legal separation by means of a divorce *a mensa et thoro* from the Ecclesiastical Courts. In the final stage, the husband would petition the House of Lords to pass a private Act of Parliament granting a divorce *a vinculo matrimonii*. Once passed, the bill would be sent to the House of Commons for approval and finally Royal Assent would be granted. A couple were then legally divorced and each party was free to remarry. This process was expensive and lengthy, which put divorce beyond the reach of most people.

Informal marriages or clandestine marriages caused their own problems. Informal marriage involved an exchange of vows between the parties without solemnisation from a legally sanctioned third party. Fleet marriages were particularly notorious in the seventeenth and early eighteenth centuries.[64] The ceremony was typically conducted by a parson in the Fleet Register, a poorly supervised chaplaincy of the Fleet Prison in London.[65] Lord Hardwicke's Marriage Act 1753 attempted to regulate marriage by only sanctioning Church of England marriages solemnised *in facie ecclesiae* according to the form established in the *Book of Common Prayer*.[66] Jewish and Quaker marriages were exempted. The 1753 Act, however, did not completely resolve the issue of clandestine marriages. Many English couples simply eloped to the Scottish border town of Gretna Green.[67]

As early as 1215, the Fourth Lateran Council had sought to discourage informal marriage by urging people to marry before a priest.[68] By the mid-sixteenth century, the Roman Catholic Church required all marriages to be celebrated by a priest before two witnesses according to the Counter-Reformation teachings of the Council of Trent.[69] However, the Church of England continued to recognise

---

62 Weil (n 60) 137.
63 Wolfram (n 61) 159.
64 R.B. Outhwaite, *Clandestine Marriage in England 1500–1850* (The Hambledon Press 1995) 95. *Hill v Turner* (1737) 25 ER 892 was a particularly notorious case where a Fleet marriage was held to be valid.
65 Probert (n 35) 186.
66 (26 Geo II c 33).
67 Samuel Menefee, *Wives for Sale* (Basil Blackwell Publisher 1981) 11.
68 James Brundage, *Sex, Law and Marriage in the Middle Ages* (Variorum 1993) ch 7, p 8.
69 Witte (n 1) 106–11.

informal marriages in the pre-Reformation tradition. If the exchange of vows was made in the present tense, then the marriage would be a contract *per verba de praesenti* and binding on the parties with similar effect to that of a typical contract.[70] On the other hand, if the exchange of vows was stated in the future tense, the marriage would be a contract *per verba de futuro*. The betrothal would not be binding on the parties unless a condition of the contract was performed or the parties consummated the relationship, in which case the duty to perform the condition would be discharged.[71]

A party who contracted *per verba de praesenti* could not remarry. If a party attempted to remarry, the second marriage would be void *ab initio* and the children of the second marriage would be declared bastards.[72] Although the *Book of Common Prayer* does not declare marriages celebrated outside of its rites and ceremonies as void, 'contract marriages' did not have the same legal authority or moral standing as a marriage solemnised in a Church of England wedding.

According to Probert, contracts *per verba de praesenti* were

> morally but not legally binding; a contract that had been established to the satisfaction of the ecclesiastical courts required the parties to marry in church; and the canonical theory that consent was central to marriage does not mean it was the only thing necessary for a marriage in eighteenth-century England and Wales.[73]

Outhwaite and Stone have argued that 'contract marriages' were popular and had the same legal authority as a formal marriage.[74] Probert suggests that in fact there is 'virtually no evidence of contracted couples living together, or of cohabiting couples who claimed to be contracted.'[75] On this basis, the contract *per verba de praesenti* was no substitute to formal marriage. In fact, she suggests that formal marriage may have been more common than others have suggested, because the poor would be motivated to formally marry by their Christian faith, the desire to maintain their reputation in the community, and pressure from the Church and the state.[76] If Probert's analysis is correct, then it suggests that informal divorce would have also been fairly uncommon.

After the introduction of the Marriage Act 1753, informal 'contract marriages' were not legally recognised by the Ecclesiastical Courts.[77] However, due to the difficulty associated with the legal process of applying for divorce, a few husbands attempted to informally divorce their wives, even if they were legally rather than informally married. Using a 'wife contract,' a husband would 'sell' his wife to

70 Probert (n 35) 27.
71 *Ibid*.
72 *Ibid*. 38.
73 *Ibid*. 66.
74 Outhwaite (n 64) 2; Stone (n 49) 76–9.
75 Probert (n 35) 122.
76 *Ibid*. 127–9.
77 Outhwaite (n 64) 84; Marriage Act 1753, s 13.

another man by a written agreement.[78] The assignment of the wife from the first husband to the second husband was said to have terminated the first marriage and initiated the second. This arrangement features in the Thomas Hardy novel *The Mayor of Casterbridge*.[79] The novel begins with the protagonist Michael Henchard selling his wife at a county fair for five guineas. According to popular belief in the eighteenth century, wife sales were a legally valid form of divorce.[80] Although the courts refused to accept this form of divorce, in some circumstances the property arrangements which flowed from the sale were recognised.[81]

Bigamy when combined with the presumption of death was another informal method of divorce. Typically, a bigamist would claim that the first spouse had died and they were free to re-marry. Prior to the enactment of the Births and Deaths Registration Act 1836,[82] it was easier for a bigamist to evade detection by the authorities, since death records were not easily accessible.[83] A popular depiction is found in Charlotte Brontë's *Jane Eyre*.[84] Mr Rochester attempts to enter into a bigamous marriage with the protagonist Jane Eyre in a church wedding. The scheme is thwarted when the solicitor Mr Briggs provides evidence of Mr Rochester's first marriage and proof that his wife is still alive. There is no evidence to suggest informal divorce practices were widespread. Instead, eighteenth-century newspapers, magazines, and literature present wife sales as sensational oddities,[85] and there are very few recorded cases of bigamy.[86]

Formal divorce increased between the early eighteenth and mid-nineteenth century. The number of divorces granted by Parliament climbed from 14 between 1700 and 1749 to 117 between 1750 and 1799, and the numbers again increased to 193 in the years 1800–57.[87] The increase has been attributed to Parliament being more inclined to grant divorce and to promote the pursuit of individual happiness rather than just seeking to protect property.[88] By the early nineteenth century, the rise of the middle class meant that divorce was no longer confined to members of the aristocracy. Dr Joseph Phillimore states:

> From an exclusive privilege for rank and station Divorce bills had become the remedy for the evils attendant on matrimony, adopted by the middle classes, by all who could command the pecuniary means, and had any reason for calling on the House to interpose its authority.[89]

---

78 Menefee (n 67) 2.
79 Thomas Hardy, *Mayor of Casterbridge* (first published 1886, Penguin 2003).
80 Menefee (n 67) 1.
81 *Ibid.* 147.
82 (6 & 7 Will IV c 86).
83 Henry Finlay, *To Have But Not to Hold* (The Federation Press 2005) 12.
84 Charlotte Brontë, *Jane Eyre* (first published 1847, Penguin 2006).
85 Menefee (n 67) 1–7.
86 Outhwaite (n 64) 2; Stone (n 49) 56–7.
87 Wolfram (n 61) 157.
88 Stone (n 49) 328.
89 HC Deb 3 June 1830, vol 24, col 1268.

For the entire period of the eighteenth century, not a single wife attempted to formally divorce her husband. The first woman to successfully apply for divorce was Jane Addison (née Campbell). She divorced her husband, Edward Addison, for committing incestuous adultery with his sister-in-law. In 1800, the Ecclesiastical Courts granted Mrs Addison a divorce *a mensa et thoro*. The peculiar facts of incestuous adultery were enough to spur Parliament into passing the Addison/Campbell Divorce Act 1801.[90] Under the Act, custody of the children was granted to Mrs Addison, with the children deemed to be wards of Chancery. Divorce bills did not normally consider the issue of child custody as there was a presumption that custody was granted to the husband.[91]

Although divorce was not exclusive to the aristocracy, it was predominantly the privilege of the wealthy. Ralph Box, a London grocer who later became a druggist, is a notable exception and he was one of the first to be granted a divorce in 1700.[92] According to Sybil Wolfram, 67.5 per cent of the husbands who were granted divorce Acts between 1750 and 1857 can be classed as being from the upper class (i.e., titled men, esquires, and gentlemen).[93] The remaining 32.5 per cent were divorces largely from the middle class and this includes clergy (6 per cent), merchants (5 per cent), physicians and surgeons (3 per cent), armed forces personnel (5 per cent), and other non-titled men (13.5 per cent).[94] The majority of the English population, especially those of the poorer classes, were effectively prevented from applying for divorce. In the early nineteenth century, many divorce cases were associated with prestige, property, and power. From 1801 to 1857, out of the 230 petitions for divorce *a vinculo matrimonii*,[95] the House of Lords granted 192.[96] Although more than three-quarters of all petitions were successful, this does not mean a private Act of Parliament was easily attainable. Some parliamentary divorces were rejected as a result of connivance or collusion.[97] The average number of divorces per year during this period was only 3.3, and the number of petitions was very low, at approximately a few dozen each decade.[98] Only divorce cases that were likely to succeed would result in petitioning, because of the time and expense.[99]

---

90 Stone (n 49) 360.
91 Wolfram (n 61) 174.
92 Stuart Anderson, 'Legislative Divorce—Law for the Aristocracy?' in Gerry Rubin and David Sugarman (eds), *Law, Economy and Society, 1750–1914: Essays in the History of English Law* (Professional Books 1984) 417.
93 Wolfram (n 61) 164.
94 *Ibid*.
95 Anderson (n 92) 415.
96 *Ibid*. This number tallies with Wolfram's figure of 193 with a starting date of 1800, as there was only one statute in 1800; Wolfram (n 61) 157.
97 Stone (n 49) 328–32.
98 Wolfram (n 61) 157.
99 A divorce *a vinculo matrimonii* proceeding would take a few years to resolve with an average cost of £700. *First Report of the Commissioners…Into the Law of Divorce* (BPP vol 40, 1852-3) 269–70.

The case of Lord and Lady Byron

During this period, there were a number of sensational divorce cases involving aristocrats, a prime minister, and even the king. An examination of these cases shall provide important insights into the legal procedure and consequences of divorce. These *causes célèbres* helped to put the issue of divorce law on a national stage and illustrate some of the problems with the existing law. Donna Andrew states, 'Thus, by the early nineteenth century, the attack on fashionable adultery, on the *beau monde* as the site of such sin, and on its corrosive effects on both law and property, was systematically and powerfully articulated.'[100] The *causes célèbres* indeed highlighted for everyone the inefficient and inaccessible legal procedure of obtaining a divorce. They also reflect the way that divorce was still dominated by the wealthy.

The case of Lord and Lady Byron provides a good illustration of informal divorce and the use of private separation agreements. Lord Byron was a famous and popular literary figure during his lifetime, and is still remembered for his romantic poetry and scandalous affairs.[101] In 1815, Lord Byron married Anne Isabella (Annabella) Milbanke (hereafter referred to as 'Lady Byron'). After only a year of marriage, the parties separated and reached an out-of-court settlement.[102] In preparing for divorce *a mensa et thoro*, Lady Byron sought the legal counsel of Dr Stephen Lushington. Divorce *a vinculo matrimonii* was almost unheard of for women at the time. In the first half of the nineteenth century, the House of Lords granted only four divorces to women on the grounds of adultery coupled with cruelty or incest,[103] but women's petitions for divorce based on adultery alone were rejected.[104] A grant of divorce *a mensa et thoro* would have entitled Lady Byron to a judicial separation from the Ecclesiastical Courts and to seek alimony from Lord Byron. It would have also prevented Lord Byron from initiating a restitution suit of conjugal rights, which might result in an order that Lady Byron return to the matrimonial home.[105]

A married woman was said to be *feme covert*, meaning that she held no common law rights to real property, since the wife's property was assigned to the husband at the time of marriage.[106] Personal property of the wife was assigned to the

---

100 Donna Andrew, '"Adultery à-la-Mode": Privilege, the Law and Attitudes to Adultery 1770–1809' (1997) 82(265) *History* 5, 23.
101 For further biographical details see Phylliss Grosskurth, *Byron: The Flawed Angel* (Hodder and Stoughton 1997).
102 Stephen Waddams, *Law, Politics and the Church of England: The Career of Stephen Lushington* (Cambridge University Press 1992) 100–1.
103 There were a total of seven divorce petitions from women between 1801 and 1850: two petitions in 1801–10, three in 1831–40, and two in 1841–50. Anderson (n 92) 415.
104 *First Report of the Commissioners...Into the Law of Divorce* (BPP vol 40, 1852-3) 256–7.
105 A restitution suit for conjugal rights was an Ecclesiastical Courts remedy that could be initiated by the husband to compel a separated wife to cohabitate with the husband. *Orme v Orme* (1824) 2 Add 382.
106 Lee Holcombe, *Wives and Property: Reform of the Married Women's Property Law in Nineteenth-Century England* (University of Toronto Press 1983) 23.

husband once they married, with the exception of paraphernalia—clothing and personal ornaments of the wife held before and during the marriage.[107] In order to circumvent this law, matrimonial property could be distributed to the wife through vesting property in a trust. *The Countess of Strathmore v Bowes* provides a good example of a married woman's property trust.[108] Lady Strathmore was one of the richest people in Britain and prior to marriage she settled her estates and personal property.[109] Lord Thurlow held that the conveyance of property by the wife is *prima facie* valid either before or after the marriage so long as notice is given to the husband, otherwise the settlement would be set aside for fraud.[110] This illustrates how married women in the eighteenth century could protect their property in equity, despite the lack of recognition under common law. Lady Byron received £300 *per annum* for her private consumption from a trust account.[111]

Adultery was interpreted to mean sexual intercourse. It was thought impractical to request explicit evidence of adultery.[112] Whilst ocular evidence was not required, other evidence of adultery must be 'strict, satisfactory and conclusive.'[113] The law applied an objective standard based on the discretion of a reasonable and just man that adultery had been committed.[114] Circumstantial evidence of adultery sufficed on its own, since it was not necessary to prove that an act of adultery was committed at a specific time or place.[115] The opportunity of committing adultery was insufficient circumstantial evidence. It was necessary to prove either an overt act of adultery or some circumstance proving the accused was inclined to take advantage of the opportunity to commit adultery and actually did so.[116] Lady Byron sought to prove that Lord Byron had an extra-marital affair with Susan Boyce. This would have been difficult to prove, because Lord Byron had legitimate reasons for seeing Boyce at the theatre and accompanying her home safely.[117] Furthermore, Lord Byron could have countered the claim of adultery and cruelty by claiming that Lady Byron's affectionate letters addressed to him after separation constituted condonation of his actions.[118]

In order to establish cruelty, Lady Byron sought to prove that her husband was frequently intoxicated and had physically abused her to the point of putting

---

107 *Robinson v Robinson* (1728) 2 Lee 593; *D'Aguilar v D'Aguilar* (1828) 1 Hag 773, 778.
108 (1789) 1 Ves Jun 22. See also R.W. Shannon, 'The Countess of Strathmore versus Bowes' (1923) 1(5) *Canadian Bar Review* 425.
109 See Rosalind Marshall, 'Bowes, Mary Eleanor, Countess of Strathmore and Kinghorne (1749–1800),' *Oxford Dictionary of National Biography* (2004) <https://doi.org/10.1093/ref:odnb/3056>.
110 *The Countess of Strathmore v Bowes* (1789) 1 Ves Jun 22, 28.
111 Waddams (n 102) 130.
112 *Williams v Williams* (1798) 1 Hag Con 299.
113 *Rix v Rix* (1777) 3 Hag Ecc 74.
114 *Loveden v Loveden* (1810) 2 Hag Con 1, 3.
115 *Grant v Grant* (1839) 2 Curt 16, 57.
116 *Harris v Harris* (1828) 2 Hag 376, 379.
117 Waddams (n 102) 111.
118 *Ibid.* 104.

her personal safety in peril.[119] *Evans v Evans* had established cruelty as a ground of divorce *a mensa et thoro*.[120] Cruelty as a ground of divorce was designed to protect the vulnerable party (usually the wife). It was judged on the basis of the reasonable apprehension of danger to life or health.[121] Sir William Scott of the London Consistory Court limited the scope of cruelty, and he did so in order to uphold the sanctity of marriage.

> For though in particular cases the repugnance of the law to dissolve the obligations of matrimonial cohabitation may operate with great severity upon individuals, yet it must be carefully remembered that the general happiness of married life is secured by its indissolubility.[122]

Cruelty remained narrowly defined. It was not necessary to prove many acts of cruelty so long as it could be proven that the act was likely to occur again.[123] Personal violence was not necessary,[124] but abusive language failed to constitute cruelty unless the words amounted to threats of bodily harm.[125] For example, in *Saunders v Saunders*, the 'gross outrage' of the husband spitting in the wife's face, the husband's 'opprobrious language,' and the dragging, pushing, and slapping of the wife was deemed to be 'gross misconduct' that constituted a reasonable apprehension of bodily injury amounting to cruelty.[126] However, cruelty did not stretch to wives who accused their husbands of quarrelling and improper language,[127] failing to communicate the risk of catching sexually transmitted infections,[128] and intoxication.[129] Similarly, the husband denying the wife access to her family did not amount to cruelty,[130] but cruelty would be found if the husband verbally or physically abused the wife's family in order to prevent access to the wife.[131] Lady Byron would have had difficulties proving cruelty, because it was limited in its definition and interpreted narrowly.

In fact, the Byrons settled their matrimonial dispute in a private separation agreement in 1816. During the Campbell Commission, Lushington stated, 'It is a constant practice to resort to separation by agreement.'[132] Lord Byron acceded to Lady Byron's demands that he would not seek a restitution of conjugal rights

---

119 *Ibid.* 111.
120 (1790) 1 Hag Con 34.
121 *Evans* (n 120) 38; *Waring v Waring* (1813) 2 Phill Ecc 132.
122 *Evans* (n 120) 35.
123 *Westmeath v Westmeath* (1826) 2 Hag Ecc (Supp) 1, 71–2.
124 *Hulme v Hulme* (1823) 2 Add 27; *Otway v Otway* (1812) 2 Phill Ecc 95.
125 *Evans* (n 120) 38; *Holden v Holden* (1810) 1 Hag Con 452, 458; *Dysart v Dysart* (1847) 1 Rob Ecc 470, 473–8.
126 (1847) 1 Rob Ecc 549, 558–9.
127 *Kenrick v Kenrick* (1831) 4 Hag Ecc 114.
128 *Ciocci v Ciocci* (1853) 1 Sp 121.
129 *Chesnutt v Chesnutt* (1854) 1 Sp 196.
130 *Neeld v Neeld* (1831) 4 Hag 263, 269.
131 *Saunders* (n 126) 558.
132 *First Report of the Commissioners…Into the Law of Divorce* (BPP vol 40, 1852–3) 297.

28 *The tripartite divorce system*

and forfeited a writ of *habeas corpus* over the custody of their daughter Ada. In exchange, Lady Byron agreed to a financial settlement with Lord Byron that satisfied his pecuniary interests. The private separation agreement safeguarded Lady Byron from the creditors of Lord Byron, which gave her the legal right of *feme sole*. Although the parties were not legally divorced, the parties effectively negotiated their own divorce *a mensa et thoro*. This method of informal divorce allowed the parties to set their own terms. The private separation agreement facilitated an expedient and relatively inexpensive way of resolving their matrimonial dispute.

The trial of Queen Caroline

The most sensational divorce case of the period involved King George IV and his estranged wife Caroline of Brunswick. In 1795, George (then the Prince of Wales) married Caroline, but only a year later the marriage had broken down and the couple separated.[133] Caroline initially stayed in England before moving to Italy. In 1820, George became King George IV upon the death of his father, King George III. In the same year, Caroline returned to England determined to claim her position as Queen Consort. The king alleged that the queen had committed adultery with her Italian servant Bartolomo Bergami during her lengthy period of separation in Italy. The procedure of divorce for the reigning sovereign was very different compared to that of his subjects. The king did not have to prove his case before the Assizes and the Ecclesiastical Courts. Instead, the House of Lords was required to pass an Act of Parliament granting the king his divorce, where the trial of Queen Caroline was a parliamentary proceeding that was judicial in nature.

At the start of the trial, the popular opinion was that the queen was guilty of adultery.[134] After 24 years of separation, it seemed very likely that the queen would have had an extra-marital affair. Although this opinion was widely held by the end of the trial, the evidence alone did not appear to be enough to support the adultery allegation.[135] The defence sought to establish that the evidence was insufficient to prove adultery. At the king's request, Prime Minister Lord Liverpool introduced the bill of pains and penalties in the House of Lords.[136] Due to the royal status of the parties, the government decided that the king should have his divorce case heard in the House of Lords at first instance, and forgo the usual practice of a jury trial in the Assizes and an inquisitorial hearing from the Ecclesiastical Courts.[137] Those in favour of the bill relied heavily on an allegation that adultery had taken place during an Italian pleasure cruise in 1816.[138] Henry

133 See Flora Fraser, *The Unruly Queen: The Life of Queen Caroline* (Macmillan Publishers 1996).
134 Waddams (n 102) 138.
135 Fraser (n 133) 443.
136 HL Deb 6 July 1820, vol 2, col 231.
137 *Ibid*. col 251.
138 The charges against the queen presented by Attorney-General Lord Gifford at the beginning of the trial focused on the alleged adulterous intercourse between the queen and Bergami in 1816.

Brougham led the defence and Lushington was one of the defence counsels. These two men later played significant roles in divorce law reform. Brougham would later advocate for the end of ecclesiastical jurisdiction over matrimonial disputes and Lushington would call for the introduction of civil divorce during the Campbell Commission.

On behalf of the defence, Lushington drew attention to the queen's age by suggesting that the accusation of adultery was preposterous for a woman so advanced in years (the queen was aged 48 in 1816).[139] He may have tried to shift attention away from innuendo to specific evidence. Lushington also suggested that the king connived at the queen's adultery by deserting his wife after a year of marriage and freely allowing her to be separated from him for 24 years.[140] Moreover, the king was notorious for his extra-marital affairs, so much so that cartoonists depicted the king in compromising positions with his mistresses.[141] Evidence of the king's own adultery would have also barred him from divorce on the ground of recrimination. However, the defence did not press this point. It would have appeared indecorous to humiliate the sovereign in the House of Lords. Although the bill barely passed the Third Reading by 108 votes to 99, the government withdrew the bill.[142] Lord Liverpool felt the bill could not proceed with a majority of nine votes, because his parliamentary majority was too small and public sentiment was too divided.[143] Furthermore, the king was deeply unpopular and the queen had popular support, with the bill likely to have been defeated in the House of Commons.[144] Lord Liverpool, who had initially been reluctant to introduce the bill, was more concerned about restoring the government's public reputation and wanted to move on from the divorce trial.[145]

Joan Perkin states the trial of Queen Caroline 'laid the groundwork for reforms concerning a mother's access to her children, and the rights of deserted wives, which were eventually to follow.'[146] She supports this claim by arguing that the trial was the first time English women mounted a public protest against husbands.[147] Any concrete impact is difficult to assess, but these events raised the issue of divorce in the popular conscience. The case certainly brought huge attention to the topic of divorce. It highlighted to the general public that the

---

The examination and cross-examination of witnesses focused on the captain and the crew of a number of ships boarded by the two. HL Deb 19 August 1820, vol 3, cols 740–74; HL Deb 21 August 1820, vol 3, cols 774–803.
139 HL Deb 26 October 1820, vol 3, cols 1186–7.
140 *Ibid.* col 1188.
141 Thomas Laqueur, 'The Queen Caroline Affair: Politics as Art in the Reign of George IV' (1982) 54(3) *Journal of Modern History* 417, 450.
142 HL Deb 10 November 1820, vol 3, cols 1744–6.
143 *Ibid.* col 1746.
144 Joan Perkin, *Women and Marriage in Nineteenth-Century England* (Routledge 1989) 36–7.
145 Norman Gash, 'Jenkinson, Robert Banks, Second Earl of Liverpool (1770–1828),' *Oxford Dictionary of National Biography* (2004) <https://doi.org/10.1093/ref:odnb/14740>.
146 Perkin (n 144) 40.
147 *Ibid.*

nobility and royalty were not immune to marital breakdowns and that it was legitimate to seek redress for matrimonial wrongdoing through the dissolution of marriage. This perhaps was a factor which increased cultural acceptance of divorce. Questions would inevitably be raised about whether the law of divorce reflected the values of English society and the effectiveness of the ecclesiastical justice system in dispensing its jurisdiction over matrimonial causes.

The reform of the Ecclesiastical Courts

The early nineteenth century saw a revival of interest in law reform with the emergence of utilitarianism, though not all reformers were utilitarians.[148] The reform of divorce law was inextricably bound up with the reform of the Ecclesiastical Courts. The English philosopher Jeremy Bentham advocated that the principle of utility be applied to the law.[149] The philosophy of utilitarianism was strongly influenced by consequentialism. According to Bentham:

> [I]t is necessary to the greatest happiness of the greatest number, that a portion of the happiness of that one be sacrificed. Reasons, indicative of this conduciveness, are reasons derived from the principle known by the name of the principle of utility: more expressively say the greatest-happiness principle. To exhibit these reasons is to draw up the account between law and happiness: to apply arithmetical calculations to the elements of happiness.[150]

Bentham supported civil divorce and favoured the Scots law of divorce that allowed for divorce on either the ground of adultery or desertion alone.[151] However, he complained that only the party who had not committed adultery was free to remarry.[152] He was also critical of the Church for exploiting religion to

---

148 Lord Brougham was a reformer, but Bentham saw his efforts for reform as half-hearted, failing to meet his standard of utilitarianism. See Jeremy Bentham, *Lord Brougham Displayed* (Robert Heward 1832); James E. Crimmins, *Utilitarian Philosophy and Politics* (Continuum 2011) 19.
149 Bentham attempted to codify English law into a comprehensive body of law known as the 'pannomion' based on utilitarian principles. Warren Swain, 'Contract Codification and the English: Some Observations from the Indian Contract Act 1872' in James Devenney and Mel Kenny (eds), *The Transformation of European Private Law: Harmonisation, Consolidation, Codification or Chaos* (Cambridge University Press 2013) 175; John Bowring (ed), *The Works of Jeremy Bentham, Volume I* (William Tait 1859) 302.
150 Philip Schofield and Jonathan Harris (eds), *'Legislator of the World': Writings on Codification, Law, and Education* (Oxford University Press 1998) 250–1.
151 Although the Scots Parliament did not pass a statute authorising divorce on the ground of adultery, the common law recognised the right to divorce as a result of the Protestant teachings of John Knox in the sixteenth century. Charles Guthrie, 'The History of Divorce in Scotland' (1910) 8(29) *The Scottish Historical Review* 39; James, Viscount of Stair, *The Institutions of the Law of Scotland: Deduced from its Originals, and Collated with the Civil, Canon, and Feudal Laws, and with the Customs of Neighbouring Nations* (University Presses of Edinburgh and Glasgow 1981) 109.
152 Mary Sokol, *Bentham, Law and Marriage: A Utilitarian Code of Law in Historical Contexts* (Continuum International Publishing Group 2011) 233.

promote its own interests.[153] Philip Schofield believes Bentham was arguing that 'God's will could not provide a standard for temporal happiness, and [Bentham was] denying the relevance of theology to morality and law.'[154]

After the restoration of the Ecclesiastical Courts in 1660, there was growing suspicion and criticism of their activities and gradual erosion of power over the next two centuries. Prior to the English Civil War, writs of prohibition were commonly used to restrain the jurisdiction of the Ecclesiastical Courts.[155] During the Interregnum, Parliament abolished the centralised Prerogative Courts of Canterbury and York and replaced them with the county-localised Probate Court.[156] The Church of England's ecclesiastical jurisdiction resumed after the Restoration, but it was frequently criticised.[157] There was a decline in the number of cases and its influence waned throughout the eighteenth century. Civilian lawyers also faced hostility. Doctors' Commons, of which the civilians were members, was 'seen as a nest of patronage and monopoly.'[158] Both complaints were justified; G.D. Squibb shows the existence of a sophisticated network of family ties that was found in the membership of Doctors' Commons.[159] A few families dominated civilian practice. Doctors' Commons remained distinct from the rest of the legal profession. Civilian lawyers held the exclusive right to practice in admiralty and ecclesiastical law, including the jurisdiction of matrimonial causes and probate of wills.[160]

Admiralty and canon law had shared roots in Roman law.[161] Following the Restoration, civil law in England was never quite the same. The ecclesiastical law became less important as applied beyond the clergy. The criminal jurisdiction of the Ecclesiastical Courts to prosecute sexual delinquency (such as pre-nuptial fornication and bastardy) fell into steep decline and had effectively broken down by 1830.[162] From the late seventeenth century, the number of admiralty suits declined, as did the number of civilians engaged in admiralty practice.[163] Many admiralty disputes were heard in the common law instead.[164]

---

153 Philip Schofield, *Utility and Democracy: The Political Thought of Jeremy Bentham* (Oxford University Press 2006) 191.
154 *Ibid.* 175.
155 R.H. Helmholz, 'Writs of Prohibition and Ecclesiastical Sanctions in the English Courts Christian' (1976) 60 *Minneapolis Law Review* 1011.
156 Veall (n 33) 193–4.
157 Complaints were levelled in Parliament against the Ecclesiastical Courts at decadal intervals in the period immediately after the Restoration. R.B. Outhwaite, *The Rise and Fall of the English Ecclesiastical Courts 1500–1860* (Cambridge University Press 2006) 104.
158 *Ibid.* 155.
159 G.D. Squibb, *Doctors' Commons: A History of the College of Advocates and Doctors of Law* (Oxford University Press 1977) 34–6.
160 Waddams (n 102) 4.
161 Peter Stein, *Roman Law in European History* (Cambridge University Press 1999) 88.
162 Outhwaite (n 157) 83–4.
163 M.J. Prichard and D.E.C. Yale (eds), *Hale and Fleetwood on Admiralty Jurisdiction* (Selden Society 1993) cxxvii–cxxxvi.
164 Warren Swain, *The Law of Contract 1670–1870* (Cambridge University Press 2015) 44–5.

32 The tripartite divorce system

The Ecclesiastical Courts had a system of procedure and rules of evidence which differed from the common law and Court of Chancery. In order to commence a matrimonial suit, the promoter (the petitioner) would apply for a citation (a judicial summons) to be issued to the respondent, then a libel (a written document detailing reasons for relief to be granted) would be submitted only once.[165] A proctor who was not involved with the case would act as an officer of the court, and privately examine the witnesses based on the allegations contained in the libel alone.[166] Generally, the testimony of a single witness was treated as insufficiently reliable,[167] but independent evidence could be used to corroborate the testimony of a single witness and establish its reliability.[168] All evidence, including testimonies, presented in the Ecclesiastical Courts had to be in writing.[169] Neither the husband nor the wife was allowed to provide evidence during the proceedings.[170] Therefore, the parties in ecclesiastical suits involving matrimonial issues could not appear as witnesses during their own trials. The common law was different. The testimony of a single witness was accepted without the need for adminicular or corroborative evidence.[171] Evidence need not be in writing. Yet even at common law there were limits on who could give evidence. The parties or those with an interest in the outcome were still excluded.[172]

The Ecclesiastical Courts survived into the nineteenth century, but in a more rational age many saw their existence as an anachronism. The reform of divorce was tied up with the abolition of the Ecclesiastical Courts' jurisdiction over matrimonial causes. There was general unhappiness with the matrimonial proceedings of Doctors' Commons. In 1828, Henry Brougham (later Lord Brougham) delivered a six-hour speech in the House of Commons calling for the reform of equity and common law.[173] In regards to the ecclesiastical jurisdiction, he criticised the Church of England's privilege to make judicial appointments in the Ecclesiastical Courts on the basis that the prelates had no legal expertise yet their decisions impacted the administration of marriage and divorce law.[174] During this period, law reform advocates presented bold and new ideas in an attempt to improve the efficiency of the justice system. However, the adopted parliamentary

---

165 Alfred Waddilove, *Digest of Cases Decided in the Court of Arches* (W. Benning and Co 1849) 31–52.
166 *Ibid*. 171.
167 Richard Burn and Robert Phillimore, *Ecclesiastical Law, Volume 3* (Sweet, Stevens, and Norton 1842) 304.
168 *Ibid*. 172.
169 Waddilove (n 165) 171.
170 *Ibid*. 364.
171 Keith Smith, 'The Trial: Adversarial Characteristics and Responsibilities; Pre-trial and Trial Procedures' in William Cornish, J. Stuart Anderson, Ray Cocks, Michael Lobban, Patrick Polden, and Keith Smith (eds), *The Oxford History of the Laws of England: Volume XIII* (Oxford University Press 2010) 86–8.
172 Evidence Act 1843 (6 & 7 Vict c 85) s 1.
173 HC Deb 7 February 1828, vol 18, cols 127–258.
174 *Ibid*. col 153.

reforms were usually half-measures that fell short of the target or simply failed.[175] For example, Lord Brougham introduced a bill that proposed to abolish the sinecure office of the Six Clerks.[176] When the watered-down bill finally passed, it failed to abolish the Six Clerks and merely stipulated that appointments continue to be made once their numbers had dropped to two.[177] The Ecclesiastical Courts were depicted as notoriously inefficient, most notably by Charles Dickens. In *David Copperfield*, Dickens describes Doctors' Commons as a 'cosey, dosey, old-fashioned, time-forgotten, sleepy-headed little family-party.'[178] Shortly after the enactment of the Matrimonial Causes Act 1857, *Punch* composed a satirical poem, 'The Divorce Bill Dissected,' rejoicing at the demise of the Ecclesiastical Courts' jurisdiction over matrimonial disputes.[179]

The divorce of the Earl of Ellenborough

The 1830 divorce of the Earl of Ellenborough drew attention to the flaws of the tripartite system of divorce and the Ecclesiastical Courts. The earl's marriage to Jane Elizabeth Digby (Lady Ellenborough) lasted only six years.[180] He alleged that his wife had an adulterous affair with Prince Schwarzenbergh in Brighton in May 1829 after becoming aware of the affair when Lady Ellenborough fell pregnant in June 1829. The earl had to prove two things in order to obtain a parliamentary divorce: first, that Lady Ellenborough had committed adultery; second, that there were no bars to divorce. Lord Chancellor Lord Lyndhurst argued that adultery was established 'beyond a doubt.'[181] He pressed this point based on the testimony of governess Margaret Steele, who deposed that Lady Ellenborough had confessed to her of the affair in Brighton. The earl was accused of connivance for being separated from his wife for a few months prior to the adultery. Lyndhurst defended the earl by arguing that he was busy discharging

---

175 See Patrick Polden, 'The Civilian Courts and the Probate, Divorce, and Admiralty Division 1' in William Cornish, J. Stuart Anderson, Ray Cocks, Michael Lobban, Patrick Polden, and Keith Smith (eds), *The Oxford History of the Laws of England: Volume XI* (Oxford University Press 2010) 704–9.
176 The Six Clerks performed administrative work in the Court of Chancery and held a number of nominal posts. Thomas Braithwaite states, 'At the time of their abolition in 1842, they were performing duties connected with the management and custody of the Records, Writs, and Rules of the Court of Chancery, and taxing of costs, were nominal Attorneys of the "Petty Bag," acting also as Comptrollers of the Hanaper, and Riding Clerk.' See Thomas Braithwaite, *The 'Six Clerks in Chancery': Their Successors in Office and the 'Houses' They Lived In: A Reminiscence* (Stevens and Haynes 1879) 13–14.
177 Chancery Regulation Act 1833 (3 & 4 Wm IV c 94). See Michael Lobban, 'Henry Brougham and Law Reform' (2000) 115 *The English Historical Review* 1184, 1197.
178 Charles Dickens, *David Copperfield* (first published 1850, Penguin 1996) 361.
179 'The Divorce Bill Dissected' *Punch* (London, 5 September 1857) 103.
180 David Steele, 'Law, Edward, First Earl of Ellenborough (1790–1871),' *Oxford Dictionary of National Biography* (2004) <https://doi.org/10.1093/ref:odnb/16143>.
181 HL Deb 17 March 1830, vol 23, col 451.

his duties as a member of the House of Lords.[182] Lawrence Stone claims that there was 'very substantial evidence of collusion' in this case.[183] However, the allegation of collusion was based on insinuations about the separation rather than any hard evidence.[184] The bill easily passed the House of Lords without a call for division.[185]

The bill faced stronger opposition in the House of Commons. Lushington believed that the evidence unequivocally suggested the existence of adultery and rejected allegations of collusion, arguing that there was no evidence to support such a claim.[186] This particular case was unusual as the earl was granted divorce *a vinculo matrimonii* after applying straight to the House of Lords on account of his parliamentary position.[187] This privilege for the nobility was not unprecedented. In 1757, Lord Powis was granted divorce *a vinculo matrimonii* from the House of Lords without ever appearing in the Assizes and the Ecclesiastical Courts.[188] Lushington noted that the tripartite system of divorce was a post-Reformation convention and not a fixed principle of law.[189] The convention appears to have first developed in the case of William Parr, Marquis of Northampton, who was granted a divorce *a mensa et thoro* from the Ecclesiastical Courts with its validity confirmed by Parliament in 1551.[190] The tripartite system of divorce was established in the case of the Duke of Norfolk in 1700.[191] Lushington used this fact to further his call for law reform by condemning the hypocrisy of the divorce law.

> [F]or forty years after the Reformation no divorce Bill had been considered by the House of Commons; all questions of divorce were decided by the House of Lords and the Ecclesiastical Courts. Then there was a complaint that to grant divorce was a violation of God's law; but if that were so, it would not be less a violation of that law that the divorce were the act of the whole Legislature.[192]

Lushington argued that divorce should be inexpensive and accessible regardless of gender or class and proposed to achieve this by abolishing the parliamentary

---

182 *Ibid.* col 452.
183 Stone (n 49) 330.
184 Although the Earl of Radnor denied imputing collusion, he suggested, 'if the parties wished for collusion, they could not have acted in a way more fit for their purpose than they, had done.' HL Deb 17 March 1830, vol 23, col 454.
185 *Ibid.* col 455.
186 HC Deb 6 April 1830, vol 23, cols 1383–5.
187 Stone (n 49) 330.
188 HC Deb 6 April 1830, vol 23, col 1387.
189 *Ibid.*
190 *First Report of the Commissioners...Into the Law of Divorce* (BPP vol 40, 1852–3) 256–7. Susan James, 'Parr, William, Marquess of Northampton (1513–1571),' *Oxford Dictionary of National Biography* (2004) <https://doi.org/10.1093/ref:odnb/21405>.
191 Wolfram (n 61) 157.
192 HC Deb 6 April 1830, vol 23, col 1387.

process of petitioning for divorce *a vinculo matrimonii*.[193] His major objection to parliamentary divorce was the huge expense and the inaptness of using a legislative procedure to facilitate what was commonly seen to be a judicial process.[194] Lushington's views would later influence the majority report of the Campbell Commission, of which he was a member, particularly its recommendation for the creation of a judicial system to hear divorce cases. He reiterated that to deny divorce to the earl in this instance would most unjustly brand him with the commission of guilt.[195]

Although Lushington received some adulation for his powerful speech, not everyone agreed with his call for divorce law reform and he was alone in pushing the issue of reform.[196] Phillimore was one of the 16 members of the House of Commons opposed to the bill. Those opposed to the bill seem to have either personally disliked the earl or genuinely believed that there were bars to divorce. For example, Joseph Hume was opposed to the bill and was forced to reject allegations that he was part of a conspiracy based on personal enmity against the Earl of Ellenborough.[197] Although Phillimore conceded that adultery was clearly established in the case, he declined to support the bill based on the bar of connivance.[198] Phillimore argued that the earl's failure to 'superintend' his young wife, who was aged 17 at the time of marriage, was evidence of connivance.[199] However, the case for divorce proved to be too strong and the bill was comfortably passed by 86 votes to 16.[200]

Parliamentarians used the Ellenborough case to publicly attack the existing law of divorce that was largely administered by the Ecclesiastical Courts. Dissent towards the divorce law was also propagated by the press and it drove popular dissatisfaction against the law. Greet De Bock states, 'Outside the field of matrimonial law, the Ellenborough affair also fuelled the demand for reform. Newspapers explicitly linked the divorce law to other gross forms of legally grounded inequality and to abuse of power.'[201] The *causes célèbres* of the trial of Queen Caroline and the divorce of the Earl of Ellenborough brought public attention to the deficiencies in the divorce law that eventually paved the way to law reform. The exclusivity of the right to divorce among the rich and powerful stirred a sense of disapprobation from the wider public.

---

193 *Ibid.* cols 1386–7.
194 *Ibid.*; Waddams (n 102) 173.
195 HC Deb 6 April 1830, vol 23, col 1387.
196 *Ibid.* cols 1387–8.
197 *Ibid.* cols 1395–6.
198 *Ibid.* col 1366.
199 *Ibid.* col 1370.
200 *Ibid.* col 1394.
201 Greet De Bock, ' "We Have to Compliment the Aristocracy on the Exhibition of their Morals": The Ellenborough Divorce Case (1830) and the Politics of Scandal in Pre-Reform London and Vormärz Vienna' (2016) 89(246) *Historical Research* 776, 796.

Royal Commission inquiry into the Ecclesiastical Courts

Shortly after the Ellenborough case, Phillimore suggested that the Royal Commission to inquire into the Ecclesiastical Courts should also investigate the law of divorce with the aim of finding a more efficient process.[202] Phillimore used the subject of divorce reform to express his wider dissatisfaction with the Ecclesiastical Courts. Although he believed that marriage should generally be indissoluble,[203] he felt it would be more expedient for the divorce *a vinculo matrimonii* cases to come under the jurisdiction of the courts rather than Parliament.[204] Solicitor-General Sir Edward Sugden opposed reform, since he was concerned it would lead to the creation of a divorce court and the extension of divorce to the poor.[205] Opposition Leader Sir Robert Peel rejected Philimore's claim that most divorce *a vinculo matrimonii* cases were subject to collusion as 'exaggerated,' and in any case he argued there was no widespread demand to change the existing divorce law.[206] Peel bluntly stated, 'The expense attendant on such proceedings must always operate as a bar to the poor.'[207] The fear that divorce law reform would lead to moral degradation, particularly among the poor, was a popularly held view among most politicians. Given the radical nature of the motion, it was not a surprise that it was overwhelmingly defeated by 45 votes to 102.[208] It would be another two decades until the law of divorce would again become subject to the serious attention of Parliament.

Although the 1832 Royal Commission to inquire into the Ecclesiastical Courts did not specifically inquire into the law of divorce, the ecclesiastical system that administered matrimonial cases was strongly criticised. The report was split into two parts. The first part was the 'Special Report' that recommended the transfer of ecclesiastical appeals to the Privy Council and the abolition of the High Court of Delegates, the highest appellate court for ecclesiastical cases.[209] Lord Brougham introduced a bill implementing these changes.[210] It was swiftly passed under the Privy Council Appeals Act 1832.[211] The speed of the enactment can be attributed to Parliament's displeasure towards the perceived incompetence of the Delegates. Lord Brougham describes the Delegates as 'not the best qualified.'[212] The choice of judges was limited to the advocates of Doctors' Commons. Court

---

202 HC Deb 3 June 1830, vol 24, col 1268.
203 HC Deb 6 April 1830, vol 23, cols 1363–4.
204 HC Deb 3 June 1830, vol 24, col 1293.
205 *Ibid.* cols 1274–6.
206 *Ibid.* cols 1286–7.
207 *Ibid.* col 1287.
208 *Ibid.* cols 1293–4.
209 *The Special and General Reports made to His Majesty by the Commissioners Appointed to Inquire into the Practice and Jurisdiction of the Ecclesiastical Courts in England and Wales* (BPP vol 24, 1831–2) 5–8.
210 HL Deb 5 July 1832, vol 14, col 78.
211 (2 & 3 Wm IV c 92).
212 HL Deb 5 July 1832, vol 14, col 79.

procedure was becoming increasingly formal and complex. Thus, the demand for a meritocratic legal profession became more important.[213]

The second part was the 'General Report' and it presented a more radical proposal—the transfer of all of the ecclesiastical jurisdiction to the two provincial courts of Canterbury and York.[214] The aim was to remove all parochial jurisdictions from archidiaconal and consistory courts.[215] Matrimonial suits were singled out as the most important area of ecclesiastical law and the Commission strongly recommended matrimonial suits be placed under the provincial courts' jurisdiction.[216] However, the General Report proposals for law reform were frustrated for another two decades. The proposed introduction of the provincial courts holding exclusive ecclesiastical jurisdiction was never implemented. Country solicitors were particularly fearful of losing business from the proposed centralisation of the Ecclesiastical Courts and resisted the proposals.[217] By the mid-nineteenth century, the power and privilege of the Ecclesiastical Courts came to an end. Parliament passed legislation stripping away its jurisdiction over matrimonial disputes,[218] probate,[219] defamation, and church brawling.[220]

Despite the theological shift in the understanding of marriage from an indissoluble sacrament into a civil contract, divorce continued to remain difficult to obtain under the laws of England. Although the procedure of divorce became more formalised into a tripartite convention in the eighteenth century, it was still very expensive, time-consuming, and inaccessible to most ordinary people. The divorce law in Georgian England followed the Reformation teaching on the dissolvability of marriage, but at the same time held onto the Catholic prohibition on divorce. Therefore, the law of divorce that emerged in the eighteenth century reflected this tension between the inconsistency of officially rejecting divorce at least on a superficial level and permitting it in rare circumstances.

Divorce was practically an exclusive privilege for the wealthy rather than a legitimate expectation for the general population. By the early nineteenth century, there was a strong push to reform the Ecclesiastical Courts that culminated into calls for divorce law reform. This was part of the wider nineteenth-century zeal for law reform, but there was also a deeper cultural shift. The *causes célèbres* did not directly lead to legal change. What they illustrated to the English public were the flaws in the law and the growing societal acceptance of divorce. The Royal Commission of 1832 helped lay down the foundations for the resulting divorce law reforms in early Victorian England.

---

213 Christopher Allen, *The Law of Evidence in Victorian England* (Cambridge University Press 1997) 3–4.
214 *The Special and General Reports made to His Majesty by the Commissioners Appointed to Inquire into the Practice and Jurisdiction of the Ecclesiastical Courts in England and Wales* (BPP vol 24, 1831–2) 21–4.
215 *Ibid*.
216 *Ibid*. 43–4.
217 Outhwaite (n 157) 147.
218 Matrimonial Causes Act 1857.
219 Court of Probate Act 1857 (20 & 21 Vict c 77).
220 Ecclesiastical Courts Jurisdiction Act 1860 (23 & 24 Vict c 32).

3 The enactment of the Matrimonial Causes Act 1857

The state of affairs in early Victorian England

By the mid-nineteenth century, there were calls for the reform of divorce law that were tied up with the wider pressure for ecclesiastical law reform. There was mistrust about the effectiveness of the Ecclesiastical Courts and many felt that divorce law could be more effectively administered without resorting to Doctors' Commons.[1] Lord Brougham had begun the call for divorce law reform in early Victorian England. This was partly based on the influence of Bentham's theory of utilitarianism.[2] However, Brougham did not go as far as Bentham in promoting law reform due to a sense of political pragmatism.[3] The time was ripe for divorce law reform with the increase in the annual average of divorce decrees in the first half of the nineteenth century. The average number of divorces granted by Parliament increased from 2.3 *per annum* in the period 1750–99 to 3.3 *per annum* in the years 1800–57.[4] This trend can be attributed to the secularisation of relationship status, and the growing acceptance of divorce as a remedy for an irreconcilable breakdown of marriage.[5]

In the first year of Queen Victoria's reign, the Marriage Act 1836 came into effect,[6] and replaced Lord Hardwicke's Marriage Act 1753.[7] This legal change introduced a secular form of marriage in civil jurisprudence and ended the Church of England monopoly on all marriages. The pressure for reform came from different individuals who all wanted change for a variety of reasons. Some of the motivations were ideological, while others were moved by more personal

---

1 R.B. Outhwaite, *The Rise and Fall of the English Ecclesiastical Courts 1500–1860* (Cambridge University Press 2006) 159–62.
2 In Lord Brougham's introductory notes to his great speech on law reform that he delivered in the House of Commons in 1828, he notes, 'The age of law reform and the age of Jeremy Bentham are one and the same.' Leon Radzinowicz, *A History of English Criminal Law and its Administration from 1750, Volume I* (Stevens and Sons 1948) 355.
3 Ben Eggleston and Dale E. Miller (eds), *The Cambridge Companion to Utilitarianism* (Cambridge University Press 2014) 50–1.
4 Sybil Wolfram, 'Divorce in England 1700–1857' (1985) 5(2) *Oxford Journal of Legal Studies* 155, 157.
5 Lawrence Stone, *Road to Divorce: England 1530–1987* (Oxford University Press 1995) 328.
6 (6 & 7 Wm IV c 85).
7 (26 Geo II c 33).

or practical concerns. These individuals came from disparate backgrounds and included women activists, intellectuals and members of the judiciary. The prominent individuals included Caroline Norton, Mr Justice Maule, John Stuart Mill and Barbara Leigh Smith Bodichon. The activism of these personalities shall be considered.

Caroline Norton and the trial of Lord Melbourne

Caroline Elizabeth Sarah Norton (née Sheridan) was a leading proponent for the reform of child and divorce law.[8] Her activism began as a result of her acrimonious separation with her husband George Norton and the subsequent loss of contact with her sons. Caroline was accused of committing adultery with Lord Melbourne after first meeting him in 1831. L.G. Mitchell states, 'The liaison was so vivid and so public, that, in April 1835, Disraeli could plausibly claim that Melbourne was using Mrs Norton as a political intermediary in negotiations with Tories.'[9] In 1836, George commenced criminal conversation proceedings for damages laid at £10,000 against Melbourne for allegedly committing adultery with Caroline. George was probably motivated by pecuniary and political reasons to initiate the suit of criminal conversation. Damages of £10,000 was an extraordinary sum of money and would have significantly helped George's precarious financial situation. Furthermore, George was a Tory MP and Melbourne was by then the Whig prime minister. If the criminal conversation suit had succeeded, the resulting scandal would have been catastrophic for the electoral prospects of the Melbourne government.

Norton v Viscount Melbourne was conducted as a criminal proceeding in the Court of Common Pleas before Lord Chief Justice Sir Nicholas Conyngham Tindal and a Middlesex special jury.[10] George Norton was represented by Sir William Follett, and Melbourne was represented by Attorney-General Sir John Campbell, who later became Lord Campbell and chaired the Campbell Commission. Caroline was a third party to the proceedings; therefore, she had no voice whatsoever in the case. She was seen, but not heard. Follett pre-emptively defended George from allegations of connivance by arguing that George was away from the matrimonial home due to his obligations as magistrate.[11] The defence decided not to press this rather reasonable explanation. Follett also presented quite dubious circumstantial evidence of adultery.

> One of the servants having gone into the room while Lord Melbourne was there, on more occasions than one found the door bolted, and had seen

---

8 See Alice Acland, *Caroline Norton* (Constable 1948); Diane Atkinson, *The Criminal Conversation of Mrs Norton* (Preface 2012); Alan Chedzoy, *A Scandalous Woman: The Story of Caroline Norton* (Allison and Busby 1992); Jane Gray Perkins, *The Life of the Honourable Mrs. Norton* (Henry Holt and Company 1909).
9 L.G. Mitchell, *Lord Melbourne 1779–1848* (Oxford University Press 1997) 222.
10 Anon, *Norton v Viscount Melbourne* (William Marshall 1836).
11 *Ibid.* 13.

kisses pass between the parties. She had seen Mrs Norton's arm round Lord Melbourne's neck—had seen her hand upon his knee, and herself kneeling in a posture. In that room Mrs Norton has been seen lying on the floor, her clothes in a position to expose her person—(Great sensation).[12]

Follett then proceeded in presenting Caroline's dirty linen to the jury. Thereupon, he pointed out marks visible on the linen that he argued were as a result of the alleged sexual intercourse between Caroline and Melbourne. The plaintiff also relied on a letter Melbourne sent to Caroline: 'How are you? (A laugh) I shall not be able to call today, but I probably shall tomorrow.'[13] It was suggested that the letter was evidence of Melbourne attempting to arrange a secret rendezvous with Caroline. Charles Dickens was covering this case as a journalist on behalf of the *Morning Chronicle*. He later parodied this piece of evidence in *The Pickwick Papers*. In the novel, Samuel Pickwick's innocuous note to Mrs Bardell is construed as a love letter which leads to the hapless Pickwick being sued for breaching a promise of marriage: 'Dear Mrs B., I shall not be at home till tomorrow. Slow coach … Don't trouble yourself about the warming-pan.'[14] However, none of the plaintiff's witnesses could testify that they directly saw any sexual acts between Caroline and Melbourne. It was later revealed that the witnesses were paid for their court testimonies and were provided accommodation by George's brother.[15] Therefore, the evidence presented was merely circumstantial, relying heavily on innuendo with no credible evidence of sexual intercourse.

Campbell had a relatively easy task defending Melbourne. He reminded the jury that their verdict must be beyond reasonable doubt and the bonds of marriage could only be dissolved if there was absolute proof of adultery.[16] These statements were aimed at demonstrating to the jury that the plaintiff's evidence was insufficient to pronounce a guilty verdict. Campbell proceeded to argue that George did not harbour suspicion of an adulterous affair between Caroline and Melbourne for many years, but rather approved of their friendship.[17] He dismissed the evidence of the witnesses as woefully unreliable and caricaturised domestic servants as 'sowers of discord.'[18] Caroline's letters written to George even up until the year of the trial were always affectionate, which he argued demonstrated that no affair took place.[19] The defence felt there was no need to call witnesses. After the Lord Chief Justice summed up the case, the jury turned around and took only a few seconds to deliver the verdict of not guilty.[20] The

12 *Ibid*. 12.
13 *Ibid*. 13.
14 Charles Dickens, *The Pickwick Papers* (first published 1836, Oxford University Press 1986) 521.
15 Kieran Dolin, *A Critical Introduction to Law and Literature* (Cambridge University Press 2007) 123.
16 Anon (n 10) 27.
17 *Ibid*. 28.
18 *Ibid*. 30.
19 *Ibid*. 34.
20 *Ibid*. 36.

jury appear to have been convinced that the law suit was motivated by greed and politics.[21] Immediately after the trial, late at night, Campbell went to the House of Commons, which was sitting, and received uproarious applause, but only from the Whig bench.[22] The Melbourne trial was inextricably linked with politics. The case against Melbourne was weak and doomed to fail. Mitchell states, 'As matters turned out, the trial proved a damp squib.'[23] Although Melbourne's reputation was immediately restored, Caroline continued to suffer irreparable reputational damage from the legal ordeal and faced ongoing personal struggles from the breakdown of the marriage.[24]

Caroline was effectively barred from petitioning for divorce *a mensa et thoro*, because her short-lived reconciliation with George would have been seen as condonation of his matrimonial offences. Caroline was also separated from her three young sons and she had no legal power to challenge George's right to child custody under common law. After the trial, Caroline campaigned for the right of mothers to the custody of their children,[25] and wrote an article advocating child law reform.[26] Under the pseudonym Pearce Stevenson, Caroline condemned the injustices suffered by mothers who were denied the right to have custody and access to their children. She strongly implored Members of Parliament to support the infant custody bill.[27] Thomas Talfourd, serjeant-at-law and MP, was so moved by Caroline's appeal that he introduced the infant custody bill in the House of Commons.[28] Caroline also sent a letter to the Bishop of Exeter, Henry Phillpotts, arguing that the special bond between mother and child is indissoluble. She urged him to use his power and influence to support the passage of the bill in the House of Lords.[29] The Infant Custody Act 1839 was subsequently passed and allowed mothers to apply to the Court of Chancery for child custody for children under the age of seven and child access for children under the age of 16.[30] The introduction of the Act weakened the husband's right to custody of the children and marked the beginning of modern child law.[31]

---

21 Atkinson (n 8) 22.
22 Perkins (n 8) 94. The House of Commons was located in the crypt of St Stephen's Church at the time after the burning of Parliament in 1834.
23 Mitchell (n 9) 224.
24 Acland (n 8) 92.
25 John Wroath, *Until They are Seven: The Origins of Women's Legal Rights* (Waterside Press 1998) 92–118.
26 Caroline Norton, *The Separation of Mother and Child by the Law of Custody of Infants, Considered* (Roake and Varty 1838).
27 Caroline Norton, *A Plain Letter to the Lord Chancellor on the Infant Custody Bill* (James Ridgway 1839).
28 HC Deb 12 June 1839, vol 48, col 157.
29 Caroline Norton, *A Letter to the Right Reverend the Lord Bishop of Exeter on the Custody of Infants* (Edward Churton 1839).
30 (2 & 3 Vict c 54).
31 Although the Court of Chancery already exercised *parens patriae* jurisdiction and heard child custody cases under the Tenures Abolition Act 1660 (12 Car 2 c 24), the Infant Custody Act 1839 significantly strengthened its power to decide more favourably towards the mother. Prior to the 1839

Caroline also played a role in challenging the divorce law, but was treated with some suspicion from other women activists. Some perceived her to be more motivated by self-interest rather than feminism. For example, Harriet Martineau once commented:

> The best friends of that cause are women who are morally as well intellectually competent to the most serious business of life, and must be clearly seen to speak from conviction of the truth, and not from personal unhappiness.[32]

It was well known that Martineau had a personal disdain for Caroline.[33] The fact that Caroline was more driven by her personal plight rather than as a result of a convicted and rational ideological motivation put her at odds with Martineau. However, George Eliot (real name Mary Ann Evans) was sympathetic to Caroline both on a personal level, towards the suffering Caroline endured at the hands of her husband, and at a political level, by supporting her campaign for the rights of married women and divorce law reform.[34]

Contemporary scholars have predominantly taken the view of Caroline's contemporary critics of her as a self-serving polemicist. Barbara Caine describes Caroline as someone 'pleading not for her sex, but rather for herself.'[35] Mary Shanley argues that Caroline recognised the right of married women to separate legal personality only to serve as a safeguard from the tyranny of the husband.[36] Whereas the Married Women's Property Committee completely rejected the doctrine of coverture and believed in the right of women to separate legal personality as an inalienable principle.[37] This outlook is further substantiated in Caroline's own actions. In 1837, Caroline asked Talfourd to withdraw the infant custody bill after George allowed her to see her children.[38] The bill only proceeded to the Second Reading and then debate resumed after the Nortons' arrangements for the children broke down. However, Mary Poovey takes a more nuanced view of Caroline's legal and political activism. She states:

> Caroline Norton could influence Parliament because much of what she said was what lawmakers expected and wanted to hear: that the home should be

---

Act, Chancery decisions on child custody were overwhelmingly in favour of the father. However, it would be misleading to characterise this period as the 'empire of the father,' because fathers did not have an absolute right to child custody. See Sarah Abramowicz, 'English Child Custody Law, 1660–1839: The Origins of Judicial Intervention in Paternal Custody' (1999) 99(5) *Columbia Law Review* 1344, 1381–91.

32 Harriet Martineau, *Harriet Martineau's Autobiography, Volume 1* (first published 1877, Cambridge University Press 2010) 401.
33 Acland (n 8) 37.
34 Anna Nardo, *George Eliot's Dialogue with John Milton* (University of Missouri Press 2003) 5.
35 Barbara Caine, *English Feminism 1780–1980* (Oxford University Press, 1997) 69.
36 Mary Shanley, *Feminism, Marriage, and the Law in Victorian England, 1850–1895* (Princeton University Press 1993) 33.
37 *Ibid.*
38 Wroath (n 25) 100–1.

kept separate from commercial and political relations, that the sexual double standard was both natural and just, that protection was a women's definitive right.[39]

Caroline's pleas for law reform based on the inferiority of the female sex may have been used as a guileful ploy to assuage the fears of male politicians towards comprehensive women's emancipation and to successfully push for married women's rights in the form of piecemeal reform.[40] It is indeed plausible that Caroline was primarily motivated by her own self-interest given her ongoing dispute with her husband, but it should not be forgotten that Caroline came from a political family, with her grandfather Richard Brinsley Sheridan serving as a Whig MP. Caroline had the political nous to convey a message that was euphonic to her predominantly male audience to achieve her personal political objectives.

George stopped paying alimony to Caroline in 1851. This was in breach of their 1848 deed of settlement, but soon after it was found to be invalid. It was a blessing in disguise, as Caroline was released from bearing liability over her own debts. Caroline retaliated by referring all her creditors to George, since the husband assumed the debt of the wife under common law. George was able to successfully defend himself at trial, but the press tarnished Caroline's reputation by opening up old wounds from the Melbourne criminal conversation trial.[41] Consequently, Caroline became vocal in her support for the introduction of civil divorce and the expansion of married women's property rights. In 1854, Caroline published *English Laws for Women in the Nineteenth Century*. In this publication, she details various injustices against women in the law including the inaccessibility of divorce and the denial of the right for married women to enter into contracts under common law.[42] However, the pamphlet was not politically successful, because too much emphasis was devoted to her personal marital plights rather than the status of women under the law.[43]

Caroline was the public face of the private suffering of many women in Victorian England. Karen Chase and Michael Levenson describe Caroline as 'the Byron of modern poetesses ... a Whig poetic mother, a public mother resolved to teach the lessons of reforms.'[44] The life of Caroline Norton inspired William Thackeray's portrayal of two characters in *The Newcomes*: Clara Pulleyn

---

39 Mary Poovey, *Uneven Developments: The Ideological Work of Gender in Mid-Victorian England* (Virago Press 1988) 84.
40 Caroline Norton, *English Laws for Women in the Nineteenth Century* (1854) 152–3; Caroline Norton, *A Letter to the Queen on Lord Chancellor Cranworth's Marriage and Divorce Bill* (Longman, Brown, Green, and Longmans 1855) 98.
41 Wroath (n 25) 121–2.
42 Caroline Norton, *English Laws for Women in the Nineteenth Century* (J. Wertheimer and Co. 1854).
43 Wroath (n 25) 123.
44 Karen Chase and Michael Levenson, *The Spectacle of Intimacy: A Public Life for the Victorian Family* (Princeton University Press 2000) 45.

Newcome, whose volatile marriage with Barnes Newcome resembles that of the Nortons, and Ethel Newcome, who adopts Caroline's traits of beauty and intelligence.[45] Kieran Dolin argues that Thackeray highlights the hypocrisy of Victorian morality in his portrayal of Clara and Barnes Newcome's marriage, where society is 'at once appalled by Barnes's conduct and requiring Clara to maintain the façade of a happy marriage.'[46]

Mr Justice Maule

Not only did the high-profile scandals of Caroline Norton bring public attention to the unsatisfactory state of the divorce law, but there were also calls for reform from the judiciary. The fact that, in 1845, a common labourer named Thomas Hall was convicted of bigamy in the Warwick Assizes after marrying again following his first wife's desertion would be unremarkable but for the somewhat sarcastic remarks by the presiding judge, Mr Justice Maule.[47]

> But the law was the same for him as it was for a rich man, and was equally open for him, through its aid, to afford relief; but, as the rich man would have done, he should also have pursued the proper means pointed out by law whereby to obtain redress of his grievances. He should have brought an action against the man who was living in the way stated with his wife, and he should have obtained damages, and then should have gone to the Ecclesiastical Court and obtained a divorce, which would have done what seemed to have been done already, and then he should have gone to the House of Lords, and, proving all his case and the preliminary proceedings, have obtained a full and complete divorce, after which he might, if he liked it, have married again. The prisoner might perhaps object to this that he had not the money to pay the expenses, which would amount to about 500 l. or 600 l.—perhaps he had not so many pence—but this did not exempt him from paying the penalty for committing a felony, of which he had been convicted. His Lordship might, perhaps, have visited the crime more lightly if the prisoner had not misrepresented himself as a bachelor to Maria Hadley, and so deceived her ... For this offence he must receive some punishment, and the sentence was, that he be imprisoned and kept to hard labour for four months, which he hoped would operate as a warning how people trifled with matrimony.[48]

---

45 Dolin (n 15) 130–1.
46 *Ibid.* 131.
47 Maule was well known for making statements of this sort; Anon, 'Sir William Henry Maule' (1858) 5 *Law Magazine* 1, 23–4.
48 *R v Hall* (1845) *The Times*, 3 April 1845 as cited in Rebecca Probert, '*R v Hall* and the changing perceptions of the crime of bigamy' (2019) 39 *Legal Studies* 1, 2.

The enactment of the 1857 Act 45

There have been various versions of the Mr Justice Maule's judgment in *R v Hall* that have exaggerated the impecunious and helpless position of Thomas Hall for the purpose of promoting divorce law reform.[49] Nevertheless, this case gained infamy for the fact that it highlighted the impracticality of obtaining a divorce for many English people due to the expense and complexity in accessing the tripartite system. The cost of divorce would be a recurring theme.[50] As things stood, informal divorce practices, such as private separation agreements, informal separations, bigamy and wife sales, were the only options available to most people.[51]

Barbara Leigh Smith Bodichon and the Law Amendment Society

In the 1850s more individuals were calling for the reform of the divorce law. In 1854, a young feminist named Barbara Leigh Smith Bodichon[52] published a provocative pamphlet calling for divorce and matrimonial property law reform.[53] She was no stranger to politics. Her father, Benjamin Leigh Smith, was a Whig politician and social reformer. Bodichon criticised the doctrine of coverture: 'A woman's body belongs to her husband; she is in his custody, and he can enforce his right by a writ of *habeas corpus.*'[54] She was also critical of the inaccessibility of divorce: 'The expenses of only a common divorce bill are between six hundred and seven hundred pounds, which makes the possibility of release from the matrimonial bond a privilege of the rich.'[55] Her efforts attracted support from the Law Amendment Society after Liberal MP Richard Monckton Milnes submitted Bodichon's pamphlet for its consideration. The society was founded by Lord Brougham in 1844[56] to support his law reform agenda,[57] and to make a case for reform through its quarterly journal *Law Review*.[58]

Bodichon's call for divorce reform was also supported by John Stuart Mill. In a letter dated November 1855, Mill strongly advocated for civil divorce to be introduced on equal terms.

---

49 The various versions include: Margaret Cole, *Marriage Past and Present* (JM Dent 1938) 55–6; O.R. McGregor, *Divorce in England* (Heinemann 1957) 15–16. See also Probert (n 48) 2.
50 HC Deb 9 February 1843 vol 66, cols 331–2 (Sir Robert Inglis).
51 Roderick Phillips, *Untying the Knot: A Short History of Divorce* (Cambridge University Press 1991) 81–92.
52 In 1857, Barbara Leigh Smith married Eugène Bodichon and took his surname. She shall hereafter be referred to as Bodichon, because she is commonly known by this name even when describing her before she was married.
53 Barbara Leigh Smith Bodichon, *A Brief Summary, in Plain Language, of the Most Important Laws Concerning Women: Together with a Few Observations Thereon* (Holyoake and Co 1856).
54 *Ibid*. 4.
55 *Ibid*. 6. The figure is supported by the findings of the Campbell Commission. See *First Report of the Commissioners...Into the Law of Divorce* (1852–3) BPP vol 40, 270.
56 Law Amendment Society, 'Report of the Personal Laws Committee (of the Law Amendment Society) on the Laws Relating to the Property of Married Women' (1856) 66 *Westminster Review* 331; Shanley (n 36) 34–5.
57 G.T. Garratt, *Lord Brougham* (Macmillan 1935) 326.
58 *Ibid*. 332.

46 *The enactment of the 1857 Act*

> My Opinion on Divorce is that though any relaxation of the irrevocability of marriage would be an improvement, nothing ought to be ultimately rested in, short of entire freedom on both sides to dissolve this like any other partnership.[59]

Mill argued that 'the happiness of both parties would be greatly promoted by a dissolution of marriage' in cases where the couple's friendship came to an end.[60] Although Mill was a peripheral voice during the campaign to reform the divorce law, he stated views held but not commonly expressed by many in society that irretrievably broken down marriages should be dissolved.

In 1856, the Law Amendment Society endorsed Bodichon's pamphlet and published a report supporting the right of married women to own property and to legally enter contracts in line with their own aim to fuse equity and common law.[61] Married women could already practically own property as a beneficiary under a trust, but the status of *feme sole* under law would give married women separate legal personality and financial independence. The Law Amendment Society believed the inconsistency between equity and common law found in matrimonial property law only made the law unnecessarily complicated[62] and supported the introduction of civil divorce with the goal of making divorce more accessible as a matter of legal equality.[63] Early feminists supported civil divorce and making divorce more accessible on the grounds of equality.[64] Bodichon along with like-minded friends Mary Howitt and Bessie Parkes established the *English Women's Journal* (1858–64) and the Langham Place Circle (1858–66) to push the cause of 'liberal feminism.'[65] Bodichon was a prominent feminist who led the nascent women's rights movement and brought attention to the legal status of women.[66]

---

59 John Stuart Mill, 'Letter 253' in Dwight Lindley and Francis Mineka (eds), *The Later Letters of John Stuart Mill* (Routledge and Kegan Paul 1972) vol 14, 500.
60 John Stuart Mill, 'On Marriage' in John Robson (ed), *Essays on Equality, Law, and Education, Collected Works* (Toronto, 1984) vol 21, 45.
61 Caroline Cornwallis, 'The Property of Married Women: Report of the Personal Laws Committee (of the Law Amendment Society) on the Laws Relating to the Property of Married Women' (1856) 66 *Westminster Review* 331.
62 Law Amendment Society, 'Fusion of Law and Equity' (1852) 16(1) *Law Review* 184.
63 Wroath (n 25) 130.
64 *Ibid.*
65 Lydia Murdoch, *Daily Life of Victorian Women* (Greenwood 2014) 8; Sheila Herstein, 'The Langham Place Circle and Feminist Periodicals of the 1860s' (1993) 26 *Victorian Periodicals Review* 24; Candida Ann Lacey (ed), *Barbara Leigh Smith Bodichon and the Langham Place Group* (Routledge 1987).
66 Joanne Conaghan, '*A Brief Summary of the Most Important Laws Concerning Women*, Barbara Leigh Smith Bodichon, 1854' in Erika Rackley and Rosemary Auchmuty (eds), *Women's Legal Landmarks: Celebrating the History of Women and Law in the UK and Ireland* (Hart Publishing 2018) 60.

The Campbell Commission

The Whig Prime Minister Lord John Russell ordered the convening of a royal commission on divorce on 10 December 1850. Its report, *The First Report of the Commissioners Appointed by Her Majesty to Enquire into the Law of Divorce, and More Particularly into the Mode of Obtaining Divorces a Vinculo Matrimonii*, was published in 1853.[67] Royal commissions had been used since the Middle Ages, but the nineteenth century was something of a golden age for the institution.[68] Lord Campbell, Dr Stephen Lushington, Baron Beaumont, Lord Redesdale, Edward Bouverie, Spencer Walpole, and William Page Wood were chosen by Home Secretary Sir George Grey to act as commissioners. Lord Redesdale was the sole dissenter and prepared his own report, while all the other commissioners supported the introduction of civil divorce in their jointly written majority report.

Lord Redesdale succeeded to his father's title in 1830, but only became active in the House of Lords from 1837. He was renowned for his reactionary views with an orthodox Protestant outlook. Redesdale opposed repeal of the corn laws, the disestablishment of the Church of Ireland, and ritualism in the Church of England.[69] Prime Minister Benjamin Disraeli described Redesdale as a man possessing 'many excellent qualities and talents, but who is narrow-minded, prejudiced, and utterly unconscious of what is going on in the country, its wishes, opinions or feelings.'[70] Redesdale was the Tory voice of the Campbell Commission and was a leading Protestant controversialist on the divorce debates along with William Gladstone and Bishop Samuel Wilberforce. William Cornish states, 'His vision of a social pestilence infecting the lower orders found a ready enough response in mid-Victorian England, linked as it was to Christian beliefs in the sanctity of marriage.'[71]

The majority commissioners were a curious mix of individuals. Some of the panel were distinguished and two would become lord chancellor. One of those

---

67 *First Report of the Commissioners...Into the Law of Divorce* (1852–3) BPP vol 40, 249.
68 Hugh Clockie and J. William Robinson, *Royal Commissions of Inquiry* (Octagon Books 1969) ch 3.
69 In 1875, Redesdale expressed his support for communion in both kinds (i.e., receiving both the bread and the wine in the Eucharist) in a debate against Henry Edward Cardinal Manning, the Roman Catholic Archbishop of Westminster, published in the *Daily Telegraph*. See Lord Redesdale and Cardinal Manning, *The Infallible Church and Communion under One Kind* (Lane and Son 1875). On 14 June 1877, he condemned a manual entitled *The Priest in Absolution* in the House of Lords. The manual was used privately by clergy of the Society of the Holy Cross, an Anglo-Catholic religious order in the Church of England. See Anon, *The Priest in Absolution: A Manual for Such as are Called unto the Higher Ministries in the English Church* (Joseph Masters 1866); HL Deb 14 June 1877, vol 234, cols 1741–5.
70 W.F. Monypenny and G.E. Buckle (eds), *The Life of Benjamin Disraeli, Earl of Beaconsfield, Volume 6* (The Macmillan Company 1920) 589.
71 William Cornish, 'Law of Persons: Family and Other Relationships' in J. Stuart Anderson, Ray Cocks, Michael Lobban, Patrick Polden, and Keith Smith (eds), *The Oxford History of the Laws of England: Volume XIII* (Oxford University Press 2010) 783.

was the chair, Lord Campbell, who was a considerable figure. He became lord chancellor of Great Britain in 1859, having served variously as a Member of Parliament, solicitor-general, attorney-general, lord chancellor of Ireland, chancellor of the Duchy of Lancaster, and chief justice of the Court of Queen's Bench.[72] He had the experience of sitting on an earlier royal commission on real property.[73] Campbell can also claim some credit as a reformer[74] and some grounding in family disputes, having acted as defence counsel to Lord Melbourne in the Norton case.[75]

Lushington had the greatest experience in matrimonial disputes of any of the commissioners. As an advocate of Doctors' Commons he had appeared in a number of high-profile cases.[76] He successfully advised Lady Byron in her application for judicial separation[77] and was counsel for Queen Caroline.[78] In 1828, Lushington was appointed as a judge in the most important English diocesan court, the London Consistory Court. He sat there for the next three decades. He was also a prominent parliamentary reformer,[79] supporting causes such as the abolition of slavery[80] and Catholic emancipation.[81] His reformist outlook underpinned the majority report of the Campbell Commission.

Some of the other authors of the majority report brought more expertise than others. Baron Beaumont was a writer and later in life commandant of the West York militia.[82] Beaumont had gained some notoriety for surviving a gunshot to his chest in a duel against Major General Lorenzo Moore on Wimbledon Common in 1832.[83] He was not formally trained in law and his role may have been to represent the laity.

Edward Bouverie had practised as a barrister and sat as Member of Parliament for Kilmarnock as a staunch Whig-Liberal.[84] His political stance made him

---

72 For his career see, Gareth Jones and Vivienne Jones, 'Campbell, John, First Baron Campbell of St Andrews (1779–1861),' *Oxford Dictionary of National Biography* (2004) <https://doi.org/10.1093/ref:odnb/4521>; J.B. Atlay, *The Victorian Chancellors, Vol 2* (Smith, Elder & Co 1908) 127–218.
73 *Copy of the First Report made to His Majesty by the Commissioners Appointed to Inquire into the Law of England Respecting Real Property* (1829) BPP vol 10, 263.
74 Notably the Libel Act 1843 (6 & 7 Vict c 96); Fatal Accidents Act 1846 (9 & 10 Vict c 93).
75 Mary Hardcastle (ed), *Life of John, Lord Campbell, Lord High Chancellor of Great Britain, Volume 2* (John Murray 1881) 82–5.
76 For a discussion of the institution, see G.D. Squibb, *Doctors' Commons* (Oxford University Press 1977).
77 Stephen Waddams, *Law, Politics and the Church of England: The Career of Stephen Lushington* (Cambridge University Press 1992) 100–34.
78 *Ibid*. 135–59.
79 He was a Member of Parliament in 1806–8 and 1820–41, with a brief absence in 1830–31.
80 Waddams (n 77) 63–99.
81 *Ibid*. 25.
82 Frederic Boase, *Modern English Biography, Volume I* (Cass 1965) 213.
83 Stephen Banks, *A Polite Exchange of Bullets: The Duel and the English Gentleman, 1750–1850* (Boydell Press 2010) 282.
84 J.P. Parry, *Democracy and Religion: Gladstone and the Liberal Party 1867–1875* (Cambridge University Press 1986) 371.

conducive to supporting divorce law reform. He became under-secretary of state for the Home Department in 1850 and would later become chairman of committees, vice-president of the Board of Trade, president of the Poor Law Board, member of the Council on Education, Church Estate commissioner, and ecclesiastical commissioner.[85] He was the youngest member of the Campbell Commission, aged just 35 at the time of the report's publication in 1853.

Spencer Walpole was a Chancery barrister and served as a Conservative Member of Parliament for Midhurst and later Cambridge University.[86] As a staunch protectionist he had opposed the repeal of the corn laws.[87] He was also a Church commissioner who believed that the Church of England should retain its privileged position. His earlier history did not suggest someone likely to side with the majority,[88] even if he did have a reputation as a man who vacillated in his opinions.[89] However, Walpole's support for the introduction of civil divorce may have been influenced by the affair between his distant cousin, Lord Horatio Walpole (later Fourth Earl of Orford) and Lady Lincoln, Susan Hamilton. The Earl of Lincoln Henry Pelham Fiennes Pelham-Clinton (later Fifth Duke of Newcastle) married Lady Lincoln in 1832.[90] The marriage was an unhappy one. Lady Lincoln had an affair in Italy with Lord Horatio Walpole in 1848 that led to her giving birth to an illegitimate son in 1849.[91] William Gladstone had travelled to Italy in 1849 and found Lady Lincoln to indeed be pregnant.[92] Lord Lincoln obtained a parliamentary divorce from the House of Lords on 14 August 1850.[93] The divorce proceedings were supported by Gladstone's testimony and the efforts of Lord Brougham.[94]

The final member of the majority, William Page Wood (later Lord Hatherley), was variously Member of Parliament for Oxford, vice-chancellor of the County Palatine of Lancaster and would later become solicitor-general and the vice-chancellor of the Chancery Court. Like Campbell he brought his experience of

---

85 G.C. Boase, 'Bouverie, Edward Pleydell (1818–1889),' *Oxford Dictionary of National Biography* (2004) <https://doi.org/10.1093/ref:odnb/3016>.
86 Derek Beales, 'Walpole, Spencer Horatio (1806–1898),' *Oxford Dictionary of National Biography* (2004) <https://doi.org/10.1093/ref:odnb/28604>.
87 *Ibid.*
88 The repeal of the corn laws has been described as 'the central rite of passage of mid-Victorians.' See K. Theodore Hoppen, *The Mid-Victorian Generation 1846–1886* (Oxford University Press 1998) 127. The majority of Conservatives opposed free trade.
89 J.R. Vincent (ed), *Disraeli, Derby and the Conservative Party: Journals and Memoirs of Edward Henry, Lord Stanley, 1849–1869* (Harvester Press 1978) 67.
90 Darrell Munsell, 'Clinton, Henry Pelham Fiennes Pelham-, Fifth Duke of Newcastle under Lyme,' *Oxford Dictionary of National Biography* (2004) <https://doi.org/10.1093/ref:odnb/5686>.
91 J. Gilliland, 'Opdebeck [née Douglas-Hamilton], Lady Susan Harriet Catherine [Other Married Name Susan Harriet Catherine Pelham-Clinton, Countess of Lincoln],' *Oxford Dictionary of National Biography* (2004) <https://doi.org/10.1093/ref:odnb/39436>.
92 Virginia Surtees, *A Beckford Inheritance: The Lady Lincoln Scandal* (Michael Russell 1977) 108–9.
93 House of Lords, *The Sessional Papers* (Vol 44, 1850) 140.
94 Surtees (n 92) 124.

earlier commissions.[95] In 1868, he would become lord chancellor. Wood was a devout high church Anglican, but he was also religiously tolerant. He supported Jewish emancipation and respected Irish disestablishment. In regards to divorce, Wood remarked in 1852,

> divorce for incompatibility of temper ... must follow on their principles. Germany and even Scotland allow it; so Scripture will not be in the way, and many persons (poor people greatly to be pitied, no doubt!) live in adultery because they have such a brute of a husband and cannot get a divorce.[96]

Wood was well aware of the hypocrisy of the existing divorce law. The existing law limited divorce with the ostensible goal of being in line with Christian teaching, yet the inaccessibility of divorce made many live in adulterous relationships *in flagrante delicto* of Christian scripture.

With the exception of the Conservative Walpole, Lord Redesdale, who wrote a dissenting report, and Baron Beaumont, whose affiliations are unknown, the majority were firmly within the Whig political tradition. This tends to suggest that the government of Lord John Russell was intent on reforms, from which it followed that Russell had a certain wariness of the established Church.[97] The backgrounds of the majority commissioners reveal a strong record and a penchant for law reform, though within the majority there were various shades of opinion. Campbell's pragmatic views are summed up by his assertion that, 'What I should like above all things would be to be in the House of Commons; to bring in Bills for the improvement of the law.'[98] The commissioners, like everyone else, were complex in their views. Lushington, for example, is described by his biographer as being 'as conservative in theology as he was radical in politics.'[99] One feature that most shared was that, as politicians, they understood the art of compromise. This may in the end explain why the report attracted support even though there were still battles ahead. The majority supported reform but they also warned:

> The dangerous extremes are, absolute and universal indissolubility on the one hand, which has been found to be productive of a general connivance at infidelity, and consequently of a general dissoluteness of matters, and on the other, a considerable facility of Divorce in cases very difficult to be

---

95 J.A. Hamilton, 'Wood, William Page, Baron Hatherley (1801–1881),' *Oxford Dictionary of National Biography* (2004) <https://doi.org/10.1093/ref:odnb/29901>; Atlay (n 72) 334–76.
96 W.R.W. Stephens (ed.), *A Memoir of the Right Hon. William Page Wood, Baron Hatherley, Volume 2* (Richard Bentley & Son 1883) 127.
97 A.J.P. Taylor, *Essays in English History* (Pelican, 1976) 72. It was the authority of the Church that worried Russell rather than religion *per se*. Russell himself had a 'broad church outlook,' John Prest, *Lord John Russell* (Macmillan 1972) 79.
98 Mary Hardcastle (ed), *Life of John, Lord Campbell, Lord High Chancellor of Great Britain, Volume 1* (John Murray 1881) 465–6.
99 Waddams (n 77) 56.

defined—a practice (to say nothing of other evil consequences) which would be at variance with the institution of marriage.[100]

Majority report

The majority considered four legal issues associated with the introduction of civil divorce:

1. the grounds for divorce;
2. the bars to divorce;
3. the terms and legal consequences of granting divorce; and
4. the judicial procedure for divorce.

The grounds for divorce before 1858 were very narrow. A divorce *a mensa et thoro* would only be granted on proof of adultery or cruelty in the Ecclesiastical Courts.[101] Adultery was seen as 'plainly so gross a violation of the marriage contract' that the innocent party should not be compelled to live with the guilty party.[102] Cruelty was narrowly interpreted but was included as a ground for divorce *a mensa et thoro* in order to protect the innocent party based on the 'duty of self-preservation.'[103] The majority were reluctant to extend the scope of cruelty, because they believed matrimonial life would teach married men and women to become better husbands and wives and to promote the moral order of civil society and the welfare of children.[104]

The majority recommended the inclusion of wilful desertion as a ground for divorce *a mensa et thoro* or an order of alimony for the innocent party if judicial separation could not be granted.[105] This mirrored Scots law, which allowed for the dissolution of marriage after four years of separation.[106] Although the majority supported divorce *a mensa et thoro* on these three grounds, they were unwilling to include further grounds, such as mere dislike, contrariety of temper, severity, neglect or voluntary arrangements. Any further relaxation of the grounds for divorce would, it was said, see a descent into a state of moral corruption similar to what hastened the decline of the Roman Empire and would engender 'the utter subversion not only of manners but of law, morality, reason, and religion, which marked the French Revolution.'[107] Susan Treggiari points out, 'To a Victorian Englishman, the simplicity of divorce in Rome must also have seemed amazing, and sometimes shocking.'[108]

---

100 *First Report of the Commissioners...Into the Law of Divorce* (1852–3) BPP vol 40, 264.
101 Leonard Shelford, *A Practical Treatise of the Law of Marriage and Divorce* (1841) 192.
102 *First Report of the Commissioners...Into the Law of Divorce* (1852–3) BPP vol 40, 264–5.
103 *Ibid.* 265.
104 *Ibid.*
105 *Ibid.* 266–7.
106 (1573) 6 Jac VI c 55.
107 *First Report of the Commissioners...Into the Law of Divorce* (1852–3) BPP vol 40, 266.
108 Susan Treggiari, 'Divorce Roman Style: How Easy and how Frequent Was It?' in Beryl Rawson (ed), *Marriage Divorce and Children in Ancient Rome* (Oxford University Press 1991) 44–5.

52   The enactment of the 1857 Act

The majority accepted the *status quo* that divorce *a vinculo matrimonii* should only be granted in cases of adultery.[109] In reality this was the only ground for a husband to divorce a wife. Wives were never found to be guilty of cruelty or wilful desertion. As was explained, cruelty was the 'tyranny of the husband' and wilful desertion was a means of protecting 'the wife from the wanton abandonment.'[110] In other respects the existing law was disadvantageous to wives. A wife not only had to prove the husband's adultery but also aggravated enormity. The majority sought to preserve the double standard,[111] because they feared granting divorce to the wife for the husband's adultery alone 'would lead to all the evils of voluntary agreement for terminating the union.'[112] The specific concern was that a husband would simply have an extra-marital affair in order to end the marriage.

The second issue concerned the bars to divorce. Divorce petitioners were required to come with clean hands.[113] This was based on a precept of Roman law found in the *Digest of Justinian* (D.48.5.14.5),[114] and it was accepted in the *Reformatio Legum Ecclesiasticarum* (De Adulteriis et Divortiis, s 17).[115] A petitioner's own adultery would bar divorce. If both parties committed adultery, each would be barred from divorce. The majority commissioners recommended retaining the other existing bars to divorce: recrimination, connivance, and condonation.[116] Recrimination referred to a situation where the petitioner effectively brought the marital problem on himself through acts of cruelty or desertion. The majority commissioners recommended the extension of recrimination. Under the existing law in a case like *Reeves v Reeves*, there was no bar on a husband seeking divorce on the ground of the wife's adultery despite his desertion to Ireland.[117] It was recommended that recrimination would be a bar when desertion and cruelty were present because they 'expose a wife to many temptations.'[118] This was later adopted in the Act, where recrimination

---

109   *First Report of the Commissioners...Into the Law of Divorce* (1852–3) BPP vol 40, 267.
110   *Ibid*.
111   See Rebecca Probert, 'The Double Standard of Morality in the Divorce and Matrimonial Causes Act 1857' (1999) 28 *Anglo-American Law Review* 73.
112   *First Report of the Commissioners...Into the Law of Divorce* (1852–3) BPP vol 40, 268.
113   *Ibid*.
114   'A judge [in a case] of adultery ought to keep before his eyes and to inquire into whether the husband by his own chaste life was also setting his wife an example of cultivating sound morals; for it appears the height of injustice that a husband should demand of his wife a purity which he does not show himself; this is something which can condemn the husband also, that the pair of them did not come to an agreement for the balancing out of their mutual offenses.' Alan Watson, Theodor Mommsen, and Paul Krueger (eds), *The Digest of Justinian, Volume 2* (University of Pennsylvania Press 1985) 322.
115   'If the person who has been convicted of adultery is able to prove the same crime against the other marriage partner, and does so before that party has proceeded to a new marriage, the equal guilt of each party shall incur equal punishment, and the former marriage between them shall remain valid.' Gerald Bray (ed), *Tudor Church Reform: The Henrician Canons of 1535 and the Reformatio Legum Ecclesiasticarum* (Boydell Press 2000) 277.
116   *First Report of the Commissioners...Into the Law of Divorce* (1852–3) BPP vol 40, 268–9.
117   (1813) 2 Phill 125.
118   *First Report of the Commissioners...Into the Law of Divorce* (1852–3) BPP vol 40, 269.

was defined as having been committed by a petitioner who, 'of having deserted or wilfully separated himself or herself from the other Party before the Adultery complained of, and without reasonable Excuse, or of such wilful Neglect or Misconduct as has conduced to the Adultery.'[119] Connivance occurred when a petitioner had acted in any manner as accessory to or conniving at the adultery of the other party, such as a husband driving his wife into prostitution. Condonation referred to the petitioner disregarding and failing to actively reprobate the other party's adultery, thereby waiving his or her right to petition for divorce. This did not mean that the petitioner approved the infidelity of the other party, nor did it mean that the petitioner had forgiven the other party. Overall, the issue of bars to divorce was largely uncontroversial.

The third issue facing the Commission concerned the legal consequences of granting divorce. In relation to divorce *a mensa et thoro*, the majority believed maintenance should be granted to the wife in order to secure her financial welfare with the amount to be determined by judicial discretion.[120] Although this recommendation supported the existing principles of alimony, a problem relating to costs had wider implications. In *Belcher v Belcher*, Sir Herbert Jenner of the Arches Court stated, 'Upon general principles the costs of the wife must be defrayed by the husband, who is presumed to possess the whole property.'[121] The presumption did not entirely reflect the reality in which a separated married woman was able to hold her own property. The doctrine of coverture was circumvented by the forming of a contract between the husband and trustees for the wife at the point of immediate separation known as a 'separate estate.'[122] In *Lord St John v Lady St John*, Lord Eldon ruled that maintenance contracts for separated married couples should be indissoluble.[123] The majority of the commissioners, having rejected the *Belcher* presumption, recognised that the wife was entitled to hold property independent of her husband in some circumstances.[124] In the decades before 1882 this was of great symbolic importance.[125]

The final issue was the judicial procedure for divorce, and it was the most radical section of the majority report. With the benefit of hindsight it can be seen as the beginning of the modern family justice system. The report recommended the creation of a secular tribunal to be invested with broad powers to implement family law.[126] This encompassed not only divorce law and matrimonial property, but also the welfare and guardianship of children. Once a married couple divorced, they would be separate legal personalities in relation to each other, and it was envisaged the children of the marriage would become wards of the

---

119 Matrimonial Causes Act 1857 (20 & 21 Vict c 85) s 31.
120 *First Report of the Commissioners...Into the Law of Divorce* (1852–3) BPP vol 40, 269.
121 (1836) 1 Curt 444.
122 Susan Staves, *Married Women's Separate Property in England, 1660–1833* (Harvard University Press 1990) 186.
123 (1805) 11 Ves Jun 525, 530.
124 *First Report of the Commissioners...Into the Law of Divorce* (1852–3) BPP vol 40, 269.
125 Married Women's Property Act 1882 (45 & 46 Vict c 75).
126 *First Report of the Commissioners...Into the Law of Divorce* (1852–3) BPP vol 40, 269–70.

54 *The enactment of the 1857 Act*

court under its absolute control. These recommendations were a reaction to the expense of the existing system: 'The great expense and the long delay of these proceedings is a grievous hardship and oppression to individuals, and they amount in many cases to a denial of justice.'[127] The reform of the legal procedure and judicial system was critical to changing divorce law. It was strongly connected to the abolition of many of the jurisdictions that were held by the Ecclesiastical Courts in the mid-nineteenth century.

Some figures were produced in support of this claim. The cost of divorce *a vinculo matrimonii* was estimated to be £700–800, even in the most favourable circumstances, but could often exceed to £1000 in a highly litigious suit.[128] The expenses included parliamentary costs (£200 alone), counsel and solicitor's fees, and charges for witnesses. Even the cost of applying for divorce *a mensa et thoro* in the London Consistory Courts was expensive, at £120–140, with the process taking about two months for an unopposed suit.[129] If the suit was opposed, then the expenses could be more than double, at £300–500, and it would take between one and three years to be resolved.[130] It was part of a wider problem. The superior courts more generally were expensive for litigants. Even the local courts, like the Court of Conscience and its successor the County Court, whilst much cheaper, were beyond the reach of many.[131]

Wolfram challenges the report's finding that £700 was the total average cost of divorce *a vinculo matrimonii*. She argues that the majority omitted to mention that the costs in a successful criminal conversation case would have been borne by the adulterer, and the damages awarded would have easily paid for the rest of the petitioner's costs in the divorce proceedings.[132] Indeed, this is an important fact that should have been disclosed in the report. Nevertheless, the figure of £700 is an accurate account of gross expenditure, and there are other primary sources that support this. In *A Practical Treatise of the Law of Marriage and Divorce*, Leonard Shelford states:

> It is understood that the expense of a common divorce bill, which has nothing peculiar in it, is between 600*l.* and 700*l.*; the middle and lower ranks of life are therefore for the most part excluded from resorting to this remedy.[133]

In Charles Dickens' *Hard Times*, Mr Bounderby informs the hapless Old Stephen that the total cost of divorce would range 'from a thousand to fifteen hundred

---

127 *Ibid.* 270.
128 *Ibid.*
129 *Ibid.*
130 *Ibid.* 269–70.
131 *Copy of the Fifth Report Made to His Majesty by the Commissioners Appointed to Inquire into the Practice and Proceedings of the Superior Courts of Common Law* (1833) BPP vol 22, 210. There was also some dissatisfaction with the size of fees in the County Court in the 1840s; Patrick Polden, *A History of the County Court 1846–1971* (Cambridge University Press 1999) 52.
132 Wolfram (n 4) 167.
133 Shelford (n 101) 201.

pound' and 'Perhaps twice the money.'[134] Although the costs are exaggerated in order to satirise the divorce process, the criticism of the expense and inaccessibility is made patently clear. In contrast, the Scottish courts solely decided the process of obtaining divorce *a vinculo matrimonii*, where the average cost of divorce in Scotland was £30 in a disputed suit and £20 for an unopposed suit.[135]

In the end the majority of the Campbell Commissioners favoured a new court,[136] since the existing courts were rejected as unsuitable.[137] The legal expertise of a judge was preferred to that of a lay jury, especially in considering the solemn issue of dissolving a marriage. Moreover, juries began to decline by the middle of the nineteenth century.[138] The Courts of Law were rejected, because the calm deliberation of judges was preferred over a jury. Although a common law court without a jury could have been chosen, they were not deemed to be the most appropriate type of court with the necessary expertise for hearing inquisitorial divorce matters. The Privy Council was essentially a final court of appeal that lacked an investigatory capacity that would be necessary for conducting divorce trials. Although the Ecclesiastical Courts already held jurisdiction over divorce *a mensa et thoro*, their matrimonial jurisdiction was in the process of being abolished. The majority seriously doubted the ability of the Ecclesiastical Courts to satisfactorily exercise jurisdiction over divorce *a vinculo matrimonii*. The majority held the Court of Chancery in esteem, but it was notoriously slow and inefficient.[139] Furthermore, the majority thought a single judge should not preside over the entire decision of granting divorce *a vinculo matrimonii*. Therefore, the majority commissioners recommended the appointment of three judges on the new divorce court comprised of a Chancery judge, a common law judge, and an Ecclesiastical Courts judge. The aim was to establish a divorce court with the principles of equitable jurisprudence, the knowledge of civil and common law, and the expertise of gathering evidence. A jury would only be called at the discretion of the court if it requested assistance in deciding questions of fact.[140] The divorce court was expected to exercise an inquisitorial role and hear applications for both divorce *a mensa et thoro* and divorce *a vinculo matrimonii*. The House of Lords was recommended as the final court of appeal.

Two miscellaneous issues were considered at the end of the report.[141] First, the majority supported allowing the guilty party in a divorce *a vinculo matrimonii*

---

134 Charles Dickens, *Hard Times* (first published 1854, Penguin 1995) 76.
135 *First Report of the Commissioners...Into the Law of Divorce* (1852–3) BPP vol 40, 325.
136 *Ibid.* 271.
137 *Ibid.* 272.
138 Joshua Getzler, 'The Fate of the Civil Jury in Late Victorian England' in John Cairns and Grant McLeod (eds), *The Dearest Birth Right of the People of England* (Hart Publishing 2002) 220–1.
139 Patrick Polden, 'The Court of Chancery, 1820–1875' in William Cornish, J. Stuart Anderson, Ray Cocks, Michael Lobban, Patrick Polden, and Keith Smith (eds), *The Oxford History of the Laws of England: Volume XI 1820–1914: English Legal System* (Oxford University Press 2010) 668.
140 Matrimonial Causes Act 1857, s 28.
141 *First Report of the Commissioners...Into the Law of Divorce* (1852–3) BPP vol 40, 273.

a right to remarry. Past experience demonstrated the difficulties of imposing a bar of marriage on the guilty party in private Acts of Parliament. In the House of Lords debate on Sir William Abdy's divorce bill, the clause to prevent Lady Abdy from remarrying was comfortably defeated without the need to call for division.[142] Second, the majority highlighted the anomalies associated with the conflicts of law between English and Scots divorce. In *Warrender v Warrender*, the House of Lords refused to recognise divorces granted by Scottish courts or indeed any foreign jurisdiction for marriages contracted in England.[143] The case was an appeal from the Court of Sessions. The appeal concerned the jurisdiction of Scottish courts to hear cases of divorce involving marriages contacted in England. A Scottish man married an English woman in England, and they lived in Scotland before returning to England. The marriage broke down, the parties secured a separate maintenance contract, and the wife left for France. It was during this time the husband accused her of committing adultery, and sought a divorce in Scotland. The problem associated with the House of Lords' decision not to recognise foreign divorce was the possible dilemma of an Englishman being legally married to two women concurrently. Lord Lyndhurst states:

> As the laws of both now stand, it would appear that Sir George Warrender may have two wives; for having been divorced in Scotland, he may marry again in that country; he may live with one wife in Scotland most lawfully, and with the other equally lawfully in England; but only bring him across the border, his English wife may proceed against him in the English courts ... again, send him to Scotland, and his Scottish wife may proceed, in the Courts in Scotland, for breach of the marriage contract entered into with her in that country.[144]

The English courts consistently refused to provide legal recognition of foreign divorces involving marriages contracted in England. This followed the principle of *lex loci contractus* in contracts law.[145] In *R v Lolley*, William Lolley unsuccessfully appealed his conviction for bigamy in the Court of Chancery from the Lancashire Assizes.[146] William and Anne Lolley were both domiciled and married in England, but later moved to Scotland for the manifest purpose of procuring a divorce under Scots law. Once the Consistorial Court of Scotland granted divorce, William returned to England and married an English woman, and was subsequently prosecuted for bigamy. Serjeants' Inn Hall upheld the defendant's bigamy conviction and ruled 'that no sentence or Act of any foreign country or state could dissolve an English marriage *a vinculo matrimonii*, for ground on

---

142 HL Deb 7 June 1816, vol 34, cols 1017–18.
143 (1835) 2 Cl & Fin 488.
144 *Warrender v Warrender* (1835) 2 Cl & Fin 488, 560.
145 Lord Mansfield states, 'I admit that there are many cases where the law of the place of the transaction shall be the rule.' *Robinson v Bland* (1760) 2 Burr 1077, 1079.
146 (1812) Russ & Ry 237.

which it was not liable to be dissolved *a vinculo matrimonii* in England.'[147] Lord Brougham was one of the judges who heard the *Warrender* case, but earlier in his career he had represented Mr Lolley. It is worth noting that Lord Brougham was at pains to mention that 'Whatever opinion I may have entertained of Lolley's case in the Court of Chancery, or privately, cannot affect my judicial opinion in this House, sitting as a member of a Court of Appeal on a case from Scotland.'[148] It would appear that Lord Brougham may not have been comfortable with the strictness of divorce law, but felt constrained by precedent to act otherwise.

This legal principle was affirmed in the case of *M'Carthy v DeCaix*.[149] The issue was whether the Danish divorce of a marriage contracted in England between a Danish man and an English woman with the parties both domiciled in Denmark should be recognised under English law. Lord Brougham declared the divorce void, and ruled that no foreign divorce could operate to dissolve or affect a marriage contracted in England.[150] The majority commissioners felt it necessary to acknowledge the conflict of law problem, but tactfully declined to provide a solution, believing it was beyond the scope of the Campbell Commission.

The majority report reflects a tension between change and continuity. The call for a new secular system of family justice was a significant change. The call for legal change was offset by the fact that the new court would follow ecclesiastical principles and precedents. Stephen Cretney argues that the Campbell Commission sought to achieve a modern and secular procedure for divorce by abolishing the matrimonial jurisdiction of the Ecclesiastical Courts, but he rejects the suggestion that the Commission initiated a legal revolution as the basic principles of the existing divorce law remained.[151] The Matrimonial Causes Act 1857 codified many of the existing grounds and bars to divorce. However, to only consider the codification of the existing law as a procedural process misses the point of the wider implications of the reform. The Act represented an ideological shift that dispelled any notions of marriage being indissoluble. It was the first step in making divorce acceptable to the wider population. Moreover, the abolition of the matrimonial disputes jurisdiction of the Ecclesiastical Courts was the last rites for Doctors' Commons, and in its place the birth of the modern family justice system.

Shanley also displays reticence in recognising the significance of the Matrimonial Causes Act 1857. She argues that Parliament's continued acceptance of a double standard between the genders for divorce *a vinculo matrimonii* reflects 'their ardent desire to change the traditional law of marriage, and the traditional status of married women, as little as possible.'[152] This perpetuates the misunderstanding that the Act was solely about continuity. It ignores the

---

147 *Ibid.* 239.
148 *Warrender v Warrender* (1835) 2 Cl & Fin 488, 567.
149 (1831) 2 Russ & My 614.
150 *M'Carthy v DeCaix* (1831) 2 Russ & My 614.
151 Stephen Cretney, *Family Law in the Twentieth Century* (Oxford University Press 2003) 162–3.
152 Shanley (n 36) 44.

significant changes recommended in the majority report that were in fact rather revolutionary beyond the issue of gender. The cessation of the tripartite process of divorce that was notorious for its expensiveness and inefficiency led to a significantly simpler, cheaper, and more accessible process of applying for divorce. Most importantly, the law created a change in the perception of divorce. It was once a remedy that was seldom granted in order to preserve the façade that marriage was indissoluble. The Act transformed marriage as a civil contract dissolvable for breach to the matrimonial bonds, albeit on limited grounds.

Minority report

Lord Redesdale objected to the majority's recommendation for the introduction of civil divorce on religious, moral, and social grounds. He argued that the dissolution of marriage was contrary to scripture. In the report he paraphrases Jesus Christ's teaching in the Gospel of Mark, 'which declare man and wife to be one flesh, and that man may not put asunder those whom God has joined together.'[153] According to the Gospel of Matthew, Jesus Christ states, 'I tell you that anyone who divorces his wife, except for sexual immorality, and marries another woman commits adultery.'[154] Based on this passage, Redesdale was initially in favour of allowing divorce *a vinculo matrimonii* and remarriage for the husband in the case of the wife being found guilty of adultery, but he later changed his position.[155] In his report he argues that an apostolic injunction against divorce exists in the Bible.[156]

Lord Redesdale cites St Paul's First Epistle to the Corinthians.

> To the married I give this command (not I, but the Lord): A wife must not separate from her husband. But if she does, she must remain unmarried or else be reconciled to her husband. And a husband must not divorce his wife.[157]

This text is an instruction directed towards Christians. It can be distinguished from the Pauline privilege, which allows a Christian convert to divorce his or her non-Christian spouse if he or she leaves the marriage.[158] Despite the introduction of secular marriage under the Marriage Act 1836, most of the English

---

153 See Mark 10:1–12. *First Report of the Commissioners…Into the Law of Divorce* (1852–3) BPP vol 40, 275.
154 Matthew 19:9.
155 *First Report of the Commissioners…Into the Law of Divorce* (1852–3) BPP vol 40, 275. Lord Redesdale once helped his friend obtain a divorce before changing his position on divorce while serving on the Campbell Commission. Lord Redesdale, *The Law of Scripture against Divorce* (Rivingtons 1856) 5.
156 *First Report of the Commissioners…Into the Law of Divorce* (1852–3) BPP vol 40, 275.
157 1 Corinthians 7:10–11.
158 1 Corinthians 7:12–15.

population were outwardly Christian in the Victorian period.[159] Christian wedding ceremonies were overwhelmingly favoured.[160] Redesdale believed that English law should follow scripture and this included outlawing divorce *a vinculo matrimonii*. He contended, 'that if a woman is guilty of adultery the husband is justified in putting her away from him, but that the marriage nevertheless remains indissoluble.'[161] This meant that whilst Redesdale supported judicial separation or divorce *a mensa et thoro*, he opposed divorce *a vinculo matrimonii* outright. On this view, a judicially separated couple were still legally married and neither was free to remarry. Crucially, Redesdale adopted a literal hermeneutic approach towards scripture. This form of theology was associated with conservative elements in the Church of England during the nineteenth century. It is based on the belief that the word of God is found within the holy writ of scripture.[162] It led Redesdale to argue that Jesus Christ abrogated the Mosaic law of divorce.[163] This gave precedence to Pauline teaching without reconciling the nuances of Jesus Christ's teaching on divorce found in the various accounts of the synoptic gospels.[164] Redesdale's conservative religious views also reflected his broader moral stance.

The majority expressed concern about the consequences of extending divorce. Redesdale went further when he suggested that civil divorce would lead to moral degradation, with many couples seeking divorce over reconciliation.[165] He believed that keeping divorce inaccessible protected the middle and lower classes from the harmful consequences, and sincerely doubted whether the wealthy had benefited from access to divorce.[166] Redesdale even went as far as to suggest that the publicity given to divorce *a vinculo martimonii* cases presented an indecorous image of English society at home and abroad, and gave the false impression that divorce was a more frequent occurrence than it actually was. Moreover, he argued that denying divorce to married couples was 'beneficial both to their morals and happiness.'[167] He claimed that the majority of remarriages were disastrous, and those separated couples who decided against remarriage have prudently avoided 'many of the evils attendant on them.'[168]

---

159 For a discussion of the place of religion in the mid-nineteenth century, see K. Theodore Hoppen, *The Mid-Victorian Generation 1846–1886* (Oxford University Press 1998) 427–71; Owen Chadwick, *The Victorian Church, Part II* (Adam and Charles Black 1970) 466–72.
160 In 1844, there were 120,009 Church of England weddings, 6,284 non-conformist weddings, 2,280 Roman Catholic weddings, 175 Jewish weddings, 55 Quaker weddings, and only 3,446 civil weddings; *Tenth Annual Report of the Registrar-General of Births, Deaths and Marriages in England* (Longman, Brown, Green, and Longmans 1852) iv.
161 *First Report of the Commissioners...Into the Law of Divorce* (1852–3) BPP vol 40, 275.
162 Adshead, Samuel Adrian Miles, *Philosophy of Religion in Nineteenth-Century England and Beyond* (Macmillan Press 2000) 68.
163 See Deuteronomy 24:1–4.
164 See Mark 10:1–12, Luke 16:16–18, Matthew 5:31–32, and Matthew 19:1–9.
165 *First Report of the Commissioners...Into the Law of Divorce* (1852–3) BPP vol 40, 276–8.
166 *Ibid*. 276.
167 *Ibid*. 277.
168 *Ibid*.

Redesdale concluded by calling for marriage to continue to be an indissoluble union, but also went further. He wanted the abolition of parliamentary divorces *a vinculo matrimonii*. The one thing he shared with the majority was the view that a new divorce court was needed, but he thought it should only be able to grant divorce *a mensa et thoro*.[169] In 1856, he published a pamphlet, *The Law of Scripture against Divorce*,[170] and in Parliament over the coming years steadfastly opposed the Matrimonial Causes Act 1857.

The initial failed attempts to introduce divorce law reform

On 13 June 1854, Lord Cranworth, as lord chancellor, introduced the matrimonial causes bill for the first time in the House of Lords, as a result of the recommendations of the Campbell Commission.[171] The bill was rather modest and proposed merely a procedural change. Lord Brougham summarised the aims of the bill.

> The two great objects of the measure must meet with universal approval—namely, the transference from the Ecclesiastical Courts of matrimonial causes, and the transference from Parliament of the function of dissolving marriages a vinculo.[172]

This included transferring jurisdiction of divorce *a mensa et thoro* to the Court of Chancery.[173] For cases of divorce *a vinculo matrimonii*, Cranworth proposed the creation of a new divorce court comprised of five judges, including the lord chancellor, the lord chief justice of the Court of Queen's Bench, the master of the rolls, and two learned civilians.[174] The suit of criminal conversation was to be retained in the Court of Common Pleas and the Court of Queen's Bench, but the action would only be allowed to proceed after a judicial separation or a divorce.[175] The bill allowed adultery of the wife alone to be a sufficient ground for the husband to divorce *a vinculo matrimonii*, but a wife would have to prove both adultery of the husband and aggravated enormity.[176] Cranworth attempted to justify the double standard by arguing that divorce would be too easily attainable for the husband 'by merely being a little profligate.'[177] Caroline found this

---

169 *Ibid.*
170 Lord Redesdale (n 155).
171 HL Deb 13 June 1854, vol 134, col 5.
172 *Ibid.* col 14.
173 *Ibid.* col 10.
174 *Ibid.* cols 8–9.
175 *Ibid.* col 23.
176 *Ibid.* col 7. Aggravated enormity referred to matrimonial offences other than adultery, including incest (*Turton v Turton* (1830) 3 Hag Ecc 338), bigamy (Ann Battersby 1840 (3 & 4 Vict c 48); Georgina Hall 1850 (3 & 14 Vict c 25)), and cruelty (*Evans v Evans* (1790) 1 Hag Con 35).
177 HL Deb 13 June 1854, vol 134, col 7.

comment 'blinded by strong prejudice,'[178] and it was also rebuked in the press.[179] Although Caroline supported the introduction of civil divorce in *A Letter to the Queen*, she was outraged by the bill's double standard.[180]

Cranworth's bill faced some opposition in the House of Lords from both sides of the debate. Lord Lyndhurst was so persuaded by *A Letter to the Queen* that he argued for the removal of the double standard, albeit unsuccessfully, in the 1857 parliamentary debates.[181] Lord St Leonards expressed his disappointment towards the bill for not going far enough, particularly the bill's failure to reconcile with the conflicting Scottish divorce law and for not abolishing criminal conversation, 'which was a disgrace to the country and civilisation.'[182] However, Lord Redesdale argued that there was no popular support for the introduction of the bill, and was concerned about the decline of moral standards if divorce was extended more easily to the poor.[183] Eventually, Cranworth withdrew the bill with the plan of later re-introducing the divorce law reform in tandem with a bill proposing to transfer jurisdiction of the probate of wills from the Ecclesiastical Courts to the Court of Chancery.[184] The reform of divorce and probate both required transferring jurisdiction away from the Ecclesiastical Courts. Therefore, it was more expedient to pass two significant pieces of legislation in a single package of law reforms in order to debate the common issue of reforming the Ecclesiastical Courts.

On 20 May 1856, Lord Cranworth introduced a divorce bill into the House of Lords for a second time.[185] During the same debate, Lord Lyndhurst put a motion to establish a select committee of the House of Lords on the divorce bill, which he later chaired.[186] This would prove to be a clever move on the part of those who wanted reform. The committee of 17 members met five times.[187] There were three distinct factions: the radicals, the conservatives, and the government. The radicals included Lord Lyndhurst, Lord St Leonards, Lord Somerhill, Lord Wyndford, and the Marquees of Lansdowne. These men supported the introduction of civil divorce and the removal of the double standards in the grounds of divorce. The conservatives included Lord Redesdale and Bishop of Oxford Samuel Wilberforce, who was nicknamed 'Soapy Sam' and best known as an opponent of Charles Darwin's theories of evolution. Wilberforce wrote

---

178 Caroline Norton, *A Letter to the Queen on Lord Chancellor Cranworth's Marriage and Divorce Bill* (Longman, Brown, Green, and Longmans 1855) 35.
179 *The Times* described Lord Cranwroth's comment as an 'unfortunate phrase.' 'The Law of Divorce,' *The Times* (London, 27 January 1857) 4.
180 Norton (n 178) 16–24.
181 Dolin (n 15) 125.
182 HL Deb 13 June 1854, vol 134, col 23.
183 *Ibid*. col 20.
184 HL Deb 10 July 1854, vol 134, col 1036.
185 HL Deb 20 May 1856, vol 142, col 401.
186 *Ibid*. cols 408–10.
187 Dorothy Stetson, *A Woman's Issue: the Politics of Family Law Reform in England* (Greenwood Press 1982) 46.

a letter to William Gladstone expressing their mutually shared belief as to 'the wickedness and destructiveness of the divorce bill.'[188] The idea of the Church marrying divorced persons was intolerable to Wilberforce as he believed this put the teachings of the Church in opposition to the law of the state.[189] These men believed that divorce was against the teachings of scripture. Lord Cranworth and Lord Campbell represented the government, and attempted to pass legislation that was seen to be an acceptable compromise.

The committee published its findings a month later. First, the committee recommended that a new tribunal to decide divorce *a vinculo matrimonii* cases should be comprised of five judges: the lord chancellor, the three chief judges of the Courts of Common Law, and the Dean of Arches. The House of Lords would hear appeals in regards to questions of law only, but not questions in respect to matters of fact.[190] Although the original bill proposed that the divorce court should consist of the lord chancellor, the lord chief justice of the Court of Queen's Bench, and a judge from the Ecclesiastical Courts, there was no fundamental difference compared with the committee's recommendation. Second, the committee unanimously decided that a separated wife who had divorced *a mensa et thoro* should be allowed to exercise control of her earnings and property, and enter into legally binding contracts as though she was *feme sole*.[191] Third, the Committee recommended extending the grounds of divorce for the wife beyond the proposal in the bill of adultery accompanied by incest to include adultery accompanied by cruelty, bigamy, or wilful desertion for four years.[192]

The radicals failed to gain support for all their demands. The select committee rejected Lyndhurst's proposal to abolish suits of criminal conversation.[193] Although Lyndhurst was frustrated that he could not convince his colleagues to allow wives to divorce on the ground of adultery alone, he accepted the compromise.[194] The opponents of change, Bishop Wilberforce and Lord Redesdale, were also disappointed and once more argued that making divorce accessible to the poor would erode the sanctity of marriage and social order.[195] For the government, Lord Cranworth was generally supportive of the committee's recommendations, but thought abolishing suits of criminal conversation would help divorce cases to be judged on their own merits and believed the topic of *feme sole* should be supported in a separate bill.[196] Lord Campbell agreed with the proposal to extend the grounds of divorce for wives, but thought that it

---

188 Reginald Wilberforce (ed), *Life of Samuel Wilberforce, with Selections from his Diary and Correspondence* (John Murray 1881) 345.
189 Standish Meacham, *Lord Bishop: The Life of Samuel Wilberforce* (Harvard University Press 1970) 262.
190 HL Deb 26 June 1856, vol 142, col 1968.
191 *Ibid.* col 1969.
192 *Ibid.* col 1976.
193 *Ibid.* cols 1971–2.
194 *Ibid.* col 1972.
195 *Ibid.* cols 1979–84.
196 *Ibid.* cols 1975–7.

was wrong to allow wives to be granted divorce for adultery alone.[197] Cretney summarises the view, held by many at the time, 'that making the divorce process more "efficient" could also be seen as making divorce "easier," and inevitably increasing the appetite for divorce and threatening the stability of family life.'[198] The House of Lords accepted the select committee's amendments.[199] The recommendations of the committee introduced important changes that shaped the character of the final 1857 Act, but opponents of reform were still a long way from giving up. Wolfram states, 'The reform was presented as purely procedural.'[200] This may have been the initial intention of the Palmerston government.[201] However, the introduction of the *feme sole* provision and the expansion of the grounds of divorce for wives made the divorce bill a more substantive measure of law reform.

The passage of the divorce bill

On 19 May 1857, Cranworth introduced the bill for a third time to its Second Reading debate in the House of Lords with the aim of 'improving the law of divorce, and of establishing on a rational footing what should be done when, unhappily, circumstances arose which naturally and justly led to a dissolution of the marriage tie.'[202] The Palmerston government was determined to get the divorce bill passed after so many years of delay as part of its domestic law reform. Allen Horstman argues that Viscount Palmerston was particularly eager to pass the divorce bill to demonstrate his political power after winning a large parliamentary majority in the election of March 1857.[203] After all, passing the bill eventually helped to further improve the reputation of the government.[204] The Palmerston government's objectives were relatively benign, with the goal of creating a new divorce court and simplifying the administrative process of applying for divorce. The government decided, perhaps wisely, given its removal would be so controversial, to retain the double standard provision in divorce. In part the retention of the double standard can be put down to political expediency. It was not even much of a gamble given the relative insignificance of those who wanted it to be abolished when set against those who opposed change.[205] Even someone like Jeremy Bentham, who held a series of radical views on marriage, thought that men and women should be treated differently.[206]

197 *Ibid.* col 1978.
198 Cretney (n 151) 163.
199 HL Deb 26 June 1856, vol 142, col 1987.
200 Wolfram (n 4) 178.
201 HL Deb 20 May 1856, vol 142, col 404.
202 HL Deb 19 May 1857, vol 145, col 494.
203 Allen Horstman, *Victorian Divorce* (St Martin's Press 1985) 77.
204 'The Divorce Bill offers one of those occasional instances in which a large majority furnishes the best answer to ingenious and plausible arguments.' *The Times* (London, 4 August 1857) 7.
205 Probert (n 111).
206 Mary Sokol, *Bentham, Law and Marriage* (Continuum International Publishing Group 2011) 126–7.

64 The enactment of the 1857 Act

The double standard may also have reflected wider and real concerns about the security of dynastic landholding, which remained an important, albeit declining, feature of nineteenth-century society.[207] The risk of women producing illegitimate children was seen to represent a threat to the orderly succession of property and justified the inclusion of the double standard. The majority of the Campbell Commission had pointed out that the effects of a wife's adultery were different in that they risked the legitimacy of the husband's offspring.[208] These factors probably do not tell the whole story. Victorian sexual morality was ever-present in these debates.[209] The Campbell Commission itself had suggested that wives could be expected to forgive a straying husband, otherwise divorce would be too readily available.[210]

Alongside these attempts at compromise, there was also fierce resistance to the introduction of civil divorce. Gladstone led the political opposition. His biographer has described Gladstone as 'a little unhinged on anything to do with the institution of marriage. Its disciplines had to be preserved at all costs.'[211] He was particularly sensitive to changing the law of divorce, because of his strong Christian belief that marriage is a divine institution governed by a spiritual rather than a temporal authority.[212] The topic of divorce provoked a strong reactionary response in Gladstone that may have been seen as hypocritical given his conspicuous support for Lord Lincoln's divorce in 1850.[213] The English prelate Henry Edward Manning seemed to have played a role in influencing Gladstone's position on divorce. According to their correspondences in 1849, Manning upheld the indissolubility of marriage, but in even stronger terms condemned remarriage.[214] In response to questions on divorce in 1889, more than three decades after the introduction of civil divorce in England, Gladstone held steadfast to the view that marriage was something unique: 'The parental and conjugal relations are joined together by the hand of the Almighty no less than the persons united by the marriage tie to another.'[215]

Church of England clergy largely opposed the change. During the debates of 1857, the Bishop of Oxford led thousands of Church of England clergymen

---

207 F.M.L. Thompson, *English Landed Society in the Nineteenth Century* (Routledge and Keegan Paul 1971).
208 *First Report of the Commissioners...Into the Law of Divorce* (1852–3) BPP vol 40, 267.
209 For an account which looks at some of the realities behind the stereotypes, see Michael Mason, *The Making of Victorian Sexuality* (Oxford University Press 1994).
210 *First Report of the Commissioners...Into the Law of Divorce* (1852–3) BPP vol 40, 268.
211 Roy Jenkins, *Gladstone* (Random House 1997) 184.
212 David Bebbington, *The Mind of Gladstone: Religion, Homer, and Politics* (Oxford University Press 2004) 140.
213 Richard Shannon, *Gladstone, Volume 1* (Hamish Hamilton 1982) 343–4.
214 Peter C. Erb (ed), *The Correspondence of Henry Edward Manning and William Ewart Gladstone, Volume 2: 1844–1853* (Oxford University Press 2013) 290–1. Henry Edward Manning was Archdeacon of Chichester in the Church of England at the time of the Lincoln case. He was ordained in the Roman Catholic Church in 1851.
215 D.C. Lathbury (ed), *Correspondence on Church and Religion of William Ewart Gladstone, Volume 2* (The Macmillan Company 1910) 361–2.

to sign a petition against the bill.[216] Other senior clergy were less resistant to change. John Bird Sumner, the Archbishop of Canterbury, supported the idea of allowing a husband to divorce his wife on the ground of adultery.[217] He justified this position based on an exception to the indissolubility of marriage in Matthew 19:9.[218] Non-conformist denominations adopted the Lutheran and Calvinist views of marriage as a dissolvable civil contract.[219] There was some opposition to reform from ordinary people. A petition signed by 16,000 women from all backgrounds was presented to the queen opposing the expansion of the grounds for divorce and separation.[220] If the divorce bill was passed, some wives feared their husbands would leave them abandoned and destitute. A further petition against the bill gained 90,000 signatures.[221]

Three major issues arose in the parliamentary debate on the divorce bill: the process of divorce, the grounds for divorce, and the bars to remarriage. Parliament sought a legal overhaul of the existing tripartite process of divorce. First, criminal conversation was abolished[222] and replaced with statutory damages.[223] Criminal conversation suits were seen as a national embarrassment.[224] Lord Lyndhurst called for their complete abolition. Others wanted to substitute an alternative which would act as a punishment for adultery.[225] The House of Lords approved a clause criminalising adultery with a married woman as a misdemeanour punishable by a pecuniary penalty, but this was initially rejected in the House of Commons.[226] After a long debate, the House of Commons, led by Attorney-General Sir Richard Bethel, amended the bill to incorporate statutory damages.[227] The amendment allowed a husband to recover statutory damages against the

---

216 The number of signatures is disputed. Joseph Henley claimed 6,000 clergymen signed the petitions; HC Deb 24 July 1857, vol 147, col 380. Gladstone claimed there were 10,000 signatures, while Samuel Warren claimed 9,000 signatures; HC Deb 4 August 1857, vol 147, col 1028.
217 HL Deb 19 May 1857, vol 145, cols 494–6; Nigel Scotland, *John Bird Sumner: Evangelical Archbishop* (Gracewing 1995) 70.
218 Nigel Scotland, 'John Bird Sumner in Parliament' (1990) 7(2) *Anvil* 141, 147.
219 Max Rheinstein, *Marriage Stability, Divorce and the Law* (University of Chicago Press 1972) 22–3.
220 HC Deb 4 August 1857, vol 147, col 1031.
221 HC Deb 30 July 1857, vol 147, col 758; HC Deb 31 July 1857, vol 147, col 870.
222 Matrimonial Causes Act 1857, s 59.
223 Matrimonial Causes Act 1857, s 33.
224 Attorney-General Sir Richard Bethel describes the action for criminal conversation as 'that most abominable proceeding ... had been held to be a great reproach to this country'; HC Deb 30 July 1857, vol 147, col 723. See Anon, 'The English Law of Divorce' (1856) 65(128) *Westminster Review* 338, 339.
225 Lord Campbell 'was impatient to see the action for criminal conversation abolished; but he should not like to see it abolished without some substitute, for otherwise that would be a state of things which would operate as an encouragement to adultery': HL Deb 25 May 1857, vol 145, col 830. Likewise, Isaac Butt states, 'The action for criminal conversation had been the scourge of adultery, and he thought that very few persons would be willing to abolish this action without some substitute being provided for it': HC Deb 18 August 1857, vol 147, col 1833.
226 HC Deb 18 August 1857, vol 147, col 1836.
227 HC Deb 21 August 1857, vol 147, col 1978.

wife's alleged adulterer in the proposed new Court for Divorce and Matrimonial Causes.[228] The trial was to be conducted according to the rules and regulations of the common law courts, which meant using a jury. An adulterer would be required to pay damages to the court to be held under a constructive trust. The presiding judge had discretion in the distribution of the damages for the welfare of children, the alimony for the wife, and the reparations for the husband. Suing the wife's alleged adulterer was no longer necessary in order to be granted a divorce. This was a significant change, which simplified the process of divorce and reduced costs.

Second, the Ecclesiastical Courts' jurisdiction over cases of divorce *a mensa et thoro* was abolished,[229] to be replaced with decrees of judicial separation under the jurisdiction of the proposed Court for Divorce and Matrimonial Causes and the Assizes.[230] Thereafter, divorce *a mensa et thoro* became officially referred to as 'judicial separation.' The transfer of jurisdiction effectively stripped the declining Ecclesiastical Courts of their last remaining jurisdiction over matrimonial disputes. Lawyers on all sides recognised that the existing ecclesiastical system of justice was problematic and had to change.[231] Some members of the House of Lords remained hostile to increasing access to judicial separation to the poorer classes,[232] and questioned the ability of the Assizes to adjudicate judicial separation and restitution of conjugal rights cases.[233] In the House of Commons there was more support for transferring jurisdiction relating to judicial separation to the Assizes, in the belief that it would facilitate greater ease of access to this remedy for the poorer classes.[234] The Assizes were seen as a suitable forum for judicial separation cases, since the court already had experience dealing with the (now to be abolished) suits for criminal conversation.

Whilst a judicial separation was no longer a prerequisite to a divorce, it continued to have significant legal consequences. A judicial separation allowed a wife to be granted the property rights of *feme sole*.[235] This came about as a result of an amendment by Lord St Leonards that aimed to protect the income and property rights of a wife from an 'unworthy husband.'[236] Earlier the same year Lord Brougham had introduced the first married women's property bill into the House of Lords to grant married women the rights of *feme sole*.[237] St Leonards' amendment was a compromise between the existing position and the full-blown

---

228 Matrimonial Causes Act 1857, s 33.
229 HL Deb 24 August 1857, vol 147, cols 2014–16, 2027–30; Matrimonial Causes Act 1857, ss 2, 7.
230 Matrimonial Causes Act 1857, ss 17, 18.
231 Outhwaite (n 1) 166.
232 HL Deb 19 May 1857, vol 145, 508–9, col 527.
233 HL Deb 24 August 1857, vol 147, col 2015.
234 HC Deb 7 August 1857, vol 147, cols 1242–67.
235 Matrimonial Causes Act 1857, ss 25 and 26.
236 HL Deb 25 May 1857, vol 147, col 800.
237 HL Deb 3 February 1857, vol 144, cols 605–19. And, in the House of Commons later the same year, HC Deb 14 May 1857, vol 145, cols 266–81.

The enactment of the 1857 Act 67

abolition of coverture in that it allowed separated married women to legally enter into contracts in their own name, create their own separate wills, and keep their own earnings.[238]

The government introduced the amendment not as an ideologically driven manoeuvre to preserve male dominance at the expense of women's rights, as previously claimed.[239] Rather, the amendment was introduced as a middle way in response to the bill introduced by Sir Erskine Perry and supported by Richard Monckton Milnes three months after Lord Brougham's bill.[240] Perry's bill proposed to remedy the perceived financial exploitation of married women found in the legal fiction of coverture by giving all women the right of *feme sole*.[241] Lord St Leonards sensed that the bill would be a highly divisive issue. The proposal undermined the longstanding doctrine of coverture by disrupting the traditional gender roles of male headship and female submission.[242] The bill was rather radical and no one in Parliament, including probably Perry himself, actually believed it would pass, but it was rather used as a political strategy to obtain more concessions on married women's property rights by drawing more publicity on this issue.[243] Therefore, Lord St Leonards successfully persuaded his colleagues to support his amendment to the divorce bill that provided the rights of *feme sole* to separated married women whilst avoiding the potentially divisive issue of coverture.[244]

Lawrence Stone argues that there was a sense of irony in the success of Lord St Leonards' proposal, because it may have inadvertently curtailed the extension of this right to all women irrespective of marital status.[245] Indeed, it would take another quarter of a century before the doctrine of coverture was completely eliminated by the Married Women's Property Act 1882. According to Hansard, Lord St Leonards described the bill that called for an extension of *feme sole* to all married women as a 'mischievous one,' and believed that his amendment was measured, 'going as far as was desirable, and so prevent a greater evil.'[246] There is some dispute as to whether Lord St Leonards actually described the bill in this way as none of the shorthand writers in the Lords gallery recorded hearing this.[247] Nevertheless, Lord St Leonards' bill was a response to the recent political exigencies that were raised in Perry's bill, introduced 11 days prior.

---

238 HL Deb 25 May 1857, vol 145, cols 806–8; Matrimonial Causes Act 1857, s 26.
239 Lee Holcombe, *Wives and Property: Reform of the Married Women's Property Law in Nineteenth-Century England* (University of Toronto Press 1983) 102; Poovey (n 39) 78–9; Shanley (n 36) 46–7.
240 Olive Anderson, 'Hansard's Hazards: An Illustration from Recent Interpretations of Married Women's Property Law and the 1857 Divorce Act' (1997) 112(449) *English Historical Review* 1202, 1209.
241 HC Deb 14 May 1857, vol 145, cols 266–81.
242 HL Deb, 25 May 1857, vol 145, col 800.
243 Anderson (n 240) 1211–12.
244 HL Deb 25 May 1857, vol 145, cols 806–8.
245 Lawrence Stone, *Road to Divorce: England 1530–1987* (Oxford University Press 1995) 376.
246 HL Deb, 25 May 1857, vol 145, col 800.
247 Anderson (n 240) 1211.

Furthermore, the grounds for judicial separation were equal for either spouse, and included the existing grounds of adultery and cruelty with the addition of wilful desertion without cause for two years.[248] This was the same as the new grounds of divorce *a vinculo matrimonii* but without the double standard. Although in hindsight judicial separation would be a stepping stone for the later reform, this further illustrates the extent to which the present legislation was built on compromise.

Third, the jurisdiction of divorce *a vinculo matrimonii* was transferred from the House of Lords to the Court for Divorce and Matrimonial Causes.[249] The Court was vested with the power to hear cases involving divorce, nullity of marriage, restitution of conjugal rights, jactitation of marriage, and all other matrimonial matters. The main aim of the government in its pursuit to reform the procedure of divorce law was the creation of a new divorce court. In Cranworth's Second Reading speech in 1857, he outlined the reasons for the changes to the process of divorce.

> [T]he law should be made to adapt itself to the practice and to what had been shown to be the wants of the community, and that a competent tribunal should be constituted, to do that which the Legislature had heretofore been in the habit of doing.[250]

There was strong support for the creation of a new divorce court in order to facilitate a cheaper and more efficient way to access divorce.[251] Determining the composition of the court proved more difficult. The Ecclesiastical Courts lost their jurisdiction over matrimonial disputes and probate but there was still some continuity. A civilian was appointed judge ordinary of the Court for Divorce and Matrimonial Causes and the Court of Probate,[252] who was also expected to be appointed as the judge of the Court of Admiralty.[253]

In order to stress the gravity of divorce, Parliament decided that the Court for Divorce and Matrimonial Causes should be comprised of the highest judicial officers in the kingdom. This included the lord chancellor, the lord chief justice of the Court of Queen's Bench, the lord chief justice of the Court of Common Pleas, the lord chief baron of the Court of Exchequer, the senior puisne judges, and the judge ordinary.[254] Three judges were required to hear

---

248 Matrimonial Causes Act 1857, s 16.
249 Matrimonial Causes Act 1857, s 6.
250 HL Deb 19 May 1857, vol 145, cols 487–8.
251 HC Deb 6 August 1857, vol 147, col 1172.
252 Matrimonial Causes Act 1857, s 9.
253 Court of Probate Act 1857, s 10. The civilians' monopoly over the Court of Admiralty ceased under the High Court of Admiralty Act 1859 (22 & 23 Vict c 6). However, after Dr Stephen Lushington retired as judge of the Court of Admiralty in 1867, he was replaced by the civilian Sir Robert Phillimore instead of the incumbent judge ordinary of the Court of Probate, Sir James Wilde.
254 Matrimonial Causes Act 1857, s 8.

divorce and nullity of marriage cases, one of whom was the judge ordinary.[255] Many were under the naïve assumption that there would only be a handful of divorce cases each year after the enactment of the bill.[256] At the time, this was not an unreasonable expectation. The government promoted the bill as merely procedural, and securing a divorce was generally seen as an extraordinary step. George Bowyer complained that the divorce court was based in London rather than the more accessible county courts.[257] Lord John Manners (coincidentally the fourth great-grandson of Lord Roos and later Seventh Duke of Rutland) expressed support for the creation of the Court for Divorce and Matrimonial Causes, but like others was reluctant to increase access, which might increase divorce amongst the poor.[258] This suited the government, which presented these changes as procedural.

The grounds for divorce in the bill largely derived from the existing law, and included adultery and acts of aggravated enormity—incest, bigamy, rape, sodomy, bestiality, cruelty, and wilful desertion of two years or more.[259] Wilful desertion as a new ground for divorce was recommended by the Campbell Commission. Lord Lyndhurst stressed the need to safeguard a wife from abandonment by a husband.[260] Divorce would allow the deserted wife to be free from a broken marriage and gain the legal rights of *feme sole*. On the other hand, there was some concern that adding wilful desertion would lead to the rise of divorce by mutual consent. Cranworth drew attention to the situation in Prussia, and he alleged that the number of collusive divorces was uncontrollable after wilful desertion was accepted as a ground for divorce.[261] Lyndhurst introduced an amendment to include wilful desertion as a ground for divorce, but this was defeated by 97 votes to 8 in the House of Lords.[262] However, the attorney-general was successful in including wilful desertion into the bill, which was eventually passed in the House of Commons.[263] There was also a proposal to include adultery in the marital home as a specific ground for divorce. This was rejected in the Lords, because of fears that a wife could trap the husband in an extra-marital affair with a mistress in the conjugal residence.[264]

The strength of the challenge to the double standard should not be overstated,[265] but there were sympathisers on both sides of the general debate. Lord Lyndhurst argued that, 'By adultery the very essence of the contract is directly violated,' and therefore there should be no distinction between the adultery

---

255 Matrimonial Causes Act 1857, s 10.
256 HC Deb 6 August 1857, vol 147, col 1162.
257 *Ibid.* col 1180–1; Matrimonial Causes Act 1857, s 12.
258 HC Deb 6 August 1857, vol 147, col 1176.
259 Matrimonial Causes Act 1857, s 27.
260 HL Deb 25 May 1857, vol 145, cols 815–17.
261 *Ibid.* col 817.
262 *Ibid.* cols 819–20.
263 HC Deb 30 July 1857, vol 147, col 722.
264 HL Deb 20 August 1857, vol 147, col 2016.
265 Probert (n 111) 85.

of the husband and the wife.[266] He repeated his objections the following year.[267] He was much influenced by Caroline Norton.[268] Although Gladstone strongly opposed the bill, he supported making divorce equally accessible. He regarded the double standard as contrary to the idea of biblical equality, and believed it was unreasonable to condemn a wife to a broken marriage unless an act of aggravated enormity was committed.[269] His opposition towards the double standard may at least in part have also been used as a ploy to encourage others to vote against the bill on the grounds that it was too radical. It was a roundabout way of stopping divorce becoming more accessible. However, the proposal to eliminate the double standard still lacked government support. Lord Cranworth argued the sin of a wife's adultery was greater than a husband's, because the wife's misdeeds could lead to 'palming spurious offspring upon the husband.'[270] In the end, the amendment for the removal of the double standard failed by 71 votes to 20 in the House of Lords,[271] and by 126 votes to 65 in the House of Commons.[272]

Finally, the issue of bars to remarriage was debated. The Bishop of Oxford proposed an amendment that would have prohibited remarriage for the adulterous party on the basis that it 'opened a path for sin, and almost certainly led the coming generation into trifling with this holy ordinance.'[273] Although the Archbishop of Canterbury supported the introduction of civil divorce, he strongly backed the amendment. He could 'neither reconcile [the remarriage of the guilty parties] to reason nor to the Divine command.'[274] Conversely, Cranworth believed that the amendment was 'inimical to morality,' because it was akin to forcing one of the separated parties to live with their partner in adultery for the rest of their lives.[275] Similarly, Sir George Grey expressed opposition to the amendment, but described it as 'tantamount to a sentence of penal celibacy.'[276] The amendment was narrowly defeated by 53 votes to 47 in the House of Lords (but succeeded among the Lords Spiritual by 13 votes to 2),[277] and it was comfortably defeated by 110 votes to 50 in the House of Commons.[278] A closely related issue to bars to remarriage was the right of clerics in the Church of England to refuse remarrying divorcees guilty of adultery. This was not only an issue about marriage law, but it also raised questions about the separation of the Church and the state. Gladstone was concerned the bill would damage that relationship by forcing the acceptance of civil divorce onto the clergy with

---

266 HL Deb 20 May 1856, vol 142, col 416.
267 HL Deb 25 May 1857, vol 145, cols 813–14.
268 Dolin (n 15) 125.
269 HC Deb 7 August 1857, vol 147, cols 1271–8.
270 HL Deb 25 May 1857, vol 145, col 813.
271 *Ibid.* cols 814–15.
272 HC Deb 7 August 1857, vol 147, col 1283.
273 HL Deb 25 May 1857, vol 145, col 823.
274 *Ibid.* col 828.
275 *Ibid.* cols 828–9.
276 HC Deb 17 August 1857, vol 147, col 1765.
277 HL Deb 25 May 1857, vol 145, cols 822–30.
278 HC Deb 17 August 1857, vol 147, cols 1760–6.

The enactment of the 1857 Act 71

legitimate objections of conscience.[279] The attorney-general viewed this position as hypocritical.

> The Church of England clergyman will reason most consecutively according to his impression of the great principle which we are about to introduce into the Bill when he says, 'I must decline to read the burial service over an unbaptized man—how can I commit to the earth 'in the sure and certain hope of a joyful resurrection' the body of a man who I know to have died in the commission of some great sin?[280]

The attorney-general was exposing the hypocrisy of the Anglican clergy who commonly buried the unbaptised dead despite having no confidence the deceased would be resurrected to eternal life.[281] Despite this, yet another compromise was put forward[282] with an amendment to allow an Anglican minister to object to the remarrying of divorcees,[283] but not to stop a marriage ceremony being performed by another clergyman in his church building.[284]

The Third Reading of the bill passed the House of Lords by 46 votes to 25 on 23 June 1857.[285] The bill was then sent to the House of Commons for consideration. The Second Reading of the bill passed the House of Commons by 208 votes to 97 on 31 July 1857.[286] The opposition did their best to delay the passage of the bill by filibustering throughout the summer of 1857. Prime Minister Palmerston made his intentions clear.

> I certainly congratulate the opponents of this Bill on the success with which they have, for ten hours, contrived to exercise their ingenuity upon three lines of a clause. If they will allow me, however, I beg to inform them that we shall return and sit here day by day, and night by night, until this Bill be concluded.[287]

His Members of Parliament remained in London throughout the summer.[288] Eventually, the Third Reading passed the House of Commons on 21 August 1857.[289] The Palmerston government gained 53 seats earlier in the year at the 1857 general election, and was able to use its increased majority to get the bill

---

279 HC Deb 31 July 1857, vol 147, col 851.
280 HC Deb 18 August 1857, vol 147, col 1806.
281 The attorney-general was alluding to a passage found in 'At the Burial of the Dead' in the *Book of Common Prayer*. The passage is said by the priest while earth is being cast onto the body for burial. *The Book of Common Prayer* (first published 1662, Cambridge University Press 2004) 332–3.
282 HC Deb 18 August 1857, vol 147, cols 1821–32.
283 Matrimonial Causes Act 1857, s 57.
284 Matrimonial Causes Act 1857, s 58.
285 HL Deb 23 June 1857, vol 146, cols 228–9.
286 HC Deb 31 July 1857, vol 147, cols 892–5.
287 HC Deb 13 August 1857, vol 147, col 1602.
288 HC Deb 4 August 1857, vol 147, cols 1021–2.
289 HC Deb 21 August 1857, vol 147, col 1999.

through the House of Commons.[290] On 24 August 1857, the House of Commons amendments were approved and the bill finally passed the House of Lords by a tiny margin of 46 votes to 44, and received Royal Assent on 28 August 1857.[291] The sister bill to the divorce legislation, the probate and letters of administration bill, was introduced on 23 February 1857, and received Royal Assent on 25 August 1857.[292]

Reflections on the reform of divorce law

The matrimonial causes bill failed to pass into law in 1854, because it was not tied to the wider legislative reform of the Ecclesiastical Courts. Only when it was attached to the reform of probate law did divorce law reform become more palatable, and was seriously considered by Parliament in 1856–7. In many ways the Matrimonial Causes Act 1857 was quite atypical. It raised fundamental issues about morality, religion, and the relationship between Church and state. In other ways it fitted into a broader pattern of law reform in the mid-nineteenth century which was much concerned with promoting the efficiency of the legal system. The Judicature Acts might be the most obvious manifestation,[293] but there were countless others including reform of procedure, pleading, and process.[294] Many of these other reforms were also the result of careful deliberation through committee reports and parliamentary debates. There were compromises there too. For example, in the face of decades of criticism the civil jury was not abolished; rather, it was sidelined.[295] Shortly after the bill passed, *Punch* wrote a satirical poem entitled 'The Divorce Bill Dissected.'

> The Divorce Bill's an Act, the Divorce Bill is Law,
> Old Pam has established a clerical raw,
> Though Gladstone protests, and Sam Wilberforce groans
> That what's good for a Duke is not good for a Jones …
>
> As regards divorce questions, *Punch* gladly reports
> We've abolished the Ecclesiastical Courts:
> All complaints matrimonial, for kill or for cure,
> Are tried in Lord Cupid-Pam's new *Cour d'Amour*.[296]

Because the Matrimonial Causes Act 1857 was a controversial piece of legislation, the need for a compromise was all the more acute. It was a clever move on

---

290 FWS Craig, *British Electoral Facts: 1832–1987* (Parliamentary Research Services 1989) 6–7.
291 HL Deb 24 August 1857, vol 147, col 2036.
292 Court of Probate Act 1857 (20 & 21 Vict c 77).
293 Cornish (n 71) 757–84.
294 *Ibid*. 569–604.
295 Michael Lobban, 'The Strange Life of the English Civil Jury, 1837–1914' in John Cairns and Grant McLeod (eds), *The Dearest Birth Right of the People of England* (Hart Publishing 2002) 173–209.
296 'The Divorce Bill Dissected,' *Punch* (London, 5 September 1857) 103.

the part of the government to present the reform as procedural.[297] In this way it could be tied into the weakening of the status of the Ecclesiastical Courts. But it also made the changes seem, at least superficially, less threatening. At the same time, the claims of Hortsman and Woodhouse that the parliamentary debates were merely procedural[298] and amounted to very little[299] rather misses the point. Whilst it is true that the legislation enacted large parts of the majority report of the Campbell Commission, the outcome was only clear in hindsight. Similarly, Wolfram states, 'The reform was presented as purely procedural.'[300] The Act has been viewed as a landmark in women's emancipation, yet its introduction is still seen as procedural.[301] Although it may have been the initial intention of the Palmerston government to introduce procedural reform, it cannot be said that the legal change was both simultaneously procedural in nature and a landmark moment.[302] The introduction of the *feme sole* provisions and the expansion of the grounds of divorce for married women were substantive law reform measures that created a legal landmark.

Although the grounds and bars to divorce largely followed the existing precedent of the ecclesiastical laws, this area of divorce law was not entirely devoid of change. Where new grounds for divorce were introduced they came with a double standard between the sexes that never existed for divorce *a mensa et thoro*. The introduction of civil divorce into the law on the one hand and the restrictions on the grounds for divorce on the other hand were the result of compromise. It matters less in the detail and more in the fact that it was through these long, often acrimonious debates that an acceptable compromise could be hammered out. Lord St Leonards' amendment, which went beyond anything suggested by the Campbell Commission, was seen in the context of the time as a radical proposal. It seems unlikely that all of those who opposed the bill saw the changes as procedural alone. An objection repeated over and over again was that the reforms would open up divorce to the poor. As Cretney has observed, 'making the divorce process more "efficient" could also be seen as making divorce "easier," and inevitably increasing the appetite for divorce and threatening the stability of family life.'[303]

The Matrimonial Causes Act 1857 commenced its operation on 11 January 1858.[304] The Court for Divorce and Matrimonial Causes heard its first case

---

297 HL Deb 20 May 1856, vol 142, col 404.
298 Horstman (n 203) 78.
299 M.K. Woodhouse, 'The Marriage and Divorce Bill of 1857' (1959) 3 *American Journal of Legal History* 260, 274–5.
300 Wolfram (n 4) 178.
301 Penelope Russell, 'Matrimonial Causes Act 1857' in Erika Rackley and Rosemary Auchmuty (eds), *Women's Legal Landmarks: Celebrating the History of Women and Law in the UK and Ireland* (Hart Publishing, 2018) 68.
302 When Lord Cranworth introduced the 1857 bill, he outlined the aim 'was to do away with the remedy of private legislation for such persons only as could afford to obtain a divorce by Act of Parliament.' HL Deb 19 May 1857, vol 145, col 494.
303 Cretney (n 151) 163.
304 'Court of Probate, Jan 11,' *The Times* (London, 12 January 1858) 9.

on 16 January 1858, when it considered Mrs Deane's application for judicial separation on the ground of her husband's adultery.[305] Within the first year of the operation of the Matrimonial Causes Act 1857, there were 253 petitions for divorce and 87 petitions for judicial separation.[306] *The Times* supported the introduction of the Act during the debates of 1857, but later conveyed a sense of shock shared by many from the unexpected volume of divorce cases.

> [S]o we do not believe that any one either of the most eager supporters or violent opponents of the Divorce Bill of 1857 had the least idea of the quantity of matrimonial misery which was silent only for want of the opportunity to express itself until certified of the fact by the crowded state of the Court of Divorce, and the enormous pressure of the suitors.[307]

The amazement was also felt by Lord Brougham, who remarked, 'Still it was a startling fact that the new Court should have granted in one day as many as, under the old system, had been granted by Parliament in three or four years.'[308] Many people were only accustomed to the tripartite process of divorce and knew of its infrequency. According to Wolfram, the annual average of divorce was about 3.3 *per annum* prior to 1857, but this unexpectedly jumped to 150 *per annum* in the years immediately after 1857.[309] Lord Redesdale felt vindicated in his opposition to the Act. He claimed, 'Everything which had occurred in the Divorce Court since it had been established had done much to lessen in the country the sanctity of the matrimonial tie.'[310] Such was the pressure of business, it soon became clear it was impractical to have three senior judges sit in every single divorce case. Lord Campbell stated it was 'a mere waste of judicial power' to call for a full court of three judges.[311] By 1860 it was decided to allow a judge ordinary sitting alone to decide divorce cases as well as those which were only concerned with separation.[312] Working out the scope of some of the new provisions, including those on desertion, would very quickly give rise to a fair amount of litigation.[313] In the end perhaps the biggest change brought about by the legislation was one of perception.[314] If the secularisation of divorce did not suddenly remove the stigma of divorce, it did begin to dispel the idea of marriage as an indissoluble union. And this alone was a significant feat.

---

305 'Court for Divorce and Matrimonial Causes, Jan 16,' *The Times* (London, 18 January 1858) 9; *Deane v Deane* (1858) 1 Sw&Tr 90.
306 Horstman (n 203) 85.
307 'London, Wednesday, 12 January, 1859,' *The Times* (London, 12 January 1859) 8.
308 HL Deb 4 July 1859, vol 154, col 563.
309 Wolfram (n 4) 158.
310 HL Deb 17 April 1860, vol 157, col 1881.
311 *Ibid.* col 1875.
312 Matrimonial Causes Act 1860 (23 & 24 Vict c 144).
313 *Ward v Ward* (1858) 1 Sw&Tr 185; *Thompson v Thompson* (1858) 1 Sw&Tr 231; *Cargill v Cargill* (1858) 1 Sw&Tr 235; *Macdonald v Macdonald* (1859) 4 Sw&Tr 242.
314 Stephen Waddams, 'English Matrimonial Law on the Eve of Reform (1828–57)' (2000) 21 *Journal of Legal History* 59, 77.

4 Divorce under the Matrimonial Causes Act 1857

GROUNDS FOR DIVORCE

Adultery

The Matrimonial Causes Act 1857 codified the grounds and bars to divorce. In order to obtain a divorce, the petitioner must have an extant valid marriage.[1] Where there were disputes about the validity of the marriage, a suit for nullity of marriage could be commenced in order to seek a declaratory decree to try its validity according to the laws of England.[2] This is a separate issue to divorce. In order to appreciate the legal development of divorce law and the eventual campaign for divorce law reform in the early twentieth century, it is necessary to provide an analysis of the grounds and bars to divorce. The Act aimed to promote marriage stability and limit divorce to a few exceptional cases. It presumed that divorce by mutual consent was objectionable by making adultery the *condition sine qua non* for all divorce decrees.[3] Adultery was interpreted strictly throughout the entire period of the Act's operation.

Adultery required evidence of sexual intercourse or indecent familiarity with a paramour. The sexual consent of the respondent or co-respondent was a necessary element in establishing adultery, otherwise the sexual act would not constitute adultery.[4] However, a wife was also required to prove aggravated enormity in order to be granted a divorce. The ground of adultery followed the precedent of parliamentary divorce and adopted the recommendation of the Campbell Commission to introduce a double standard for divorce.[5] A wife was required to prove either one of the following: incest, bigamy, rape, sodomy, bestiality, cruelty, or desertion of at least two years.[6] The ecclesiastical precedents were largely followed for cases of adultery and aggravated enormity.

---

1 Matrimonial Causes Act 1857, s 31.
2 Matrimonial Causes Act 1857, s 10; *Simonin (falsely called Mallac) v Mallac* (1860) 2 Sw&Tr 67.
3 Matrimonial Causes Act 1857, s 27.
4 *Long v Long and Johnson* (1890) 15 PD 218.
5 *First Report of the Commissioners…Into the Law of Divorce* (1852–3) BPP vol 40, 267–8.
6 Matrimonial Causes Act 1857, s 27.

In nearly all cases, an inference from evidence of inclination and opportunity to commit adultery was sufficient to prove the ground of adultery.[7] This could be established through evidence of 'indecent familiarity,' which refers to any suggestive sexual acts without actual penetration (such as kissing and mutual masturbation).[8] The fact that the parties had not consummated the marriage was immaterial to a divorce proceeding.[9] Ocular evidence of sexual intercourse was not necessary.[10] There was no requirement to identify the respondent's adulterer, which meant it was possible for the co-respondent to be found guilty of adultery without the respondent receiving the same verdict[11] and vice versa.[12]

Even if ocular evidence could be provided, this alone was not always sufficient to establish that adultery had occurred. In *Alexander v Alexander and Amos*, the husband sent a 12-year-old boy to climb up a ladder that led up to a bedroom window. The boy witnessed the wife having sexual intercourse with the co-respondent.[13] The Court disbelieved the allegation and rejected the husband's petition for divorce. It found it unbelievable that the wife would have committed adultery based on her humble background, lack of education, and the absence of prior suspicion of infidelity.[14] However, an inference from evidence of inclination and opportunity to commit adultery was adequate to establish the ground of adultery. In *Wales v Wales and Cullen*, a barman saw the wife kissing the co-respondent on numerous occasions, and once witnessed the wife in a petticoat together with the co-respondent, who had taken off his boots in a bedroom.[15] The Court accepted the inference of the witness testimony.

The complexity of divorce law caused a great deal of public misperception. This is illustrated in the case of *Crawford v Crawford and Dilke (The Queen's Proctor Intervening)*.[16] Sir Charles Dilke was a rising star in the Liberal Party, who was popularly touted as a possible replacement for William Gladstone as party leader.[17] In 1886, Donald Crawford, a Scottish Liberal MP, accused his colleague Dilke of committing adultery with his wife Virginia Crawford. Virginia confessed to committing adultery, which was accepted by the trial judge, who granted Donald a decree *nisi*. However, it was not proven at trial that Dilke was her paramour, merely the fact that Virginia was guilty of committing adultery with an unknown party. In fact, the suit against Dilke was dismissed and Donald

---

7 *Loveden v Loveden* (1810) 2 Hag Con 1; *Allen v Allen and Bell* [1894] P 248.
8 *Boddy v Boddy and Grover* (1860) 30 LJ(PA&M) 23; *Wales v Wales and Cullen* (1900) P 63.
9 *Patrick v Patrick* (1810) 3 Phill Ecc 496; *Waters v Waters and Gentel* (1875) 33 LT 579.
10 *Rix v Rix* (1777) 3 Hag Ecc 74; *Alexander v Alexander and Amos* (1860) 2 Sw&Tr 95.
11 In *Long v Long and Johnson* (1890) 15 PD 218, the respondent did not consent to sexual intercourse with the co-respondent. Therefore, the respondent was found not guilty of adultery, but a finding was made against the co-respondent where he was ordered to pay damages.
12 *Crawford v Crawford and Dilke (The Queen's Proctor Intervening)* (1886) 11 PD 150.
13 (1860) 2 Sw&Tr 95.
14 *Ibid*.
15 [1900] P 63.
16 (1886) 11 PD 150.
17 Roy Jenkins, *Sir Charles Dilke: A Victorian Tragedy* (Collins 1958) 208–14.

was ordered to pay his costs.[18] Although Dilke was not found guilty of adultery, the popular perception was that he had had an extra-marital affair with Virginia.[19]

In order to extricate himself, Dilke welcomed the intervention of the Queen's Proctor.[20] The burden of proving that Dilke and Virginia did not commit adultery rested on the Proctor. However, the Proctor failed to find fresh evidence to prove that Virginia did not commit adultery, thus the application to strike out the decree *nisi* was rejected.[21] This vindicated public opinion that Dilke was an adulterer, despite the fact that the Proctor never made such a claim.[22] Kali Israel states, 'The lack of clear-cut evidence and of any *positive* verdict in the Crawford-Dilke "case" have assured its long-term survival as a site for fiction and guesswork…'[23] Although Dilke was not legally found to have committed adultery with Virginia, the outcome did not vindicate his innocence and aspersions were cast on his perceived sexual impropriety. The scandal thus brought to an end any political aspirations Dilke may have had for high office.

Petitioners presented various types of evidence to the Court in order to prove the ground of adultery. Venereal disease was one type of evidence occasionally used to claim divorce, because it not only proved adultery but also cruelty. In *Gleen v Gleen*, the wife was granted a divorce by proving that the husband had committed adultery during his time as a sergeant in the Coldstream Guards.[24] The husband's army medical history sheet showed that he was admitted to hospital for a venereal illness. Another type of evidence was proving parentage of a child born outside of wedlock. There was a legal presumption in favour of legitimacy that could be rebutted by contrary evidence.[25] If sufficient doubt emerged about the legitimacy of the child, then a decree *nisi* could be issued for the duration of nine months to align with the period of a woman's pregnancy,[26] thereby allowing the Court to investigate the claim of illegitimacy.

In practice, however, it was difficult for parties to attempt to prove that a child was born out of wedlock, because of the challenge of establishing credible evidence. This problem is illustrated in the House of Lords judgment of *Russell v Russell*.[27] The Honourable John Hugo Russell, the heir to the Third Baron Ampthill, petitioned for divorce on the grounds of his wife Christabel's adultery. The case was atypical and particularly scandalous for involving members of the aristocracy, allegations of adultery, and a mystery over the child's parentage. At trial, the husband claimed that he could not be the father to the child that was

---

18 *Crawford v Crawford and Dilke (The Queen's Proctor Intervening)* (1886) 11 PD 150.
19 Jenkins (n 17) 243–5.
20 *Ibid*. 246–7.
21 *Crawford v Crawford and Dilke (The Queen's Proctor Intervening)* (1886) 11 PD 150, 158.
22 Kali Israel, *Names and Stories: Emilia Dilke and Victorian Culture* (Oxford University Press 1999) 206–9.
23 *Ibid*. 206.
24 (1900) 17 TLR 60.
25 *Bosvile v The Attorney-General* (1887) 12 PD 177, 181.
26 *Hetherington v Hetherington* (1887) 12 PD 112.
27 [1924] AC 687.

78 Divorce under the 1857 Act

born of the wife, because he did not have sexual intercourse with the wife at the time of conception.[28] A jury was invited to infer whether adultery had occurred with one of the 30 men that the husband suspected of having an extra-marital affair with the wife, and whether the child bore any physical resemblance to the husband.[29] The jury failed to reach a unanimous verdict after an eight-day trial. A retrial was called lasting 11 days that attracted a lot of publicity.[30] This time the second jury found the wife guilty of adultery with an unknown party and a decree *nisi* was granted to the husband. The wife appealed and the House of Lords ruled that spouses were not allowed to present evidence themselves on whether sexual intercourse had occurred.[31] In regards to the material facts, the House of Lords held there was insufficient admissible evidence to rebut the presumption of legitimacy, and therefore the decree *nisi* was rescinded.[32] The High Court granted a declaration of legitimacy to the child of the marriage.[33] The challenge of providing evidence of adultery limited the numbers of successful divorce petitioners, even more so from the already narrow grounds of divorce.

Certain types of evidence were privileged. In a divorce suit, a medical practitioner was not compelled to produce letters detailing health records or medical symptoms communicated from the respondent.[34] Since a divorce suit was understood to be a civil proceeding, communication relayed between the client and the solicitor was also privileged.[35] However, there was an exception to the rule in the case of the client assailing the solicitor's character for perverting the course of justice. In such a case, the solicitor would be entitled to defend himself and the rules of privilege would not apply.[36] Similarly, the petitioner was not entitled to rely upon privilege to prevent the Queen's Proctor's admission of material facts that were not adduced at trial.[37]

Witnesses were often called to testify the commission of adulterous acts. The evidence of the husband or the wife alone without corroboration was generally not accepted, because the spouses were deemed highly likely to give false, deceptive, or misleading testimony.[38] For this reason, confessions were also generally

---

28 *Russell v Russell* [1924] P 1, 8.
29 The Court held discretion on allowing contested matters of fact to be tried by a jury. Matrimonial Causes Act 1857, s 28.
30 See Stephen Cretney, '"Disgusted, Buckingham Palace…": The Judicial Proceedings (Regulation of Reports) Act 1926' (1997) 9(1) *Child and Family Law Quarterly* 43, 49–53; Lucy Bland, '"Hunnish Scenes" and a "Virgin Birth": a 1920s Case of Sexual and Bodily Ignorance' (2012) 73(1) *History Workshop Journal* 118.
31 *Russell v Russell* [1924] AC 687.
32 *Ibid.*
33 *Russell (GDE) (By his Guardian) v The Attorney-General* (1926) *The Times*, 29 July 1926.
34 *Witt v Witt and Klindworth* (1862) 3 Sw&Tr 143; overturned *Atkinson v Atkinson* (1825) 2 Add 468.
35 *Branford v Branford and Sheppard (The Queen's Proctor Intervening)* (1879) 4 PD 72.
36 *Crawford v Crawford and Dilke (The Queen's Proctor Intervening)* (1886) 11 PD 150.
37 *Lambart v Lambart (The King's Proctor Showing Cause)* (1907) 51 Sol Jo 345. The client admitted adultery to the King's Proctor, but argued her solicitor encouraged her to deny it at trial.
38 *Curtis v Curtis* (1905) 21 TLR 676; *Getty v Getty* [1907] P 314.

viewed with deep suspicion. In *Robinson v Robinson and Lane*, husband Henry Robinson unsuccessfully attempted to admit his wife Isabella Robinson's diary containing confessions of adultery with Edward Lane.[39] Cockburn CJ found the evidence unreliable as 'sound sense and judgment were wanting to correct a too vivid imagination and too ardent passions.'[40] The confessions in the wife's diary were deemed to be a work of imaginative fiction rather than a reliable admission of guilt. Emma Summerscale states, 'In a court of law, the value of Isabella's diary was dubious … it was a work of anticipation as much as memory—it was provisional and unsteady, existing at the edge of thought and act, wish and deed.'[41] The Court closely scrutinised the testimony of sole witnesses, since their evidence could not be corroborated and the Court was deeply suspicious of collusion.[42] The divorce petition was dismissed due to a lack of credible evidence of adultery.

'Loose women' or prostitutes were considered a particularly untrustworthy source of evidence.[43] Likewise, paid detectives and private investigators were distrusted. In *Sopwith v Sopwith*, the wife and her parents hired a private detective to investigate the husband's extra-marital affair.[44] The detective witnessed the husband kissing his maid and a figure of the couple undressing after peeping through the husband's bedroom keyhole. Cresswell J rejected the wife's petition for divorce.

> But when a man sets up as a hired discoverer of supposed delinquencies, when the amount of his pay depends upon the extent of his employment, and the extent of his employment depends upon the discoveries he is able to make, then that man becomes a most dangerous instrument.[45]

The Court considered the financial inducement of detectives as sufficient reason to be suspicious towards the credibility of their testimonies. The strict definition of adultery became an important reason for the extension of the grounds for divorce under the Matrimonial Causes Act 1937.[46] Adultery could be proven based on circumstantial evidence, but ultimately it was a fact-finding exercise that had to be proven usually before a jury.

Incest

A double standard prevailed in the grounds of divorce between husbands and wives. Adultery of a husband alone was not sufficient for a wife to be

---

39 (1859) 1 Sw&Tr 362.
40 *Ibid*.
41 Emma Summerscale, *Mrs Robinson's Disgrace: The Private Diary of a Victorian Lady* (Bloomsbury 2012) 225.
42 *Evans v Evans* (1844) 1 Rob Ecc 165; *Simmons v Simmons* (1847) 1 Rob Ecc 566.
43 *Ginger v Ginger* (1865) LR 1 P&D 37.
44 (1859) 4 Sw&Tr 243.
45 *Ibid*. 247.
46 (1 Ed VIII & 1 Geo VI c 57).

granted a divorce; the wife also had to prove an aggravated statutory offence until the introduction of the Matrimonial Causes Act 1923.[47] The Courts generally interpreted these statutory offences more broadly than adultery. There were three categories of aggravated statutory offence under section 27 of the Matrimonial Causes Act 1857: sexual offences, cruelty, and desertion. Sexual offences were viewed as non-normative sexual practices, which included incest, bigamy, rape, sodomy, and bestiality. All of these category offences were seen as such morally repugnant acts that they justified divorce to a limited number of married women.

Incestuous adultery was statutorily defined 'to mean Adultery committed by a Husband with a Woman with whom if his Wife were dead he could not lawfully contract Marriage by reason of her being within the prohibited Degrees of Consanguinity or Affinity.'[48] This definition was not found in the Campbell Commission majority report or the 1854 divorce bill, but was later introduced in the 1856 divorce bill as the specifics of the forthcoming legislation were being seriously considered and finalised.[49] Prior to the introduction of the 1857 Act, the legal position of incest was more legally ambiguous. In 1563, Archbishop Matthew Parker published the 'Table of Kindred and Affinity,' which listed 30 prohibited relationships that had been included in the *Book of Common Prayer* since 1603.[50] The table not only prohibits relations of consanguinity, but also relations of affinity between in-laws. This was an adoption of the Levitical prohibition of marrying a deceased brother's wife that Henry VIII used as a ground to annul his marriage with Catherine of Aragon in 1533.[51] Incest was briefly criminalised in 1650 during the Interregnum, but after the Restoration the statute was repealed in 1661.[52] It was not until the early twentieth century that incest was again criminalised.[53]

Marriages of affinity prior to 1835 were voidable (though not void *ab initio*) in the Ecclesiastical Courts.[54] During the early nineteenth century, incestuous adultery was a legal ground of divorce *a vinculo matrimonii* for married women. In Mrs Addison's case of 1801, the House of Lords at the behest of Lord Thurlow granted its first divorce *a vinculo matrimonii* to a female petitioner, Jane Addison (née Campbell), on the ground of her husband Edward Addison's incestuous adultery with her sister.[55] The precedent of granting divorce to a female

---

47 (13 & 14 Geo V c 19).
48 Matrimonial Causes Act 1857, s 27.
49 HL Deb 26 June 1856, vol 142, col 1976.
50 Brian Connolly, *Domestic Intimacies: Incest and the Liberal Subject in Nineteenth-Century America* (University of Pennsylvania Press 2014) 54.
51 Leviticus 18:16 and 20:21. Compare Deuteronomy 25:5–10.
52 Peter Bowsher, 'Incest—Should Incest between Consenting Adults be a Crime?' (2015) 3 *Criminal Law Review* 208.
53 Incest Act 1908 (8 Ed VII c 45).
54 Sybil Wolfram, 'Divorce in England 1700–1857' (1985) 5(2) *Oxford Journal of Legal Studies* 155, 161.
55 Jane Addison (41 Geo III c 102); James Campbell (41 Geo III c 119).

petitioner on the ground of the husband's incestuous adultery with his sister-in-law was followed in *Mrs Turton's Case* of 1831.[56] Lord Brougham reasoned that the precedent should be followed to preserve the innocence of relationships between close relatives and uphold the sanctity of marriage.[57]

Lord Lyndhurst's Act[58] recognised existing marriages of affinity between the husband and the deceased wife's sister,[59] but prohibited the recognition of subsequent marriages of affinity and declared such marriages as being 'within prohibited degrees hereafter to be absolutely void.'[60] Relations of affinity were seen to rupture the stability of the family unit by destabilising marriages and complicating the law of succession surrounding the legitimacy of children.[61] This Act ended any ambiguity about the legitimacy of marriages of affinity. Under the 1857 Act, the definition of incest was interpreted broadly in case law. This extended the legal ground of divorce for the wife. The husband could be found to have committed adultery with either a consanguine relative or a relation of affinity.[62]

In *Vicars v Vicars*, Naomi Vicars petitioned for divorce on the ground of her husband James Vicars' incestuous adultery.[63] The Court granted Naomi a divorce after finding that James had a sexual relationship with his biological daughter Mary Ann Vicars, who was born from another relationship. Therefore, the case established that consanguineous relationships outside of wedlock constituted the ground of incestuous adultery. However, sexual intercourse between the husband and his mother-in-law[64] or sister-in-law prior to marriage was an insufficient ground to establish incestuous adultery.[65] In order to establish incestuous adultery involving relations of affinity, the sexual relationship must have taken place during the marriage.[66] The Deceased Wife's Sister's Marriage Act 1907 lifted the prohibition against marriages between a man and his deceased wife's sister.[67] Nonetheless, incestuous adultery between a husband and a relation of affinity (particularly a sister-in-law) continued to exist as a special ground of divorce for women.

> Notwithstanding anything contained in this Act or the Matrimonial Causes Act, 1857, it shall not be lawful for a man to marry the sister of his divorced

---

56 *Turton v Turton* (1830) 3 Hag Ecc 338; Louisa Turton (1 & 2 W IV c 35).
57 John Fraser Macqueen, *A Practical Treatise on the Law of Marriage, Divorce, and Legitimacy: As Administered in the Divorce Court and in the House of Lords* (W. Maxwell 1860) 40.
58 Marriage Act 1835 (5 & 6 Will IV c 54).
59 Marriage Act 1835, s 1.
60 Marriage Act 1835, s 2.
61 HL Deb 1 June 1835, vol 28, cols 203–7.
62 Matrimonial Causes Act 1857, s 27.
63 (1858) *The Times*, 4 December 1858.
64 *Wing v Taylor (falsely calling herself Wing)* (1861) 2 Sw&Tr 278.
65 *Pagani v Pagani and Vining* (1866) LR 1 P&D 223.
66 Matrimonial Causes Act 1857, s 27. Until 28 August 1907, if the parties attempted to solemnise such relationships, it would be declared a void marriage.
67 (7 Ed VII c 47).

wife, or of his wife by whom he has been divorced, during the lifetime of such wife.[68]

Bigamy

Bigamy was statutorily defined 'to mean Marriage of any Person, being married, to any other Person during the Life of the former Husband or Wife, whether the Second Marriage shall have taken place within the Dominions of Her Majesty or elsewhere.'[69] If the husband was found to be a bigamist, the first wife would be eligible to divorce and the second 'wife' would have the relief of nullity. Bigamy was first criminalised under English law in 1603 with the maximum penalty of death.[70] Bigamy was again criminalised but with a penalty of imprisonment in 1828[71] and 1861.[72] Prior to 1857, just two women were successfully granted divorce *a vinculo matrimonii* for bigamy with adultery: Mrs Battersby in 1840 and Mrs Hall in 1850.[73] As the number of divorces increased after 1857, bigamy became more uncommon.[74] John Fraser Macqueen accurately predicted that bigamy would decline in England as a result of introducing civil divorce. He based this on the very low numbers of bigamy cases in Scotland, where the existence of civil divorce generally encouraged most couples to obtain a formal divorce before remarrying.[75]

Under the 1857 Act, three elements needed to be satisfied in order to establish bigamy with adultery as a matrimonial cause. First, the second marriage must have taken place anywhere in the world.[76] Therefore, the law of bigamy was one of the few English laws that operated extraterritorially. It is important to note that only English divorces were legally recognised unless the parties were legitimately domiciled in a foreign jurisdiction and they were not colluding to evade the laws of England.[77] Second, the adultery and bigamy must have been with the same woman, where the chronological order of the offences were not material.[78]

---

68 Deceased Wife's Sister's Marriage Act 1907, s 2. According to s 5, sister was defined to also include a half-sister.
69 Matrimonial Causes Act 1857, s 27.
70 Bigamy Act 1603 (1 Jac I c 11).
71 Offences Against the Person Act 1828 (9 Geo IV c 31) s 22.
72 Offences Against the Person Act 1861 (24 & 25 Vict c 100) s 57.
73 Ann Battersby (3 & 4 Vict c 48); Georgina Hall (13 & 14 Vict c 25). These two cases along with *Mrs Addison's Case* and *Mrs Turton's Case* were the only four cases where a married woman was successfully granted a divorce *a vinculo matrimonii* prior to 1857.
74 Lawrence Stone, *Road to Divorce* (Oxford University Press 1995) 387.
75 According to Macqueen, there were 83 convictions for bigamy in England and only two convictions for bigamy in Scotland in 1854. Macqueen (n 57) 34.
76 *Trial of Earl Russell* [1901] AC 446.
77 *Shaw v Gould* (1868) LR 3 HL 55; *Bonaparte v Bonaparte* (1892) P 402, 409–11. The legal principle also applied to irregular marriages of English couples formalised in a foreign jurisdiction; *Lawford (Otherwise Davies) v Davies* (1878) 4 PD 61.
78 In *Horne v Horne* (1858) 2 Sw&Tr 48, the wife was successful in her divorce petition on the ground of the husband's adultery with desertion but not for adultery with bigamy, because though the husband entered into a second marriage he did not consummate the relationship. See also

Third, the second marriage would have been a legally valid marriage but for the existence of the former marriage.[79]

The *Trial of Earl Russell* was a high-profile bigamous adultery case.[80] The Second Earl Russell's first marriage to Mabel Edith Scott in 1890 rapidly broke down and soon after the parties separated.[81] Mabel accused the earl of committing homosexual acts with another man in order to extort money from him, but her application for judicial separation was disbelieved and dismissed.[82] During the earl's time at Balliol College, Oxford University in 1885, he was expelled for allegedly having an improper relationship with another man.[83] The 'Oxford Incident' was used by Mabel to cast aspersions and insinuations on the earl's sexuality and the propriety of his character.[84] Mabel then filed an order for restitution of conjugal rights. The earl responded with a petition for judicial separation on the ground of cruelty which rested on Mabel publicly making allegations that she knew to be completely untrue. Although the earl was initially granted an order for judicial separation at trial, the Court of Appeal set aside the ruling as the definition of cruelty was not satisfied.[85] Mabel subsequently abandoned her own appeal for restitution of conjugal rights.

Ellam v Ellam (1889) 61 LT 338; *Sparrow v Sparrow* (1913) 30 TLR 47; *Lucid v Lucid* (1921) 39 TLR 111.
79 In *Burt v Burt* (1860) 2 Sw&Tr 88, the husband left the wife for Australia. He entered into a second marriage according to a Church of Scotland (Presbyterian) wedding ceremony in Melbourne. Since there was no formal legal documentation of the marriage under Australian law, the wife's petition for divorce on the ground of the husband's adultery with bigamy was rejected.
80 [1901] AC 446.
81 The Second Earl Russell was the eldest son of Prime Minister Lord John Russell and elder brother of the philosopher Bertrand Russell.
82 Mabel accused the earl of having committed acts of sodomy with a mathematics teacher named Herbert Roberts and also with a boy on board the earl's yacht, but the jury found that the earl was not guilty of cruelty to his wife. After the trial, the earl sued his mother-in-law, Lady Selina Scott, and the sailors who crewed his yacht for criminal libel for their testimony that he had engaged in sexual impropriety and unnatural offences. They were all subsequently found guilty of criminal libel and sentenced to eight months' imprisonment. See 'The Charge Against Lady Scott' *The Times* (London, 13 October 1896) 10; 'Central Criminal Court, Jan 8' *The Times* (London, 9 January 1897) 10; Caroline Moorehead, *Bertrand Russell* (Sinclair-Stevenson 1992) 45.
83 The master of Balliol College, Benjamin Jowett, was displeased with the earl's friendship with the poet Lionel Johnson, who later became a close friend of Oscar Wilde. Jowett expelled the earl for allegedly writing a scandalous letter, but the details have remained mired in mystery. The earl vigorously denied any wrongdoing in his autobiography. Earl Russell, *My Life and Adventures* (Cassell 1923) 107–10; Gail Savage, '"... Equality from the Masculine Point of View...": The 2nd Earl Russell and Divorce Law Reform in England' (1996) 16 *Russell: The Journal of Bertrand Russell Studies* 67, 68; Peter Bartrip, 'A Talent to Alienate: The 2nd Earl (Frank) Russell (1865–1931)' (2012–13) 32 *Russell: The Journal of Bertrand Russell Studies* 101, 106; Ann Sumner Holmes, '"Don't Frighten the Horses": the Russell Divorce Case' in George Robb and Nancy Erber (eds), *Disorder in the Court: Trials and Sexual Conflict at the Turn of the Century* (New York University Press 1999) 142–3.
84 Bartrip (n 83) 108.
85 *Russell v Russell* [1895] P 315. Affirmed by the House of Lords in *Russell v Russell* [1897] AC 395.

84 *Divorce under the 1857 Act*

The earl then met Mollie Cooke and sought to marry her notwithstanding the fact that he was still legally married to Mabel.[86] Consequently, the earl and Mollie left for America in an attempt to evade English law. On 14 April 1900, the earl obtained a divorce from the State of Nevada. On the next day, he married Mollie at the Riverside Hotel in Reno.[87] On their return to England, the earl was arrested and pleaded guilty to bigamy.[88] There was a legal presumption against a change of domicile and a person could not have more than one domicile.[89] In order to prove a change of domicile, it was necessary to unequivocally demonstrate that there was a settled purpose of making another foreign jurisdiction the principal and permanent home in order to constitute the *animus manendi* ('the intention of remaining').[90] The earl's domicile of origin was England and his brief time in America did not rebut this presumption. Lord Halsbury who prosecuted the case was particularly disdainful towards the earl and outraged that a peer had committed the offence of bigamy.[91] The earl was sentenced to three months' imprisonment.[92] However, Mabel successfully petitioned for divorce on the ground of his bigamous adultery. The earl subsequently became a leading campaigner for divorce law reform. He established the 'Society for Promoting Reforms in Marriage and Divorce Laws in England' in 1902,[93] published a book on divorce law reform,[94] and testified before the Gorell Commission in 1910 calling for the abolition of the double standard between the genders in the grounds for divorce and the expansion of the grounds of divorce.[95]

Rape

Rape was listed as one of the grounds for divorce available to a wife, but it was merely stated and not defined.[96] The rape concerned was by a husband of a woman other than his wife. In the eyes of the law, it was legally impossible for the husband to rape his wife.[97] The origins of the marital rape exemption can be

---

86 Ian Watson, 'Mollie, Countess Russell' (2003) 23 *Russell: The Journal of Bertrand Russell Studies* 65, 65–8.
87 Reno later became synonymous with Nevada's liberal divorce laws in the early twentieth century. See 'The Mechanics of a Reno Divorce are Simple and Swift' *Life* (New York, 21 June 1937) 34–40.
88 Russell (n 83) 281–3.
89 *Aikman v Aikman* (1861) 3 Macq 854; *The Lauderdale Peerage* (1885) 10 App Cas 692; *Winans v Attorney-General* [1904] AC 287.
90 *Moorhouse and Wife v Lord and Others* (1863) 10 HL Cas 272; *Goulder v Goulder* [1892] P 240; *Re Martin, Loustalan v Loustalan* [1900] P 211.
91 Russell (n 83) 283–5.
92 Rupert Furneaux, *Tried By Their Peers* (Cassell 1959) 193.
93 Stephen Cretney, *Family Law in the Twentieth Century* (Oxford University Press 2003) 205.
94 Earl Russell, *Divorce* (Heinemann 1912).
95 *Minutes of Evidence Taken Before the Royal Commission on Divorce and Matrimonial Causes, Volume 3* (Cd 6481, 1912) 450–5.
96 Matrimonial Causes Act 1857, s 27.
97 The marital rape exemption was abolished in *R v R* [1992] 1 AC 599. See Jonathan Herring, 'No More Having and Holding: The Abolition of the Marital Rape Exemption' in Stephen Gilmore,

traced to the writings of seventeenth-century jurist Sir Matthew Hale.[98] Prior to 1857, there were no successful petitions for divorce on the ground of rape. After 1857, cases involving divorce on the ground of rape were still very rare. Rape must be proven *de novo*, even if a criminal conviction already existed for the offence.[99] Rape was generally understood to mean 'any penetration' (i.e., vaginal, oral, and anal intercourse) without consent and against the victim's will.[100] Hence, marital rape was not a matrimonial cause, because the element of consent necessary to prove adultery could not be established. Someone found guilty of rape would also be found to have committed adultery.[101] There were even reported rape cases that involved female victims below the age of consent. In these sorts of cases, the Court found that rape was committed irrespective of consent.[102]

Sexual misconduct falling short of penetration may have nevertheless constituted either cruelty or rape. The definition of rape as a matrimonial offence was different from the criminal law meaning. It was interpreted more broadly to encompass sexual activity without consent and it did not necessarily have to involve penetration. In *Thompson v Thompson*, the husband's indecent assault of two young girls had so severely affected the wife's health that it was deemed to be cruelty.[103] In *Coffey v Coffey*, the wife was granted a divorce after the husband attempted to commit unlawful carnal knowledge with a girl under the age of 13 that was deemed to constitute the matrimonial definition of rape.[104] In *Bosworthick v Bosworthick*, the husband was found to have committed a series of indecent assaults on six girls under the age of 13.[105] Barnes J granted the wife divorce, and followed both *Coffey* and *Thompson* by ruling that the charges of rape and cruelty were established.[106] Sexual misconduct and impropriety were deemed to be offensive to the marriage. Therefore, rape was given a broad interpretation for the purposes of establishing matrimonial cause.

Jonathan Herring, and Rebecca Probert (eds), *Landmark Cases in Family Law* (Hart Publishing 2011) 225–39.

98 Matthew Hale, *The History of the Pleas of the Crown, Volume 1* (Nutt 1736) 629.
99 *Virgo v Virgo* (1893) 69 LT 460. The husband was found to have had sexual intercourse with the daughter of the marriage. A doctor testified that the girl was vaginally penetrated and this was decisive evidence in proving the charge of rape. The husband was found to have committed both incestuous adultery and rape. The Court granted the wife divorce.
100 *Ibid*. 461.
101 *Thompson v Thompson* (1901) 85 LT 172.
102 Under the Criminal Law Amendment Act 1885 (48 & 49 Vict c 69), it was an offence to have carnal knowledge with a girl under the age of 13 (s 4) and a girl above the age of 13 and below the age of 16 (s 5(1)). The age of consent was raised to 16 from 13 under s 4 of the Offences Against the Person Act 1875 (38 & 39 Vict c 94).
103 (1901) 85 LT 172.
104 [1898] P 169.
105 (1901) 86 LT 121.
106 *Ibid*. 122.

Unnatural offences

Sodomy and bestiality were both classed as 'unnatural offences,'[107] and were statutorily undefined grounds.[108] There were no recorded cases of bestiality as a matrimonial cause. Prior to 1857, sodomy as a matrimonial cause only applied to homosexual activity between the husband and another man. The definition of sodomy did not include anal intercourse between a man and a woman, since it would have been classed as cruelty. In *Geils v Geils*, the wife failed to prove on the evidence that her husband had committed or attempted to commit an act of sodomy towards her.[109] Sodomy was described as an 'unnatural crime,' which would have constituted an act of cruelty if proven in this case.[110] Merely attempting to commit sodomy was a ground for divorce *a mensa et thoro*.[111] In *Mogg v Mogg*, the husband's criminal conviction of assault and attempts to persuade an apprentice lad 'to take indecent liberties with his person' (though not expressly sodomy) was enough to allow the wife to successfully petition for divorce *a mensa et thoro* on the ground of cruelty.[112] There were no divorce cases of actual sodomy between men as a matrimonial cause, since sodomy was a capital offence until 1861 and thereafter remained a serious crime.[113]

The law of divorce changed after 1857 to include sodomy as a ground of divorce for the wife.[114] All allegations of unnatural offences had to be fully corroborated due to the heinous nature of the charge.[115] Attempting to commit or actually committing sodomy was a ground of divorce.[116] If evidence demonstrated that the husband forced the wife to receive a sodomitical act, then the wife was entitled to petition for divorce.[117] Conversely, if the wife was a consenting party to an act of sodomy, then she would not be able to petition for divorce solely on that offence.[118] Therefore, consent to an act of sodomy was critical in determining whether or not a divorce suit would be successful.

---

107 William Rayden, *Practice and Law in the Divorce Division of the High Court of Justice and On Appeal Therefrom* (Butterworth 1910) 62.
108 Matrimonial Causes Act 1857, s 27.
109 (1848) 6 NC 97, 147–64.
110 *Ibid*. 164.
111 *Bromley v Bromley* (1793) 2 Add 158. The decree was granted based on the husband's criminal conviction for assault and intent to commit sodomy with another man.
112 (1824) 2 Add 292.
113 Buggery Act 1533 (25 Hen VIII c 6); Offences Against the Person Act 1828. The Offences Against the Person Act 1861 abolished capital punishment for sodomy though it was still a criminal offence with the penalty of imprisonment of at least ten years. See Sean Brady, *Masculinity and Male Homosexuality in Britain, 1861–1913* (Palgrave Macmillan 2005) 85–118.
114 Matrimonial Causes Act 1857, s 27.
115 *N v N* (1862) 3 Sw&Tr 234, 238. In a judicial separation suit, the wife deposed that the husband twice committed acts of sodomy towards her, but he denied it on oath. No further supporting evidence was presented to the Court and the charge was dismissed.
116 *Ibid*. 234.
117 *C v C* (1905) 22 TLR 26.
118 *Statham v Statham* (1929) P 131.

Although the definition of adultery was rather narrow, it was possible for a married woman to claim that the husband committed one of the sexual offences in order to be granted a divorce. However, aggravated sexual offences were such extraordinary grounds to prove that they were eventually abolished under the Matrimonial Causes Act 1923.

Cruelty

An analysis of the decisions on cruelty as a matrimonial cause reveals divergence of opinion among the judiciary over the scope of cruelty. A narrow interpretation prevailed and therefore pressure was placed on Parliament to abolish cruelty as a matrimonial cause under the Matrimonial Causes Act 1923. Cruelty was defined as 'Adultery coupled with such cruelty as without Adultery would have entitled her to a Divorce *a Mensa et Thoro*.'[119] This was a reference to the legal definition of cruelty as a matrimonial cause found in the ecclesiastical laws. In particular, cruelty must be such that it would have granted a party a divorce *a mensa et thoro*. Despite the enactment of the Matrimonial Causes Act 1857, the case law throughout the nineteenth century generally held a consistently narrow legal construction of cruelty.

The legal definition of cruelty was not as clear as adultery. Cresswell J states, 'There can be no doubt about the meaning of adultery, when stated as the ground of a petition, but cruelty in ordinary language is an ambiguous term.'[120] In *Russell v Russell*,[121] the House of Lords by a slim majority of five to four affirmed the majority Court of Appeal decision that in order to establish the charge of cruelty, 'there must be actual danger to life, or limb, or to health, bodily or mental, or a reasonable apprehension of it.'[122] The majority argued that this meaning avoided defining cruelty too broadly and imprecisely. As Lord Shand states, 'I should say the law would be involved in much confusion and uncertainty.'[123] Moreover, Lord Herschell felt that matrimonial misconduct was as old as matrimony itself and there was no reason to deviate from settled ecclesiastical principles.[124] The majority decision was based on a landmark ecclesiastical case concerning the definition of cruelty.[125] In *Evans v Evans*, Lord Stowell established a narrow definition of cruelty.

> In the present case it is hardly necessary for me to define it; because the facts here complained of are such as fall within the most restricted definition of

---

119 Matrimonial Causes Act, s 27.
120 *Suggate v Suggate* (1859) 1 Sw&Tr 489.
121 [1897] AC 395.
122 *Russell v Russell* [1895] P 315, 322.
123 *Russell v Russell* [1897] AC 395, 464.
124 *Ibid.* 461.
125 The Court was obliged to follow the principles of the Ecclesiastical Courts according to the Matrimonial Causes Act 1857, s 22.

cruelty: they affect not only the comfort, but they affect the health and even the life of the party.[126]

The minority judgment argued that actual harm or reasonable apprehension of actual harm was only a category of cruelty that did not definitively limit the scope of cruelty.[127] Instead, the definition of cruelty could be extended to the conduct of the wife or husband being such as to make continued cohabitation and exercise of conjugal duties unbearable or impossible.[128]

The majority judgment was better supported by precedents, because Lord Stowell affirmed existing legal notions of cruelty.[129] According to William Blackstone, it was not only permissible but also expected of the husband to carry out moderate correction of the wife.

> For, as he is to answer for her misbehaviour, the law thought it reasonable to intrust him with this power of restraining her, by domestic chastisement, in the same moderation that a man is allowed to correct his apprentices or children; for whom the master or parent is also liable in some cases to answer.[130]

This was the legal context of Lord Stowell's decision making. It explains why cruelty was narrowly construed. This definition was followed in subsequent cases, which affirmed that mere words do not establish cruelty,[131] and imputing danger of bodily harm sufficiently proves the charge of cruelty.[132]

Cruelty was assessed objectively based on what a reasonable person would consider to constitute cruelty for each case.[133] Cruelty to one party may not necessarily be cruelty to another. Either the husband or the wife could be found to have committed cruelty.[134] It was not easy to establish actual cruelty. A single grievous act of cruelty could have been sufficient in itself to establish the matrimonial cause though such cases were seldom successful.[135] It was more typical to show a series of minor acts of cruelty in order to establish cumulative cruelty.[136] However, the acts of cruelty must have been sustained over a significant period of

---

126 (1790) 1 Hag Con 35.
127 *Russell v Russell* [1897] AC 395, 436.
128 *Ibid.* 438.
129 Stone (n 74) 203
130 William Blackstone, *Commentaries on the Laws of England, Volume 1* (1753) 444.
131 *Milford v Milford* (1866) LR 1 P&D 295, 299; *Russell v Russell* [1895] P 315, 317.
132 *Otway v Otway* (1812) 2 Phill 95.
133 *Tomkins v Tomkins* (1858) 1 Sw&Tr 168.
134 The husband could only obtain a judicial separation for the wife's cruelty towards him. *White v White* (1859) 1 Sw&Tr 591; *Prichard v Prichard* (1864) 3 Sw&Tr 523; *Forth v Forth* (1867) 16 LT 574.
135 In *Reeves v Reeves* (1862) 3 Sw&Tr 139, the husband kicked the wife on the leg leaving her with a lasting wound and she was subsequently granted a divorce. In *Smallwood v Smallwood* (1861) 2 Sw&Tr 397, however, the husband almost strangled the wife to death, but since it did not leave any lasting wound the petition for judicial separation was dismissed.
136 *Waddell v Waddell* (1862) 2 Sw&Tr 584.

time, otherwise they may be deemed to be only acts of the moment that present no real danger to life, health, or happiness of the parties.[137] The law of evidence allowed for parties to present a wide range of evidence. A decree of judicial separation on the ground of cruelty[138] or a certificate of a prior summary conviction for cruelty was accepted as *prima facie* evidence of cruelty.[139] Moreover, a party was entitled to ask a witness whether the wife made a complaint about the husband.[140] There were some probative limits to proving cruelty. An act of cruelty of which particulars had not been pleaded was not admissible, but evidence of violent demeanour and language not pleaded may be admissible.[141]

Cruelty was not just physical acts of domestic violence. Wilfully and recklessly communicating a venereal disease to the other spouse constituted cruelty.[142] The petitioner held the burden of proving that he or she was indeed infected and ignorant of the fact that the respondent hosted a sexually transmitted infection.[143] Medical evidence of venereal disease was given high probative value.[144] However, a mere skin infection alone would not constitute cruelty unless it was presented as evidence in conjunction with other acts of cruelty.[145] Venereal disease was commonly transmitted from the husband to the wife. In fact, 82 per cent of all divorce petitions that cited venereal disease were claimed by wives between 1858 and 1901.[146] The recognition of venereal disease as a form of cruelty gave married women an increased likelihood of obtaining a divorce. Gail Savage states in regards to venereal disease, 'The Divorce Court readily granted the wife both a divorce and custody of the children.'[147] Once the transmission of venereal disease was proven, then adultery could be inextricably linked to this act of cruelty. Female prostitutes were the subject of concern in the Contagious Diseases Acts, whereas married men were presumed by the Divorce Court to infect their wives and bring venereal disease into the matrimonial home.[148] The suffragette Christabel Pankhurst even remarked in 1913 that women should not enter into marriage without knowing the risks of contracting venereal diseases from their husbands.[149]

---

137 *Plowden v Plowden* (1870) 23 LT 266.
138 *Bland v Bland* (1866) LR 1 P&D 237.
139 *Judd v Judd* [1907] P 241, 243.
140 *Berry v Berry and Carpenter* (1898) 78 LT 688.
141 *Jewell v Jewell* (1862) 2 Sw&Tr 573.
142 *Squires v Squires* (1864) 3 Sw&Tr 541; *Boardman v Boardman (The Queen's Proctor Intervening)* (1866) LR 1 P&D 233.
143 *Brown v Brown* (1865) LR 1 P&D 46.
144 *Morphett v Morphett* (1869) LR 1 PD 702.
145 *Chesnutt v Chesnutt* (1854) 1 Sp Ecc & Ad 196, 200–1.
146 Gail Savage, '"The Wilful Communication of a Loathsome Disease": Marital Conflict and Veneral Disease in Victorian England' (1990) 34(1) *Victorian Studies* 35, 48.
147 Gail Savage, '"…the Instrument of an Animal Function": Marital Rape and Sexual Cruelty in the Divorce Court, 1858–1908' in Lucy Delap, Ben Griffin, and Abigail Wills (eds), *The Politics of Domestic Authority in Britain since 1800* (Palgrave Macmillan 2009) 46.
148 Savage (n 146) 49–50.
149 Lesley Hall (ed), *Outspoken Women: An Anthology of Women's Writing on Sex, 1870–1960* (Routledge 2005) 41; June Purvis, *Christabel Pankhurst: A Biography* (Routledge 2018) 333.

90 Divorce under the 1857 Act

Aside from venereal disease, the Divorce Court was very reluctant to declare non-physical or indirect harm as cruelty. The physical abuse of a child of the marriage did not constitute cruelty as a matrimonial offence unless there was evidence of direct harm to the health of the other spouse.[150] Drunkenness was not an offence that alone constituted cruelty.[151] However, acts of cruelty committed by the respondent while inebriated entitled the petitioner to receive either divorce or judicial separation.[152] Similarly, insanity did not in itself constitute cruelty unless there was actual physical harm.[153] Divorce or judicial separation may follow, but the question of sanity was not a relevant consideration in itself.[154] The Court was primarily concerned with *actus reus*, because it was not necessary to establish *mens rea* in order to prove cruelty as a matrimonial offence.[155] Cruelty was aimed at protecting the vulnerable spouse rather than punishing the cruel spouse, thus it was enough for the petitioner to prove that the respondent had committed acts of cruelty in order to establish a matrimonial cause.[156]

Constructive cruelty was a way for the Divorce Court to circumvent the strict interpretation of actual cruelty. It referred to a continuous course of non-physical conduct intended to break down the health of the other spouse.[157] This included ongoing bullying,[158] harmful insulting conduct,[159] continued threats to abandon the wife and children for another woman,[160] and the deterioration of the wife's health as a result of the husband's criminal conviction.[161] However, neglect and want of affection towards another spouse in itself did not constitute constructive cruelty.[162] Therefore, acts rather than omissions could be classed as evidence of constructive cruelty. Threats of physical violence if reasonably apprehended could constitute constructive cruelty.[163] False accusations of committing a sexual offence did not constitute cruelty in itself, but could be presented as evidence of cumulative cruelty.[164] A wife was able to obtain a judicial separation or a divorce *a mensa et*

---

150 *Birch v Birch* (1873) 42 LJ(P&M) 23.
151 *Chesnutt v Chesnutt* (1854) 1 Sp Ecc & Ad 196; *Hudson v Hudson* (1863) 3 Sw&Tr 314; *Walker v Walker* (1898) 77 LT 715.
152 *Marsh v Marsh* (1858) 1 Sw&Tr 313; *Power v Power* (1865) 34 LJ(PA&M) 137; *Walker v Walker* (1898) 77 LT 715.
153 *Hall v Hall* (1864) 3 Sw&Tr 347.
154 *Hanbury v Hanbury* [1892] P 222.
155 *Mens rea* in cruelty first appears as a necessary element to prove in the judgment of Lord Denning in *Westall v Westall* (1949) 65 TLR 337.
156 *Hanbury v Hanbury* [1892] P 222, 224.
157 *Holden v Holden* (1810) 1 Hag Con 453; *Suggate v Suggate* (1859) 1 Sw&Tr 489; *Birch v Birch* (1873) 42 LJ(P&M) 23.
158 *Kelly v Kelly* (1870) 22 LT 308; *Mytton v Mytton* (1886) 11 PD 141.
159 *Bethune v Bethune* [1891] P 205; *Walmesley v Walmesley* (1893) 69 LT 152.
160 *Le Couteur v Le Couteur* (1896) *The Times*, 2 March 1896.
161 *Thompson v Thompson* (1901) 85 LT 172.
162 *Neeld v Neeld* (1831) 4 Hag Ecc 263; *Hudson v Hudson* (1863) 3 Sw&Tr 314.
163 *D'Aguilar v D'Aguilar* (1794) 1 Hag Ecc 773; *Bostock v Bostock* (1858) 1 Sw&Tr 221; *Knight v Knight* (1865) 4 Sw&Tr 103; *Sarkies v Sarkies* (1884) *The Times*, 28 June 1884; *Barrett v Barrett* (1903) 20 TLR 73.
164 *Durant v Durant* (1825) 1 Hag Ecc 733; *Gale v Gale* (1852) 2 Rob Ecc 421; *Russell v Russell* [1897] AC 395; *Walker v Walker* (1898) 77 LT 715; *Jeapes v Jeapes* (1903) 89 LT 74.

thoro for gross insult. These included giving the public the impression that the wife was a prostitute,[165] and spitting in the wife's face.[166] However, the House of Lords in *Russell v Russell* felt that constructive cruelty was being interpreted too widely and rejected the argument that insults constituted cruelty.[167] Despite the fact that the Probate, Divorce and Admiralty (PDA) Division gradually expanded the scope of cruelty, the House of Lords applied a strict interpretation that reflected the conservative values of the Matrimonial Causes Act 1857.

Desertion

Desertion as a matrimonial cause was statutorily defined as 'Adultery coupled with Desertion, without reasonable Excuse, for Two Years or upwards.'[168] The 1856 Select Committee had initially proposed four years of desertion, but this period was seen as too long and it was halved to two years.[169] Prior to 1857, desertion was not a ground of divorce *a mensa et thoro*. Rather, it could be either used as evidence to prove recrimination in order to bar divorce or as a ground for restitution of conjugal rights. Desertion involved a situation where the respondent had wilfully lived apart from the petitioner either without the consent[170] or against the will of the petitioner.[171] Moreover, the separation was without cause or reasonable excuse for at least two years.[172] Although desertion gave married women an extra ground of aggravated enormity, it was rather complicated to prove. Once again it was a reason that was used to justify the abolition of the double standard under the Matrimonial Causes Act 1923.

Three elements were required to prove desertion: intention, evidence, and length of desertion. In regards to intention, it had to be ascertained either from fact[173] or an inference of fact.[174] Intention was evinced once its commencement

---

165 *Milner v Milner* (1861) 4 Sw&Tr 240. The husband verbally abused the wife in public, then pushed her against a wall and thrust his umbrella into her anus. A passer-by took her for a prostitute and seized hold of her leg.
166 *D'Aguilar v D'Aguilar* (1794) 1 Hag Ecc 773.
167 [1897] AC 395.
168 Matrimonial Causes Act 1857, s 27.
169 HL Deb 26 June 1856, vol 42, col 1970.
170 *Smith v Smith* (1859) 1 Sw&Tr 359; *Buckmaster v Buckmaster* (1869) LR 1 P&D 713; *Parkinson v Parkinson* (1869) LR 2 P&D 25; *Taylor v Taylor* (1881) 44 LT 31; *Dagg v Dagg and Speake* (1882) 7 PD 17.
171 *Fitzgerald v Fitzgerald* (1869) LR 1 P&D 694; *Townsend v Townsend* (1873) LR 3 P&D 129; *Henty v Henty* (1875) 33 LT 263.
172 *Thompson v Thompson* (1858) 1 Sw&Tr 231; *Ousey v Ousey and Atkinson* (1874) LR 3 P&D 223; *Williamson v Williamson and Bates* (1882) 7 PD 76; *Mackenzie v Mackenzie* [1895] AC 384; *Synge v Synge* (1900) P 180.
173 In *French-Brewster v French-Brewster and Gore* (1889) 62 LT 609, a jury was called to determine a question of fact whether the husband was honestly intending to resume cohabitation with the wife or to deprive the wife the right to divorce by interrupting the two years of separation. The jury found the latter to be true, and the Court granted divorce to the wife.
174 In *Lawrence v Lawrence* (1862) 2 Sw&Tr 575, the husband cohabitated with the wife for four years in England before leaving her for the next three years to work in the Commissariat in China. In 1859, a court martial found him guilty of embezzlement and he wrote letters to the wife

could be fixed at a certain time or event.[175] Merely living apart did not constitute desertion unless there was an intention to abandon the other party.[176] Desertion could still arise even if the deserting party failed to return due to imprisonment. In *Drew v Drew*, the husband told the wife that he was going to Ireland for a week's shooting trip, but absconded to Australia in order to avoid embezzlement charges.[177] He was arrested in Sydney, then extradited back to England. The Court ruled that his imprisonment did not break the length of desertion. Moreover, a fear of criminal prosecution was not an acceptable excuse for desertion. In *Wynne v Wynne*, the Court found that the husband's desertion of the wife due to financial difficulties and prosecution from his creditors did not exonerate him from his actions.[178] Therefore, the PDA Division provided married women some further scope of factually proving desertion.

Evidence of desertion was judged against the parties' positions and circumstances in life.[179] There were quite a number of ways that the Court could reject claims of desertion. Neglecting or refusing to pay the other spouse a financial allowance did not constitute desertion in itself.[180] Similarly, a deed of separation was only *prima facie* evidence of separation by mutual consent. This did not constitute desertion unless the parties resumed and broke cohabitation.[181] Desertion could not be found where parties who once cohabitated were already separated by mutual consent.[182] However, desertion could be found in other ways. Desertion at the outset of the marriage was recognised as an exception to the cohabitation rule, and either divorce[183] or nullity of marriage could be granted.[184] Moreover, a financial allowance given by the respondent to the petitioner while separated did not exculpate a party from the charge of desertion.[185]

The length of desertion had to be at least two years.[186] If two years had not yet elapsed, the Court could either grant a judicial separation or an adjournment until it was possible to grant a divorce, or request the filing of a fresh petition.[187]

---

expressing no intention of returning to the matrimonial home. He subsequently committed adultery. The letters were construed as evidence of desertion, and the wife was granted a divorce.

175 *Gatehouse v Gatehouse* (1867) LR 1 P&D 331; *Stickland v Stickland* (1876) 35 LT 767.
176 *Ward v Ward* (1858) 1 Sw&Tr 185.
177 (1888) 13 PD 97.
178 [1898] P 18.
179 *Williams v Williams* (1864) 3 Sw&Tr 547.
180 *Pape v Pape* (1887) 20 QBD 76.
181 *Cock v Cock* (1864) 3 Sw&Tr 514.
182 *Fitzgerald v Fitzgerald* (1869) LR 1 P&D 694; *Pape v Pape* (1887) 20 QBD 76; *R v Leresche and Another, Justices of Lancashire* [1891] 2 QB 418; *Bradshaw v Bradshaw* [1897] P 24; *Kay v Kay* [1904] P 382.
183 *De Laubenque v De Laubenque* [1899] P 42.
184 *Du Terreaux v Du Terreaux* (1859) 1 Sw&Tr 555.
185 *Macdonald v Macdonald* (1859) 4 Sw&Tr 242; *Nott v Nott* (1866) LR 1 P&D 251; *Yeatman v Yeatman* (1868) LR 1 P&D 489.
186 The set of circumstances demonstrating desertion must be proven to have existed throughout that period. *Kay v Kay* [1904] P 382, 395; *Dodd v Dodd* [1906] P 189, 194.
187 *Kettlewell v Kettlewell* (1880) 41 LT 737; *Knapp v Knapp* (1880) 6 PD 10; *Wood v Wood* (1887) 13 PD 22; *Lapington v Lapington* (1888) 14 PD 21; *Kay v Kay* [1904] P 382.

Desertion could arise if the respondent was separated from the petitioner beyond their mutually agreed period.[188] A husband who clandestinely lived with another woman and occasionally visited his wife without sexual intercourse could be found guilty of desertion.[189] The length of desertion would continue if the respondent failed to accept a reasonable offer to return to the matrimonial home from the petitioner.[190] Moreover, a *bona fide* offer to return did not ameliorate the respondent of the matrimonial offence.[191]

Desertion could have been brought to an end in a number of ways. Intermittent sexual intercourse between the spouses broke the length of desertion.[192] If the wife refused the husband's *bona fide* offer to return to the matrimonial home, then the separation would have ceased to constitute desertion.[193] The most significant barrier to proving desertion came unintentionally as a result of the introduction of the Summary Jurisdiction (Married Women) Act 1895.[194] Magistrates' orders of non-cohabitation under this Act were held to have ended the length of desertion.[195] This denied many married women the right to divorce.[196] The piecemeal reform aimed at improving access to the family justice system among the poor failed to solve the more substantive issue of discrimination against married women seeking divorce.

The Divorce Court occasionally recognised constructive desertion in a similar fashion to the way it dealt with constructive cruelty. This was a way of circumventing the issue of actual desertion. It is evident that the Divorce Court exercised its judicial discretion in mitigating the strictures of the Matrimonial Causes Act 1857. Constructive desertion could be found in cases where the respondent's bad conduct caused the petitioner to leave the matrimonial home.[197] In an ordinary case of desertion, the respondent has left the matrimonial home with the intention of abandoning the petitioner. In a case of constructive desertion, however, the petitioner has left the matrimonial home as a result of the respondent's bad conduct. Therefore, the respondent would be said to have evinced an intention to desert the petitioner through his bad conduct despite remaining in the matrimonial home. A good illustration of this involves a scenario where the husband has made cohabitation intolerable for the wife. For example, the husband could be found to have committed desertion if the wife left the matrimonial home as

---

188 *Basing v Basing* (1864) 3 Sw&Tr 516. The wife agreed for the husband to go to Australia ahead of her. Once in Australia, the husband was found to have deserted the wife by never sending back money and committing adultery.
189 *Garcia v Garcia* (1888) 13 PD 216.
190 *Gibson v Gibson* (1859) 29 LJ(P&M) 25; *Pizzala v Pizzala* (1896) 12 TLR 451.
191 *Cargill v Cargill* (1858) 1 Sw&Tr 235.
192 *Farmer v Farmer* (1884) 9 PD 245.
193 *Lodge v Lodge* (1890) 15 PD 159.
194 (58 & 59 Vict c 39).
195 *Dodd v Dodd* [1906] P 189; *Harriman v Harriman* (1909) P 123.
196 *Dodd v Dodd* [1906] P 189.
197 *Graves v Graves* (1864) 3 Sw&Tr 350; *Dickinson v Dickinson* (1889) 62 LT 330; *Pizzala v Pizzala* (1896) 12 TLR 451; *Koch v Koch* [1899] P 221; *Sickert v Sickert* [1899] P 278.

a result of reasonably suspecting that the husband was having an extra-marital relationship,[198] or the wife refused to live with the adulterer.[199] However, the husband could not be found to have committed desertion by merely living with another woman unless it could be proven to make cohabitation intolerable.[200]

An unsuccessful petition for divorce or judicial separation on the ground of constructive desertion could become a suit for restitution of conjugal rights.[201] Consequently, the petitioner had to come to the Court with strong evidence of desertion or else face a serious risk of being ordered to resume cohabitation with the respondent. The petitioner from 1884 onwards could easily resolve this by simply refusing to follow a restitution of conjugal rights order, thereby being found to have committed desertion him or herself.[202] Despite the recognition of constructive desertion, it was still rather difficult for the petitioner to prove that the respondent committed desertion. The heavy burden of proving aggravated enormity later became a strong reason for the abolition of the double standard in the grounds of divorce between the genders.[203]

Statutory damages

The Matrimonial Causes Act 1857 introduced a number of reforms to court orders. Statutory damages replaced the Assizes' jurisdiction over criminal conversation.[204] Moreover, separation orders and restitution of conjugal rights orders replaced the Ecclesiastical Courts' legal consideration over divorce *a mensa et thoro*. The Divorce Court mitigated the harshness of a strict interpretation of the Matrimonial Causes Act 1857 as case law developed over time. However, statutory change proved to be the most significant factor in promoting piecemeal reform that provided greater latitude to the Court. Piecemeal reform did not satisfactorily ameliorate wider dissatisfaction with these court orders. Therefore, a campaign to reform the divorce laws arose in the early twentieth century.

Statutory damages initially followed the principles of awarding criminal conversation in the common law courts.[205] The idea of the paramour indemnifying the husband for the loss of consortium to the wife and injury suffered from the adulterous relationship persisted throughout the Victorian period. However, the judicial discretion to grant statutory damages and the decision of whom to award it became broader over time. The Divorce Court sought to limit the remedy to reflect changing values and to provide for the welfare of the family. Just as was the case for criminal conversation trials, parties had the right to demand a jury for

---

198 *Dallas v Dallas* (1874) 43 LJ(P&M) 87.
199 *Dickinson v Dickinson* (1890) 62 LT 330.
200 *Ward v Ward* (1858) 1 Sw&Tr 185.
201 *Kay v Kay* [1904] P 382.
202 Matrimonial Causes Act 1884 (47 & 48 Vict c 68) s 5.
203 Matrimonial Causes Act 1923.
204 Lord Halsbury (ed), *The Laws of England: Volume XVI* (Butterworth 1911) 542–3.
205 Matrimonial Causes Act 1857, s 33.

trials of statutory damages.[206] A guilty co-respondent could be ordered to pay the legal costs for the proceedings.[207] The Court had the power to order that the co-respondent pay statutory damages to the husband petitioner where adultery was found but a divorce decree was refused for whatever reason.[208] In fact, statutory damages could still be awarded even if the spouses had reconciled and the divorce decree was rescinded.[209]

Unlike criminal conversation, statutory damages were compensatory rather than punitive relief for the sole benefit of the husband. Costs were determined by a judge and damages were always assessed by a jury until the passing of the Juries Act 1918, which allowed the Court to try an action without a jury.[210] The Court could direct all or part-payment of damages to provide for the benefit of the children of the marriage and for the payment of spousal maintenance to the wife.[211] In *Mozley Stark v Mozley Stark*, the Court of Appeal expanded the beneficiaries of statutory damages to include holding co-respondents responsible for paying child maintenance until the age of 21, which was hitherto limited to the parents.[212] Judicial discretion was exercised rather widely in distributing statutory damages. In *Meyern v Meyern and Myers*, the Court ordered that the statutory damages of £5000 be split among the family members: £1500 to the husband for compensation, £1500 to the youngest child of the marriage (aged five) for child maintenance, and £2000 to the wife for spousal maintenance on the condition that she never marry the co-respondent and she live a life of chastity.[213] However, there were still limits to statutory damages. It could only be sought within the lifetime of the co-respondent. In *Brydges v Brydges and Wood*, the Court of Appeal held a petitioner could not recover statutory damages from the estate of a deceased co-respondent.[214]

The first consideration for assessing damages for adultery was the value of the loss of the wife as a result of the adultery. In *Bell v Bell and Marquis of Anglesey*, Cresswell J stated, 'It has always been considered that the only question was, of the loss to the husband of the society of the wife.'[215] Statutory damages were awarded in circumstances where the co-respondent had prolonged the loss of the wife's consortium. In *Evans v Evans and Platts*, the jury found that the wife committed adultery with her solicitor for a period of about 12 months.[216]

---

206 Matrimonial Causes Act 1857, s 28.
207 Matrimonial Causes Act 1857, s 34.
208 *Bremner v Bremner and Brett* (1864) 3 Sw&Tr 378, 380; *Grosvenor v Grosvenor* (1886) 34 WR 140; *Story v Story and O'Connor* (1887) 12 PD 196, 198; *Waudby v Waudby and Bowland* [1902] P 85.
209 *Quartermaine v Quartermaine and Gleinster* [1911] P 180.
210 (8 & 9 Geo V c 23).
211 Matrimonial Causes Act 1857, s 34.
212 [1910] P 190. See also *Thomasset v Thomasset* [1894] P 295.
213 (1876) LR 2 PD 254.
214 [1909] P 187.
215 (1858) 1 Sw&Tr 565, 566.
216 [1899] P 195.

96   *Divorce under the 1857 Act*

Although the wife and the husband were separated prior to the adultery,[217] Jeune J held that the material element was the fact that the co-respondent's ongoing adultery rendered reconciliation impossible and inflicted an intolerable insult upon the petitioner that was considered worse than the breaking-up of the matrimonial home.[218]

The second consideration was assessing the value of the injury inflicted upon the feelings of the husband. In *Bell v Bell and Marquis of Anglesey*, the wife was found to have committed adultery with the co-respondent, the Marquis of Anglesey. The jury found in favour of the husband and awarded him £10,000. This was twice the amount he had sought. Cresswell J had directed the jury to consider 'the marquis taking advantage perhaps of the prestige of his rank, in making a vain woman false to her duty to her husband.'[219] This established a precedent that the wealth and status of the co-respondent compared with the petitioner was a relevant consideration in assessing statutory damages, but this was later disputed.[220] As the case law developed, the co-respondent's status became less important. Juries were directed that they were not to punish the co-respondent in awarding statutory damages, but to compensate the husband for the loss sustained.[221] Statutory damages could vary widely, but juries often awarded a higher sum than the amount sought by the petitioner.[222] Furthermore, a separation deed agreed between the parties did not bar a husband seeking relief from a co-respondent who had committed adultery with the wife, but it could be a relevant factor in mitigating damages.[223]

A co-respondent's ignorance of the wife's marital status was not an accepted excuse and it did not bar a claim for statutory damages against the co-respondent. However, this was a relevant consideration in reducing the assessment of statutory damages and costs. In practice, many judges did not award costs against

---

217 This is in contrast to the judgment in *Malcomson v Givins* (1873) *The Times*, 27 February 1873. Hannen J found that the claim for statutory damages was based on the husband's loss of consortium, but dismissed the claim in the case because of the fact that the husband and wife had lived separately.

218 *Evans v Evans and Platts* [1899] P 195, 198–9.

219 *Bell v Bell and Marquis of Anglesey* (1858) 1 Sw&Tr 565, 567.

220 In *Keyse v Keyse* (1886) 11 PD 100, 103, Hannen J stated, 'The only question is what damage the petitioner has sustained, and the damage he has sustained is the same whether the co-respondent is a rich man or a poor man.'

221 *Ibid.* 101; *Comyn v Comyn and Humphreys* (1860) 32 LJ(P) 210; *Darbishire v Darbishire* (1890) 62 LT 664; *Evans v Evans and Platts* [1899] P 195, 202; *Butterworth v Butterworth and Englefield* [1920] P 126, 139.

222 In *Bell v Bell and Marquis of Anglesey* (1858) 1 Sw&Tr 565, £5000 was sought but £10,000 was granted. In *Izard v Izard and Leslie* (1889) 14 PD 45, £5000 was awarded. In *Beckett v Beckett* [1901] P 85, an unspecified amount was sought by the petitioner that was less than the £400 that was granted.

223 *Izard v Izard and Leslie* (1889) 14 PD 45, 46–7. This was not the situation for criminal conversation cases that were heard prior to the Matrimonial Causes Act 1857, since a separation agreement barred a husband from seeking damages as a result of the perception that the husband had given licence or assent to the wife's adultery. See *Weedon v Timbrell* (1793) 5 TR 357; *Winter v Henn* (1831) 4 Car & P 494.

ignorant co-respondents though an order of statutory damages could still be made. There were some cases where judges did award a petitioner costs. The law was contested on this issue. On 14 June 1858, Cresswell J delivered two contrasting judgments. In *Teagle v Teagle and Nottingham*, the Court refused to award costs against the co-respondent on the basis that there was no proof that he was aware of the marital status of the wife.[224] However, in *Badcock v Badcock and Chamberlain*, the Court held that costs can be awarded against the co-respondent when it can be established that the co-respondent knew that the wife was married but persisted in committing adultery.[225] This principle was affirmed in *Learmouth v Learmouth and Austin*, Butt J held that as a general rule a co-respondent who continued an adulterous relationship after initial ignorance can be ordered to pay costs.[226]

BARS TO DIVORCE

Collusion

The Divorce Court interpreted bars to divorce strictly in accordance with the Matrimonial Causes Act 1857, which denied many petitioners from being granted relief. Since the grounds for divorce were already narrow, the bars to divorce compounded this situation and invigorated the divorce law reform movement in the early twentieth century. Divorce petitioners were expected to come to the Court with 'clean hands, a real grievance and present wrong.'[227] The bars to divorce were based on the principles of equity. The Divorce Court viewed its role as the keeper of morality and justice.[228] Therefore, it refused to grant divorce to a petitioner for perceived acts of immorality. Stephen Cretney explains the policy rationale—'that a petitioner should be an innocent person labouring under an intolerable grievance.'[229]

There were two types of bars to divorce: absolute and discretionary. Absolute bars included collusion, connivance, and condonation. They operated with strict liability and could not be rebutted if the act in question was proven. Discretionary bars encompassed the petitioner's adultery, recrimination, and unreasonable delay. The petitioner could have exonerated him or herself despite committing the act in question provided a satisfactory defence could be made. Therefore, the equitable doctrine of 'those seeking equity must do equity'

---

224 (1858) 1 Sw&Tr 188. Followed in *Priske v Priske and Goldby* (1860) 4 Sw&Tr 238.
225 (1858) 1 Sw&Tr 189.
226 (1889) 62 LT 608. However, Butt J did not order costs against the co-respondent due to the special facts in this case.
227 Rayden (n 107) 88.
228 In *Constantinidi v Constantinidi and Lance* [1905] P 253, 278, Stirling LJ states, 'the Court should endeavour to promote virtue and morality and to discourage vice and immorality.'
229 Cretney (n 93) 193.

98 Divorce under the 1857 Act

prevailed, or, as A.P. Herbert humorously puts it, 'A dirty dog will get no dinner from the Courts.'[230]

Collusion referred to a divorce suit involving an agreement between the parties or their agents for one of the spouses to commit adultery or give the appearance that adultery was committed.[231] It was used to expedite the legal process in order to obtain a divorce decree. The definition of collusion has its origins in the Ecclesiastical Courts. In *Crewe v Crewe*, Lord Stowell states:

> Collusion, as applied to this subject, is an agreement between the parties for one to commit, or appear to commit, a fact of adultery, in order that the other may obtain a remedy at law as for a real injury.[232]

The Matrimonial Causes Act 1857 does not define collusion, though it is mentioned under sections 29, 30, and 31 as a reason to dismiss a petition. Thus, the Courts constructed their own meaning rather strictly. Collusion was an absolute bar to divorce in order to prevent the married parties manipulating the law. Parties were required to make full disclosure of the material facts in order to prevent divorce by mutual consent. The Court was barred from granting a judicial separation or divorce to both of the spouses upon finding collusion.[233] However, a new suit free from collusion could be initiated afterwards.[234] The findings of fact in the first suit continued to be valid based on *res judicata* estoppel.[235] The Queen's Proctor was responsible for investigating cases of suspected collusion.

The Court was faced with three types of collusion: the suppression of information, sham cases, and obnoxious agreements.[236] A collusion case could feature different types of collusion at the same time. First, the suppression of information involved the parties agreeing to suppress relevant information that may be deleterious to successfully obtaining a divorce. This included suppressing evidence

---

230 A.P. Herbert, *Uncommon Law* (Methuen 1935) 335.
231 *Churchward v Churchward and Holliday (The Queen's Proctor Intervening)* [1895] P 7 contains the most definitive definition of collusion in the Victorian period.
232 *Crewe v Crewe* (1800) 3 Hag Ecc 123, 129–30.
233 This was based on the principles of equity. In *Butler v Butler and Burnham (The Queen's Proctor Intervening)* (1890) 15 PD 66, 75, Lopes LJ states, 'Now what is the object of this special provision with regard to collusion? I think that its object is to compel the parties to come into the Court of Divorce with clean hands.'
234 *Churchward v Churchward and Holliday (The Queen's Proctor Intervening)* [1895] P 7, 32.
235 *Butler v Butler* [1894] P 25. *Res judicata* refers to the preclusion of a matter being retried in a new suit as the matter has already been judged.
236 The three types of collusion are identified in *Churchward v Churchward and Holliday (The Queen's Proctor Intervening)* [1895] P 7, 17. In a treatise published in 1860, Macqueen omits suppression of information, but recognises the other two types of collusion; see Macqueen (n 57) 67. In *Jessop v Jessop (The Queen's Proctor Intervening)* (1861) 2 Sw&Tr 301, 303, Cresswell J also lists only two types of collusion and omits suppression of information. This seems to suggest that suppression of information was a later addition as a type of collusion.

of connivance,[237] obnoxious agreements,[238] and the petitioner's adultery.[239] Collusion was not found if the petitioner had asked the respondent to furnish evidence of adultery in order to adduce for trial.[240] Initially, suppressing information was not a bar to divorce in itself unless material facts of the petitioner committing a matrimonial offence were withheld.[241] However, this was later overturned in *Butler v Butler and Burnham (The Queen's Proctor Intervening)*.[242] The Court of Appeal ruled that the Court has the right to demand full disclosure by barring relief to parties who had suppressed relevant information.[243] In this case, the parties and their solicitors signed an agreement that the wife should give evidence of the husband's adultery and cruelty. The husband agreed to withdraw his petition against the wife for adultery after the first day of the trial. The trial judge was made aware of this agreement on the following day, but allowed the trial to continue. The jury found that the husband was guilty of adultery and cruelty; thus, the wife was granted a decree *nisi*. The Queen's Proctor alleged that the parties suppressed information and were guilty of collusion. Another jury was called to determine the questions of fact. The jury found that the parties had suppressed information. Therefore, the Court rescinded the decree *nisi* and dismissed both petitions based on collusion.

Second, sham cases referred to the parties agreeing to present a fabricated story in order to be granted a divorce.[244] Hotel divorces were the classic example of collusion involving the parties putting forward a false case, and became more common during the Interwar period. The respondent would book a hotel with another person who would play the role of paramour and give the appearance that adultery was committed. The Court harboured strong suspicions of collusion when the case involved adultery having taken place in a hotel. In *Todd v Todd*, the husband fulfilled a promise to his estranged wife through the agency of his sister that he would let her get a divorce by booking a hotel in Paris in order to give the appearance that he had committed adultery.[245] The Court found that the wife had acted in concert with the husband to form an obnoxious agreement for the express purpose of allowing her to petition for divorce based on false evidence of the husband's adultery. Therefore, collusion was found and the wife's petition for divorce on the grounds of adultery and desertion was dismissed.

---

237 *Hunt v Hunt and Wright* (1877) 47 LJ(P) 22.
238 *Barnes v Barnes and Grimwade (The Queen's Proctor Intervening)* (1867) LR 1 P&D 505; *Butler v Butler and Burnham (The Queen's Proctor Intervening)* (1890) 15 PD 66; *Churchward v Churchward and Holliday (The Queen's Proctor Intervening)* [1895] P 7.
239 *Apted v Apted and Bliss* [1930] P 246, 262.
240 *Laidler v Laidler* (1920) 36 TLR 510.
241 *Alexandre v Alexandre* (1870) LR 2 P&D 164.
242 (1890) 15 PD 66.
243 *Ibid.* 71–2.
244 The Ecclesiastical Courts first recognised sham cases as a type of collusion in *Crewe v Crewe* (1800) 3 Hag Ecc 123.
245 (1866) LR 1 P&D 121.

100 Divorce under the 1857 Act

Third, obnoxious agreements were bargains made between the parties prior to the suit that the Court found repugnant. Cretney states, 'This type of collusion caused great difficulty because it raised the question of how far the parties could go in agreeing the consequences of ending their marriage.'[246] Although what constituted obnoxious agreements could be open to subjective interpretation, the Courts consistently barred relief if there was some sort of bargain for one of the parties not to defend.[247] Even if the agreement was fully disclosed to the Court and there was no proof of deceit or omission of evidence, the Court was entitled to reject the petition.[248] Evidence of the petitioner's and the respondent's desires to take active steps to obtain a divorce did not necessarily make them guilty of collusion for this fact alone.[249] In *Churchward v Churchward and Holliday (The Queen's Proctor Intervening)*, the husband agreed to petition for divorce against the wife and not to claim damages against the co-respondent so long as she agreed to settle money on the child of the marriage and pay the costs of the suit.[250] Jeune J states, 'I must say that a divorce suit ought not, in my judgment, to be made the stipulated price of any pecuniary consideration.'[251] Therefore, the financial bargaining was deemed to have been an obnoxious agreement and an act of collusion. The possible broad interpretation of obnoxious agreements was certainly a factor in deterring couples from making financial and parenting agreements. The bar of collusion as demonstrated was rather broad and it caused a great deal of antipathy among couples mutually agreeing to divorce. There were calls for the expansion of the grounds for divorce in the Interwar period as the issue of collusion coincided with the rise of hotel divorces.

Connivance

Connivance is a term derived from the Latin *connivere*, meaning 'to wink at,' and referred to the petitioner acting in a way that was conducive to the respondent's commission of adultery.[252] The Court must be satisfied 'whether or not the Petitioner has been in any Manner accessory to or conniving at the Adultery,'[253] and had to determine whether the petition could be dismissed for

246 Cretney (n 93) 187.
247 *Todd v Todd* (1866) LR 1 P&D 121; *Barnes v Barnes and Grimwade (The Queen's Proctor Intervening)* (1867) LR 1 P&D 505; *Butler v Butler and Burnham (The Queen's Proctor Intervening)* (1890) 15 PD 66; *Churchward v Churchward and Holliday (The Queen's Proctor Intervening)* [1895] P 7.
248 *Butler v Butler and Burnham (The Queen's Proctor Intervening)* (1890) 15 PD 66; *Churchward v Churchward and Holliday (The Queen's Proctor Intervening)* [1895] P 7.
249 In *Harris v Harris and Lambert* (1862) 4 Sw&Tr 232, collusion was not found after the respondent gave a photograph to the petitioner's solicitor for the purposes of identification during the Court proceedings. In *Malley v Malley* (1909) 25 TLR 662, there was no collusion after the respondent's sister gave £100 to the petitioner in order to financially assist her suit.
250 [1895] P 7.
251 *Ibid.* 32.
252 Cretney (n 93) 181.
253 Matrimonial Causes Act 1857, s 29.

connivance.²⁵⁴ The main similarity between connivance and collusion was that the parties had brought about the commission of a matrimonial offence with the intention of being granted a divorce. The main difference between the two bars was that collusion involved an active collaboration between the parties, while connivance was solely concerned with the petitioner's role in tacitly conspiring at the respondent's matrimonial offences. Therefore, connivance existed in all cases of collusion, since the petitioner must connive at the adultery of the respondent for the collusive scheme to work.²⁵⁵ The finding of connivance compelled the Court to dismiss a petition for the dissolution of marriage, even if a future petition found that the respondent had subsequently committed adultery.²⁵⁶ Similarly to collusion, connivance frustrated many married couples from divorce by mutual consent. The question of connivance would be considered after failing to find collusion.

The law held a presumption against the existence of connivance.²⁵⁷ In order to establish connivance, it must have been shown that the petitioner held an intention by willing consent to connive at the adultery of the respondent,²⁵⁸ and was aware that adultery would follow from the conniving.²⁵⁹ The House of Lords later extended the scope of connivance to include acquiescence by wilfully abstaining.²⁶⁰ However, the petitioner would not be found to have committed connivance in these circumstances: executing a deed of separation before the adultery,²⁶¹ cases where there was a lack of consent to the adultery,²⁶² and evidence of intolerance after the adultery.²⁶³ Moreover, the petitioner would not be found to have connived at the respondent's adultery by delaying the petition in order to gather evidence for a suit without giving notice to the respondent.²⁶⁴

There were two types of connivance. The first was to give effect to the principle of *volenti non fit injuria*.²⁶⁵ This legal maxim is predominantly associated with tort law, namely the defence of voluntary assumption of risk.²⁶⁶ In regards to the law of divorce, *volenti* operated similarly to the equitable bar of acquiescence—in particular, the petitioner giving licence to the respondent to

---

254 Matrimonial Causes Act 1857, s 30.
255 *Todd v Todd* (1866) LR 1 P&D 121.
256 *Gipps v Gipps and Hume* (1864) 11 HLC 1, 28–9.
257 *Glennie v Glennie and Bowles* (1862) 32 LJ(PA&M) 17; *Marris v Marris and Burke (The Queen's Proctor Intervening)* (1862) 2 Sw&Tr 530; *Ross v Ross* (1869) LR 1 P&D 734.
258 *Allen v Allen and D'Arcy* (1859) 30 LJ(PA&M) 2, 4.
259 *Glennie v Glennie and Bowles* (1862) 32 LJ(PA&M) 17.
260 *Gipps v Gipps and Hume* (1864) 11 HLC 1, 14.
261 *Ross v Ross* (1869) LR 1 P&D 734.
262 *Marris v Marris and Burke (The Queen's Proctor Intervening)* (1862) 2 Sw&Tr 530.
263 *Glennie v Glennie and Bowles* (1862) 32 LJ(PA&M) 17.
264 *Reeves v Reeves* (1813) 2 Phill 125.
265 *Rogers v Rogers* (1830) 3 Hag Ecc 57; *Glennie v Glennie and Bowles* (1862) 32 LJ(PA&M) 17; *Gipps v Gipps and Hume* (1864) 11 HLC 1, 25. See also *First Report of the Commissioners…Into the Law of Divorce* (1852–3) BPP vol 40, 269.
266 Edwin Peel and James Goudkamp, *Winfield and Jolowicz on Tort* (19th edn, Thomson Reuters 2014) 787–91.

102 *Divorce under the 1857 Act*

commit adultery whether through express or implied acceptance.[267] The equivalent of *volenti* connivance and unreasonable delay in the law of equity are acquiescence and laches respectively. These two equitable bars significantly overlap with each other.[268] In *Boulting v Boulting*, the wife discovered that the husband commenced an adulterous affair a year after the marriage began.[269] For 17 years, she did not rebuke the husband for continuing his adulterous relationship. The Court found that she had not only acquiesced but also wilfully consented to the husband's adultery. Cresswell J held that the circumstances surrounding the connivance affect whether or not the Court will exercise its discretion against divorce for unreasonable delay.[270] Thus connivance was proven and the petition refused.

The second type of connivance was to give effect to the principle of clean hands.[271] This was similar to the rationale behind collusion that barred petitioners to relief for their own misdeeds. In regards to connivance, this referred to the petitioner's own matrimonial offences being seen as conniving at the adultery of the respondent. In *Gipps v Gipps and Hume*, the husband on discovering the adultery of the wife demanded £3000 from the co-respondent in exchange for the petition not to include a claim for damages.[272] Both parties agreed and performed those terms. The husband later demanded a further £4000 bond from the co-respondent in exchange for the withdrawal of the petition, but the co-respondent refused. The House of Lords found that the petitioner's bargain with the co-respondent and acquiescence by wilfully abstaining towards the wife's adultery constituted connivance.[273] Therefore, the appeal was dismissed and the decree of the Court for Divorce and Matrimonial Causes to bar relief was upheld.[274] Lord Westbury dismissed the appeal on the ground of clean hands by affirming the trial judgment of Cresswell J that the petitioner knew that adultery would occur and allowed it to continue in order to extort more money from the co-respondent.[275] On the other hand, Lord Chelmsford and Lord Wensleydale held that this was a case of *volenti* connivance based on the petitioner's acquiescence of the adultery. Lord Chelmsford, finding *volenti* connivance proven,

---

267 *Boulting v Boulting* (1864) 3 Sw&Tr 329, 335.
268 Sarah Worthington, *Equity* (2nd edn, Oxford University Press 2006) 105–6.
269 (1864) 3 Sw&Tr 329.
270 *Ibid*. 336.
271 The majority report of the Campbell Commission states, 'When one of them has connived at the guilt of the other, that connivance involves criminality ... and therefore, in point of law, as well as in point of morals, it bars relief on account of adultery which itself has occasioned or allowed to take place.' *First Report of the Commissioners...Into the Law of Divorce* (1852–3) BPP vol 40, 268–9.
272 (1864) 11 HLC 1.
273 *Ibid*.
274 *Gipps v Gipps and Hume* (1863) 3 Sw&Tr 116.
275 In *Gipps v Gipps and Hume* (1864) 11 HLC 1, 22, Lord Westbury states, 'My Lords ... for if ever there be a court in which it is incumbent to hold up the maxim that a man who seeks relief shall come with clean hands, it is undoubtedly the Court of Divorce.'

agreed with the orders of Lord Westbury and dismissed the appeal.[276] However, Lord Wensleydale in dissent disputed the decree of Cresswell J. He ruled *volenti* connivance was not sufficiently established according to the wife's lack of consent to the adultery.[277] This case highlighted the overlap between the two types of connivance, and that clean hands connivance was more difficult to prove than *volenti* connivance. It also demonstrated the multiple ways the Court could frustrate mutually consenting couples from divorcing, which later led to the call for divorce law reform.

Condonation

Condonation referred to the petitioner forgiving the matrimonial offence and reinstating the status of the respondent.[278] It was distinct from both connivance and collusion, because the acts of conniving and colluding must have occurred before the adultery. On the other hand, condonation could only occur after the adultery. The rationale behind condonation was that a petitioner could not condemn and condone a respondent at the same time, or 'blow hot and cold.'[279] This notion was similar to equitable estoppel, where the plaintiff is barred from pursuing a remedy when he or she has waived his or her rights to the claim based on a statement of an existing fact.[280] This encouraged separated parties who wanted to apply for divorce not to attempt reconciliation, which had an adverse influence to a broken-down marriage. This was part of the reason behind the expansion of the grounds for divorce under the Matrimonial Causes Act 1937, so that parties may attempt reconciliation without being barred from divorce.

The Court had to satisfy itself of the existence of condonation.[281] This was subject to the condition, whether express or implied, that the offending party had promised no further matrimonial offences would occur.[282] Otherwise, evidence proving that there was a specific agreement to the contrary should displace the belief of condonation.[283] A petition dismissed for condonation barred the granting of a divorce decree and judicial separation.[284] Condonation was supposed to restore the status of the spouses prior to the adultery by expunging

---

276 *Ibid.* 27–32.
277 *Ibid.* 22–7.
278 In *Cramp v Cramp and Freeman* [1920] P 158, 162, McCardie J states, 'It seems to me to be vital to remember that the forgiveness of condonation may be a wholly different thing to the forgiveness spoken of by ordinary men and women.'
279 *Hall v Hall and Kay* (1891) 64 LT 837, 838, per Jeune J.
280 *Jorden v Money* (1854) 5 HLC 185. See also *Durant v Durant* (1825) 1 Hag Ecc 733 for comparison with ecclesiastical notions of condonation in divorce law.
281 Matrimonial Causes Act 1857, s 29.
282 *Cooke v Cooke* (1863) 3 Sw&Tr 126; *Dent v Dent* (1865) 4 Sw&Tr 105; *Blandford v Blandford* (1883) 8 PD 19.
283 In *Rose v Rose* (1883) 8 PD 98, the Court held that the deed of separation was satisfactory evidence of condonation. In contrast to *Dowling v Dowling* (1898) P 228, condonation was not established since the petitioner failed to plead the deed of separation.
284 Matrimonial Causes Act 1857, s 30.

all matrimonial offences that the offended spouse knew or believed to have existed.[285] The law did not hold a presumption for knowledge and condonation of a matrimonial offence.[286] The commission of a matrimonial offence after an order of judicial separation could be used as evidence in a divorce suit, but not offences committed prior to the order.[287] Therefore, condonation had to be proven either through express or implied evidence, where a jury could be called to decide whether or not condonation occurred as a matter of fact.[288]

Evidence of express condonation included an agreement, but not mere words of forgiveness. In *Rose v Rose*, the husband committed acts of cruelty towards the wife resulting in the separation of the parties.[289] In the deed of separation, both parties agreed that neither should initiate proceedings based on matrimonial offences committed prior to signing the deed. After signing the deed, the husband subsequently committed adultery and the wife filed for divorce. The Court of Appeal unanimously held that that the deed of separation was satisfactory evidence of condonation. Thus the husband's cruelty was not revived and the wife could only obtain a judicial separation.

In *Keats v Keats and Montezuma*, on the other hand, the wife was found to have committed adultery with the co-respondent, who was a Spanish musician, during a stay in Brighton.[290] The husband initially expressed words of forgiveness to the wife, but he soon after filed for divorce. Cresswell J held that mere words do not constitute condonation.

> A party may 'forgive' in the sense of not meaning to bear ill will, or not seeking to punish, without at all meaning to restore to the original position. If you have a clerk or a servant who has robbed you, you might forgive him, and say, 'I forgive you,' without having the slightest intention of replacing him in your service, or of restoring him to the position he had forfeited.[291]

There not only must be an intention to forgive the offending party, but also that the intention has been manifested in a restoration of the *status quo* prior to the matrimonial offence.[292] These elements were absent in *Keats*, but were found in *Rose*.

It was more typical to prove implied condonation, because of the difficulty of proving express condonation. The popular way of proving implied condonation

---

285 *Peacock v Peacock* (1858) 1 Sw&Tr 183; *Keats v Keats and Montezuma* (1859) 1 Sw&Tr 334; *Dempster v Dempster* (1861) 2 Sw&Tr 438; *Ellis v Ellis and Smith* (1865) 4 Sw&Tr 154; *Hall v Hall and Kay* (1891) 64 LT 837.
286 *Durant v Durant* (1825) 1 Hag Ecc 733.
287 *Green v Green* (1873) LR 3 P&D 121.
288 *Peacock v Peacock* (1858) 1 Sw&Tr 183.
289 (1883) 8 PD 98.
290 (1859) 1 Sw&Tr 334.
291 *Ibid*. 346.
292 *Ibid*. 348. Condonation is also known as 'to restore as between the spouses the *status quo ante*'; see Lord Halsbury (ed), *The Laws of England: Volume XVI* (Butterworth 1911) 489.

was through inferring forgiveness of a matrimonial offence from a resumption of sexual intercourse between the parties after the adultery. However, sexual intercourse between the spouses did not in itself completely prove the condoning of a matrimonial offence. In *Hall v Hall and Kay*, the wife confessed adultery to the husband and they slept together for the following two nights, but then the husband sent the wife to her mother and began to initiate divorce proceedings.[293] Jeune J found that there was no condonation, because there was no intention from the set of circumstances to reinstate the place of the wife.[294] In *Keats v Keats and Montezuma*, Cresswell J found that there was no condonation in cases where the wife is put in a vulnerable position and has had to endure a conjugal relationship.[295] Cresswell J explains, 'The wife is hardly her own mistress; she may not have the option of going away; she may have no place to go to; no person to receive her; no funds to support her.'[296] Until the introduction of the Married Women's Property Act 1882,[297] the wife did not have the right of *feme sole* and could not legally enter into contracts or own most types of property in her own name. Consequently, married women were more likely to be financially insecure. Even after the introduction of the Act, women were generally still financially dependent on their husbands. On the other hand, McCardie J in *Cramp v Cramp and Freeman* held that the husband's repeated connubial intercourse with the wife after knowledge of her adultery 'must be conclusively presumed to have condoned her offence.'[298] The Court elicited less sympathy for the husband's refutation of condonation in those circumstances.[299]

Condonation was only conditional forgiveness. The condoned offence could be revived by a subsequent matrimonial offence.[300] There was a legal presumption that the offending party not only promised to cease any further matrimonial offences, but also resumed cohabitation and reinstated the position of the offending spouse.[301] Furthermore, there was a presumption that the offending party had given full disclosure of all matrimonial offences to the offended party.[302] Otherwise the original offence would be revived on the discovery of the

---

293 (1891) 64 LT 837.
294 *Ibid.* 838.
295 (1859) 1 Sw&Tr 334
296 *Ibid.* 347.
297 45 & 46 Vict, c 75.
298 [1920] P 158, 171.
299 In *Cramp v Cramp and Freeman* [1920] P 158, 170, McCardie J states, 'A man cannot, I think, use the body of his wife for sexual ends and announce to her at the same time that he will not forgive her adultery, but will present a petition to dissolve the matrimonial bond.'
300 *Wilton v Wilton and Chamberlain* (1859) 1 Sw&Tr 563; *Palmer v Palmer* (1860) 2 Sw&Tr 61; *Furness v Furness* (1860) 2 Sw&Tr 63.
301 *Keats v Keats and Montezuma* (1859) 1 Sw&Tr 334, 346; *Blandford v Blandford* (1888) 8 PD 19, 20; *Cramp v Cramp and Freeman* [1920] P 158, 169.
302 In *Dent v Dent* (1865) 4 Sw&Tr 105, 107, Wilde J states, '"Condonation" is a strictly technical word. It had its origin, and so far as I know its entire use, in the Ecclesiastical Courts, and it means "forgiveness with a condition."'

undisclosed offences.[303] The subsequent matrimonial offence did not have to be of the same nature as the original offence.[304] It could be less than what would normally be required to successfully file a petition in order to revive the condoned offence.[305] Disobedience to an order for restitution of conjugal rights could revive a condoned offence.[306] If the offending party subsequently committed adultery with another person, the first paramour in the condoned offence had to be made co-respondent in a petition along with the second paramour.[307]

The absolute bars to divorce shut the prospects of divorce for many people. Since adultery was the only ground of divorce that both the husband and the wife had to prove, the absolute bars of collusion, connivance, and condonation applied in all divorce suits. This was a major reason for the expansion of the grounds for divorce beyond adultery under the Matrimonial Causes Act 1937.

Petitioner's adultery

The petitioner's adultery without reasonable excuse was generally treated as an absolute bar to divorce irrespective of whether the petitioner was the husband or the wife. According to section 31 of the Matrimonial Causes Act 1857, 'the Court shall not be bound to pronounce such Decree if it shall find that the Petitioner has during the Marriage been guilty of Adultery.' However, if it could be proven that the adultery of the petitioner was condoned, innocent or unwilling, the Court could have exercised its discretion whether to bar or grant divorce. Furthermore, the respondent's conduct was sometimes a factor in the Court's exercise of its discretion, despite the fact that the bar pertained to the petitioner's own misconduct. In *Lautour v Her Majesty's Proctor*, the House of Lords held that the Court's discretion in cases of the petitioner's adultery should be rarely exercised.[308] The position had changed by the twentieth century and it was more common to find this discretion exercised. This fits with the broader liberalisation of divorce in the early twentieth century from both the judiciary and Parliament.

The rationale behind the exercise of the Court's discretion in cases involving the petitioner's adultery was to deny the petitioner divorce for committing the same matrimonial offence as the respondent. An exception was made which

---

303 *Dempster v Dempster* (1861) 2 Sw&Tr 438.
304 In *Newsome v Newsome* (1871) LR 2 P&D 306, adultery revived incestuous adultery. In *Blandford v Blandford* (1888) 8 PD 19, adultery revived cruelty and desertion. In *Houghton v Houghton* [1903] P 150 and *Copsey v Copsey and Erney* [1905] P 94, desertion revived adultery.
305 In *Bostock v Bostock* (1858) 1 Sw&Tr 221, the husband's threats of violence against the wife revived his condoned cruelty. In *Cooke v Cooke* (1863) 3 Sw&Tr 126, the husband refused to restore the conjugal status of the wife on resumption of cohabitation. In *Newsome v Newsome* (1871) LR 2 P&D 306, the husband's subsequent adultery revived his previous condoned incestuous adultery.
306 *Paine v Paine* [1903] P 263.
307 *Bernstein v Bernstein* [1893] P 292.
308 (1864) 10 HLC 685.

allowed a petitioner to present an extenuating reason, namely condoned, innocent, and unwilling adultery, in order to show that his or her adultery should not be seen with the same moral culpability as the respondent's adultery. Although it may seem counter-intuitive to deny divorce to a couple where both parties have committed adultery against each other, the Court adopted the equitable principle of clean hands. The majority report of the Campbell Commission asserted that neither party in such a case should be granted relief: 'When both parties are in the same guilt, neither can claim the vindication of a law which each has broken, nor reasonably complain of the breach of a contract which each has violated.'[309]

Courts barred relief in most cases involving a petitioner's adultery.[310] Cases involving a petitioner's single act[311] or repeated acts of adultery without reasonable excuse led to the dismissal of the petitioner's suit.[312] Moreover, drunkenness was not a reasonable excuse for the petitioner's adultery.[313] It was essential that the petitioner had disclosed his or her own adultery at the start of the trial for any chance that the Court may exercise its discretion in the petitioner's favour.[314] Even then it was exceptionally hard for most petitioners to convince the Court that their divorce applications should not be barred. In *Clarke v Clarke and Clarke*, the wife deserted the husband for eight months and during her absence the husband committed a single act of adultery.[315] Two years later, the wife was discovered having an adulterous relationship with her brother-in-law. As a consequence of the husband's single act of adultery, the Court barred him from ever seeking relief for the wife's incestuous adultery. Therefore, it was simple enough just to show that the petitioner had committed adultery for the bar to operate.

Recrimination and unreasonable delay

Both recrimination and unreasonable delay were discretionary bars, but not many cases involved petitioners being barred on these grounds. Recrimination existed as a bar in the Ecclesiastical Courts. It was statutorily defined as a petitioner who 'of having deserted or wilfully separated himself or herself from the other Party before the Adultery complained of, and without reasonable Excuse, or of such wilful Neglect or Misconduct as has conduced to the Adultery.'[316] Although the bar of recrimination could apply to either the husband or the wife, it was typically applied against the husband. This was because husbands were involved in the

---

309 *First Report of the Commissioners...Into the Law of Divorce* (1852–3) BPP vol 40, 268.
310 Cretney (n 93) 193. Cretney states that there were only 64 cases where the Court had exercised its discretion in favour of the petitioner within the first 50 years of the Court's existence.
311 *Clarke v Clarke and Clarke* (1865) 34 LJ(PA&M) 94; *Craven v Craven and Robinson* (1909) 26 TLR 4.
312 *Youell v Youell, Terrass and Burleigh (The Queen's Proctor Intervening)* (1875) 33 LT 578.
313 *Hutchinson v Hutchinson and Barker* (1866) 14 LT 338; *Grosvenor v Grosvenor* (1885) 34 WR 140.
314 *Woltereck v Woltereck and Walters* [1912] P 201; *Habra v Habra and Habal* [1914] P 100.
315 (1865) 34 LJ(PA&M) 94.
316 Matrimonial Causes Act 1857, s 31.

majority of desertion and cruelty cases. The rationale behind the bar of recrimination was that the petitioner had caused the respondent so much grief through wilful acts of desertion or cruelty that the petitioner had effectively brought the matrimonial offence onto him or herself. The recriminating act of the petitioner must have occurred prior to the alleged adultery of the respondent.[317] A petitioner who was found guilty of committing either desertion[318] or cruelty would not necessarily be barred from being granted a judicial separation or divorce for those actions in themselves.[319] In order to bar a petitioner to divorce for recrimination, it must be proven that the respondent was conduced to commit adultery as a result of the petitioner's desertion[320] or cruelty.[321] Recrimination was limited based on the exercise of judicial discretion, which turned heavily on the judge's interpretation of the facts.

Unreasonable delay can be compared to the equitable bar of laches, particularly the principle of *vigilantibus non dormientibus aequitas subvenit* (equity aids the vigilant, not the ones who sleep [on their rights]).[322] Under section 31 of the Matrimonial Causes Act 1857, the Court was not bound to grant a divorce if a petitioner was found 'guilty of unreasonable delay in presenting or prosecuting such Petition.' Generally, a delay of two years after the petitioner first gains knowledge of misconduct was deemed to constitute unreasonable delay.[323] This was in line with the length for desertion. However, the Court accepted reasonable excuses for delay, hence why unreasonable delay was a discretionary bar. The most common excuse was impecuniosity,[324] but other excuses included ignorance of the law,[325] tolerating acts of cruelty,[326] employment demands,[327] a deed of separation mistakenly thought to have been executed,[328] the insanity of the respondent,[329]

---

317 *Ousey v Ousey and Atkinson* (1874) LR 3 P&D 223.
318 *Duplany v Duplany (Cohen intervening)* [1892] P 53; *Synge v Synge* [1900] P 180.
319 *Badham v Badham and Gorst* (1890) 62 LT 663; *Forsyth v Forsyth, Eccles and Foster* (1890) 63 LT 263; *Sergent v Sergent and Weaver* (1891) 64 LT 236.
320 *Baylis v Baylis* (1867) LR 1 P&D 395; *Ousey v Ousey and Atkinson* (1874) LR 3 P&D 223.
321 *Pearman v Pearman and Burgess* (1860) 1 Sw&Tr 601; *Edwards v Edwards and Francis* [1894] P 33; *Pryor v Pryor, Cowie and Macdonald* [1900] P 157; *Squire v Squire and O'Callaghan* [1905] P 4.
322 *Boulting v Boulting* (1864) 3 Sw&Tr 329, 337. Wilde J employed the language of the equitable maxim by ruling that the petitioner's delay indicated that she had 'slumbered with sufficient comfort.'
323 *Nicholson v Nicholson* (1873) LR 3 P&D 53; *Mason v Mason and McClune* (1882) 7 PD 233; *Faulkes v Faulkes and Stainton* (1891) 64 LT 834; *Brougham v Brougham (The Queen's Proctor Intervening)* [1895] P 288.
324 *Harrison v Harrison* (1864) 3 Sw&Tr 362; *Edwards v Edwards and Doncaster* (1900) 17 TLR 38.
325 *Tollemache v Tollemache* (1859) 1 Sw&Tr 557. In 1837, an English man married a Scottish woman in Gretna Green and the matrimony was solemnised in the Anglican parish of St George's, Hanover Square in London. In 1841, the wife was found to have committed adultery. The Scottish Court of Sessions granted the wife divorce. Unbeknownst to the parties, they were still legally married under English law.
326 *Green v Green* (1873) LR 3 P&D 121.
327 *Davies v Davies and Hughes* (1863) 3 Sw&Tr 221.
328 *Beauclerk v Beauclerk* [1895] P 220.
329 *Johnson v Johnson (by her guardian ad litem)* [1901] P 193.

and the wellbeing of immediate family members in cases involving the incest of the respondent.[330] The Court harboured suspicion towards a petitioner's delay if a suit was initiated soon after settling a deed of separation, because the petitioner was viewed as adequately safeguarded through the private arrangements.[331] The bar of unreasonable delay was not a major concern for the Court. There was a wide range of excuses for reasonable delay and the bar was seldom applied.

The bars to divorce remained consistent and denied many couples a divorce decree. Although there was some loosening of the discretionary bar of petitioner's adultery in the early twentieth century, it was necessary to introduce legislative reform in order to change the grounds for divorce.[332] Piecemeal legislation, such as the Summary Jurisdiction (Married Women) Act 1895, failed to address the wider problem of the restricted nature of both the grounds and bars to divorce. Moreover, the double standard in the aggravated statutory offences aroused agitation from feminists and law reformers. In spite of the double standard in the grounds for divorce, married women made up 40 per cent of all divorce petitioners in the period between 1858 and 1900.[333] Therefore, the expansion of the grounds of adultery for wives under the Matrimonial Causes Act 1857 had actually made divorce significantly easier for married women.

The judiciary applied the divorce laws conservatively throughout the nineteenth century, but there were subtle developments in judicial interpretation. The judges ordinary of the Court for Divorce and Matrimonial Causes generally upheld the ecclesiastical precedents and principles. The judiciary was still anchored in the conservative morality of mid-Victorian England. However, the late Victorian PDA Division under Sir Charles Butt and Lord St Helier had begun to grant divorce on slightly broader grounds. The Divorce Court had developed a robust family justice system and began to display some confidence in deviating from ecclesiastical law. These judgments recognised the acute challenges of strictly applying the Matrimonial Causes Act 1857 to each individual case, and some degree of flexibility was recognised in their decision making. The exposure to the practical realities of divorcing had encouraged the PDA Division to be more flexible in its application of divorce law. This is in contrast to the narrow doctrinal approach of the House of Lords and Court of Appeal on the rare occasions when they heard divorce appeals. However, the judiciary felt compelled to follow conservative precedents, because of statutory obligation to follow ecclesiastical principles and the overwhelming body of ecclesiastical precedents. The limits to judicial activism are evident in the above analysis of the grounds and bars to divorce. Even those who wanted law reform in the early twentieth century were bound to follow the conservative precedents. Lord Gorell was a notable campaigner for divorce reform. During his time as the president of the PDA Division, he felt bound to follow precedent and denied a married woman divorce despite his call for a radical overhaul of the divorce laws.[334]

---

330 *Newman v Newman* (1870) LR 2 P&D 57.
331 *Matthews v Matthews* (1859) 1 Sw&Tr 499.
332 Matrimonial Causes Act 1923; Matrimonial Causes Act 1937.
333 Cretney (n 93) 169.
334 *Dodd v Dodd* [1906] P 189.

5 The divorce courts

The Cresswell court: Establishing the Divorce Court

The Matrimonial Causes Act 1857, which commenced on 1 January 1858, introduced a new secular judicial system and legal procedure for divorce.[1] The Act dispelled any illusions that divorce was to be solely decided by Christian dogma. As decades passed, the statute law was increasingly influenced by secular jurisprudence. By around the turn of the twentieth century, a good deal of the foundations of divorce law had been eroded. Judges were forced to appeal to public reason and the contemporary values of society to justify their decisions in the eyes of the public. This shift also began to inspire piecemeal reform in the late nineteenth century, but this would ultimately prove to be unsatisfactory by the early twentieth century. These changes did not happen overnight. In the years immediately following the 1857 Act, the Divorce Court continued to follow the pre-1858 ecclesiastical principles and some of its processes along with precedents.[2]

Judgments in respect to the grounds and bars to divorce were narrow as a result of the Divorce Court's heavy reliance on ecclesiastical precedents. Procedure was inquisitorial rather than adversarial, as was the case in the Ecclesiastical Courts. The effect of the introduction of civil divorce reflected this nature of change and continuity. Although civil divorce suddenly became more available as a judicial procedure, the Divorce Court was still only accessible in London. Moreover, England still had one of the lowest rates of divorce compared with other Western nations in the late nineteenth century.[3] Gail Savage states, 'Favoring the affluent and those who lived in London, the court remained beyond the reach of the bulk of the population.'[4] Change did not take place immediately, but rather took time to manifest itself as the divorce law developed.

---

1 Matrimonial Causes Act 1857, s 1.
2 Matrimonial Causes Act 1857, s 33.
3 In 1890, the annual divorce rate was more than 16 times greater in France (6557 divorce decrees) than England (400 divorce decrees). Gail Savage, 'Divorce and the Law in England and France Prior to the First World War' (1988) 21(3) *Journal of Social History* 499, 510.
4 Gail Savage, 'The Operation of the 1857 Divorce Act, 1860–1910 a Research Note' (1983) 16(4) *Journal of Social History* 103, 104.

The Court for Divorce and Matrimonial Causes' adoption of the inquisitorial system of the Ecclesiastical Courts placed a heavy demand on the family justice system.[5] The Divorce Court was not limited to the evidence presented by the parties, but had a duty to search for the truthfulness of a petition and investigate any bars to divorce.[6] Individual judges in the Divorce Court, when compared with other courts, played a significant and disproportionate role in interpreting the 1857 Act. At any given time, there was only one judge ordinary in the Court for Divorce and Matrimonial Causes and two judges in the Probate, Divorce and Admiralty (PDA) Division of the High Court. This meant that judges had considerable leeway in applying the law to the facts and were able to exercise their discretion more widely in the late Victorian court. Therefore, each judge of the Divorce Court warrants special attention. However, judicial power was not unfettered. Judges still had to apply the Act, otherwise their decisions would be appealed, though this was uncommon in the family law jurisdiction.

The first judge ordinary, Sir Cresswell Cresswell, formally commenced on 11 January 1858.[7] Although a confirmed bachelor, Cresswell's appointment to the Court for Divorce and Matrimonial Causes proved to be a prudent choice. His common law background and reputation as an effective administrator of justice on the Court of Common Pleas were key factors in his appointment.[8] Stephen Lushington and Richard Bethell were initially considered for the position of judge ordinary, but Lord Cranworth felt that Lushington was unsuitable as he wanted the new court to detach itself from the Ecclesiastical Courts and Bethell, who helped pass the Matrimonial Causes Act 1857, declined the position as he did not want others to think that he had supported the legislation for personal benefit.[9] Cresswell provided the much-needed strong leadership to the nascent Court. Hundreds of cases came before the Court each year and Cresswell heard over 1000 cases during his five years as judge ordinary. He played a vital role in establishing court procedure and a workable law of evidence.

Cresswell promoted a conservative interpretation of the Matrimonial Causes Act 1857. There are a number of examples. His conservative approach was sometimes a matter of statutory interpretation. Cresswell held that it was unlawful for an Englishman, whether naturalised or native, to marry his deceased wife's sister in *Mette v Mette*.[10] This was a simple application of section 27 of the Matrimonial Causes Act 1857 that prohibited the legal recognition of relationships of affinity. Cresswell also placed great weight on existing procedures as a means of keeping the law within narrow bounds. For example, he held that a foreign ceremony of

---

5 Matrimonial Causes Act 1857, s 22.
6 Matrimonial Causes Act 1860 (23 & 24 Vict c 144) s 7.
7 'Court of Probate, Jan 11' *The Times* (London, 12 January 1858) 9.
8 Joshua Getzler, 'Cresswell, Sir Cresswell (1793–1863),' *Oxford Dictionary of National Biography* (2004) <https://doi.org/10.1093/ref:odnb/6673>.
9 Gail Savage, '"What Will Most Tend towards Morality": Sir Cresswell Cresswell and the Divorce Court, 1858–1863' in James Gregory, Daniel J.R. Grey, and Annika Bautz (eds), *Judgment in the Victorian Age* (Routledge 2019) 101–2.
10 (1859) 1 Sw&Tr 416.

marriage was only valid if it was consistent with English marriage law in *Brook v Brook*.[11] Similarly in *Tollemache v Tollemache*, Cresswell ruled that the Scottish courts and consequently any foreign legal jurisdiction could not dissolve an English marriage.[12] These cases followed the existing precedents against the recognition of foreign decisions on the legality of marriage and divorce of English couples. Cresswell also followed existing ecclesiastical precedents, because case law on divorce had not yet developed and the practice and procedure of the civilians was familiar.

Introduction of the Queen's Proctor

It soon became evident that the Divorce Court was unable to effectively discharge its inquisitorial role, because the 1857 Act provided no investigatory mechanism. John Fraser Macqueen argued that the Divorce Court was failing to investigate the merits of divorce claims, particularly possible imputations against a petitioner in undefended cases.[13] Similarly, Lord Brougham wrote a letter to the Law Amendment Society highlighting the same concern: 'No sufficient security is provided, hardly any security at all, against the frauds which may be practiced by parties acting in collusion to obtain a divorce.'[14] In order to solve the problem and allow the Divorce Court to exercise its inquisitorial role, the office of Queen's Proctor was established.[15] There were great expectations for this newly established office. Cresswell described the Queen's Proctor as 'guardian of the public morals, for the purpose of preventing a misapplication of the statute constituting this Court.'[16]

The origins of the Queen's Proctor are disputed. Gail Savage states:

> Legislation passed in 1861 empowered the treasury solicitor, acting in the capacity of proctor, to investigate divorce cases based on collusion between the spouses or those brought by spouses whose own misconduct debarred them from the relief provided by divorce.[17]

Savage is referring to the Matrimonial Causes Act 1860 as the source of legal authority that established the office of the Queen's Proctor. Stephen Cretney on the other hand claims that the office of the Queen's Proctor is 'of some antiquity.'[18]

---

11 (1857–8) 3 Sm & G 481.
12 (1859) 1 Sw&Tr 557.
13 John Fraser Macqueen, *A Practical Treatise on the Law of Marriage, Divorce, and Legitimacy: As Administered in the Divorce Court and in the House of Lords* (W. Maxwell 1860) 46.
14 'The Law of Divorce' *The Spectator* (London, 18 December 1858) 1314.
15 The gender of the reigning monarch determined whether the office was referred to either as Queen's or King's Proctor. I have chosen to use 'Queen's Proctor' as Queen Victoria was the reigning monarch for all of the second half of the nineteenth century.
16 *Gethin v Gethin (The Queen's Proctor Intervening)* (1862) 2 Sw&Tr 560, 562–3.
17 Gail Savage, 'The Divorce Court and the Queen's/King's Proctor: Legal Patriarchy and the Sanctity of Marriage in England, 1861–1937' (1989) 24(1) *Historical Papers* 210, 211.
18 Stephen Cretney, *Family Law in the Twentieth Century* (Oxford University Press 2003) 178.

Both are right. The origins of the proctor can be traced to late Roman antiquity with the office of *procurator*, and its subsequent adoption in the medieval civilian courts (e.g., the Ecclesiastical Courts and the Admiralty Court).[19] Yet it was the Matrimonial Causes Act 1860 which revived the old office of Queen's Proctor in the Court for Divorce and Matrimonial Causes. This was achieved as a result of two amendments. First, divorce became a two-stage process. If the Court was satisfied that the grounds of divorce were sufficiently established, a decree *nisi* would be granted for a period of three months[20] (this period was extended to six months in 1866).[21] Second, the Queen's Proctor was given the responsibility of investigating whether there were any bars to divorce between the time of granting the decree *nisi* and the making of divorce absolute, and to intervene in the suit should evidence emerge that divorce should not be made absolute.[22] The Queen's Proctor could only act on the direction of the attorney-general, and the Court could not compel the attorney-general to issue his fiat.[23] The Court would only grant a divorce absolute once the petitioner's claim survived the decree *nisi* process with impunity.

Cresswell heard the first Queen's Proctor intervention in *Drummond v Drummond (The Queen's Proctor Intervening)*.[24] The Queen's Proctor successfully demonstrated that the petitioner committed adultery which led to the petitioner being barred to relief. The Queen's Proctor would play a prominent role in divorce until the mid-twentieth century.[25] Petitioners had to be careful not to disclose any evidence that may lead to the intervention of the Queen's Proctor. A case resting on the evidence of a single witness or that was undefended would almost inevitably lead to the Queen's Proctor's investigation for collusion.

The Queen's Proctor was responsible for investigating all petitioners in undefended cases after a grant of decree *nisi* and to intervene in suits where collusion was reasonably suspected.[26] The Queen's Proctor was usually overzealous in its investigations and would examine every single case that warranted an inkling of attention.[27] The Queen's Proctor investigated most divorce cases, but only intervened in less than 5 per cent of all divorce cases between 1858 and 1910.[28]

---

19 James Brundage, *Medieval Canon Law* (Routledge 1995) 107.
20 Matrimonial Causes Act 1860, s 7.
21 Matrimonial Causes Act 1866 (29 & 30 Vict c 32) s 3.
22 Matrimonial Causes Act 1860, s 7.
23 *Jackson v Jackson* [1910] P 230.
24 (1861) 2 Sw&Tr 269. See Deborah Cohen, *Family Secrets: Shame and Privacy in Modern Britain* (Oxford University Press 2013) 56–63.
25 Cretney (n 18) 169.
26 Matrimonial Causes Act 1860, s 7.
27 In *Hyman v Hyman and Goldman (The King's Proctor Showing Cause)* [1904] P 403, the King's Proctor discovered that the petitioner and respondent had resumed marital cohabitation, thus the decree *nisi* was rescinded for condonation of adultery. However, the Court still ordered the co-respondent to indemnify the petitioner for the costs of the King's Proctor's intervention. See also *Matrimonial Causes Act 1878* (41 & 42 Vict c 19) s 2.
28 *Report of the Royal Commission on Divorce and Matrimonial Causes* (Cmd 6478, 1912) 54.

Cresswell played an important role in clarifying the grounds and bars to divorce under the Matrimonial Causes Act 1857. Many of the provisions of the Act were not clearly defined, thus the Court was required to exercise some discretion. Cresswell generally adopted a narrow interpretation of the Act, which reflected the sensitivity of keeping the Court in line with the ecclesiastical legal precedents. His conservative profile and judicial abilities helped to ease public concern about the introduction of civil divorce. *The Spectator* was concerned with the moral effect from the publication of divorce cases,[29] but was uncertain 'as to the actual effect upon society, produced by Sir Cresswell Cresswell's Court.'[30] On the other hand, Cresswell developed an early reputation as the 'Confessor-General of England' according to *The Times*.[31]

The judgments of Cresswell demonstrate his desire to secularise the Court, but also to keep the Court in line with ecclesiastical precedents. In regards to the former, Cresswell shifted the understanding of marriage as a civil union under English law rather than as a Christian sacramental ordinance of holy matrimony. Cresswell achieved this in *Hope v Hope* by declaring that canon law was not part of the common law.[32] Yet, at the same time, Cresswell was still inclined to follow ecclesiastical precedents when interpreting the law of divorce. In *Tomkins v Tomkins*,[33] Cresswell adopted the narrow definition of cruelty as actual or a reasonable apprehension of bodily harm established by Lord Stowell in *Evans v Evans*.[34]

There were gaps in the existing law and a new procedure. Important rules of evidence for proving adultery were also introduced. Cresswell created a presumption against accepting the evidence of a paid detective in *Sopwith v Sopwith*.[35] He also held that confessions of a respondent could not be used as evidence against the co-respondent in *Iredale v Ford and Bramworth*.[36] Furthermore, Cresswell clarified the meaning of some important concepts in divorce law. Here he was making new law. In *Ward v Ward*, Cresswell ruled that in order to prove desertion, the deserting party must have separated from the other spouse without consent or condonation.[37] Merely living with someone else was not sufficient evidence in itself. The length of desertion of two years was specified under section 27 of the Matrimonial Causes Act 1857. However, issues of intention and evidence were left to the judiciary to decide. The Court also had to clarify the meaning of condonation, which remained undefined in the statute.[38] In *Keats v*

---

29 'The Teachings of the Divorce Court' *The Spectator* (London, 31 December 1859) 1333.
30 'The Return on Divorce and Matrimonial Causes' *The Spectator* (London, 16 March 1861) 275.
31 The article went onto convey a sense of indignity felt by many from the Court's exposure of the matrimonial discord and immoral behaviour of the middle class. 'Sir Cresswell Cresswell is Holding Up a Mirror to the Age' *The Times* (London, 12 December 1859) 8.
32 (1858) 1 Sw&Tr 94.
33 (1858) 1 Sw&Tr 168.
34 (1790) 1 Hag Con 34.
35 (1859) 4 Sw&Tr 243.
36 (1859) 1 Sw&Tr 305.
37 (1858) 1 Sw&Tr 185.
38 Matrimonial Causes Act 1857, s 29.

Keats and Montezuma, Cresswell held that condonation was not just mere words of forgiveness, but also involved actively restoring the relationship of the parties prior to the matrimonial offence.[39]

The legacy of Cresswell

Cresswell was seriously injured after being knocked down by a frightened horse while riding down Constitution Hill in London.[40] Soon after, he experienced heart failure and died on 29 July 1863 at the age of 69.[41] Cresswell was universally acclaimed as an assiduous and laudable judge ordinary. This was very important to the Court for Divorce and Matrimonial Causes, because Cresswell gave early confidence to the new secular tribunal and legal procedure for trying divorce matters. The lord chief justice of England, Sir Alexander Cockburn, commended Creswell as 'so eminently distinguished and able a Judge.'[42] *The Spectator* expressed sadness at his passing.

> So when Sir Cresswell Cresswell died everybody felt that he had lost, as it were, a public friend—a man who was perpetually giving one the best advice, and most politely illustrating his remarks from one's neighbour's conduct and not one's own— which is just the contrary to what one's private friends do.[43]

The Times went further and compared Cresswell as equal to the judicial stature of Lord Mansfield.[44] Although this is debateable, Cresswell indeed exceeded the expectations of many by giving confidence to the public in the new Court and establishing the foundational precedents of civil divorce law. At the beginning of the twentieth century, Cresswell was recognised as one of the greatest judges of the Victorian era for his contributions to divorce law.[45]

The Wilde court: Developing the law

Sir James Plaisted Wilde succeeded Cresswell as judge ordinary on 28 August 1863.[46] At the time of Wilde's appointment, the press was sanguine that Wilde would meet the high standard set by his predecessor. *The Spectator* stated:

---

39 (1859) 1 Sw&Tr 334.
40 'Serious Accident to Sir Cresswell Cresswell' *The Times* (London, 20 July 1863) 11.
41 'The Late Sir Cresswell Cresswell' *The Times* (London, 31 July 1863) 7.
42 HL Deb 26 April 1860, vol 158, col 132.
43 'The New Judges' *The Spectator* (London, 15 August 1863) 2369.
44 'The Late Sir Cresswell Cresswell' *The Times* (London, 31 July 1863) 7. See also 'When the Unexpected News of Sir Cresswell Cresswell's Sudden Death' *The Times* (London, 12 August 1863) 8.
45 Edward Manson, *Builders of Our Law During the Reign of Queen Victoria* (2nd edn, Horace Cox 1904) 124–31.
46 J.M. Rigg, 'Wilde, James Plaisted, Baron Penzance (1816–1899),' *Oxford Dictionary of National Biography* (2004) <https://doi.org/10.1093/ref:odnb/29397>.

116   *The divorce courts*

He has on all occasions of difficulty shown himself a jurist, and has preferred to rest his decisions on principle rather than on precedent. If in addition to this philosophical temper and grasp of mind (which after all makes the difference between a great and a good judge) we find in a man that command of temper and courtesy of manner which no one can deny to Baron Wilde, it will be admitted that the public has good reasons to hope that the administration of justice in the Divorce Court will not suffer at his hands.[47]

Wilde did not disappoint and his judgments came to be well regarded. He followed Cresswell's conservative interpretation of the Matrimonial Causes Act 1857. Wilde's most famous judgment was *Hyde v Hyde and Woodmansee*, where he defined marriage as 'the voluntary union for life of one man and one woman, to the exclusion of all others.'[48] The legal definition was upheld for nearly 150 years, most recently in *Wilkinson v Kitzinger*, until it was extended to include same-sex couples under the Marriage (Same Sex Couples) Act 2013.[49] Wilde was also known for presiding over the sensational Mordaunt divorce trial in 1870: *Mordaunt v Mordaunt, Cole and Johnstone*.[50] The case was initiated by Sir Charles Mordaunt, who petitioned for divorce on the ground of the adultery of his wife Lady Mordaunt (Harriet Moncreiffe). He alleged that his wife had committed adultery with a number of men, most notably the Prince of Wales, Albert Edward (later Edward VII). Lady Mordaunt was also fearful that her infant daughter contracted venereal disease from one of her sexual liaisons.[51] Upon receipt of the citation, the Moncreiffe family deposed that Harriet was insane and unfit to proceed with the trial. Consequently, Lady Mordaunt's father, Sir Thomas Moncreiffe, was appointed guardian *ad litem*. At the trial, a jury found that Harriet was in a state of mental disorder. Therefore, she was declared unfit and unable to answer the petition.

Wilde ordered a stay of proceedings until Lady Mordaunt recovered her mental capacity, which was upheld on appeal by the full bench of the Court for Divorce and Matrimonial Causes. In 1872, Charles, seeing that Lady Mordaunt's mental condition had deteriorated, indefinitely proceeded to appeal to the House of Lord. In 1874, the House of Lords unanimously held that insanity of either the husband or the wife was not a bar to divorce.[52] Insanity was ruled not be a bar to divorce, because divorce was held to be a civil proceeding with the aim of relieving the petitioner rather than as a criminal prosecution of the respondent. The House of Lords overturned Wilde's decision and the petition was remitted

47 'The New Judges' *The Spectator* (London, 15 August 1863) 2369.
48 (1866) LR 1 P&D 130, 133.
49 [2006] EWHC 2022 (Fam). The president of the Family Division, Sir Mark Potter, relied on Wilde's definition of marriage to reject the recognition of a same-sex marriage that took place in Canada.
50 *The Lady Mordaunt Divorce Case* (Temple Publishing Offices 1870).
51 *Ibid*. 11; Gail Savage, '"The Wilful Communication of a Loathsome Disease": Marital Conflict and Venereal Disease in Victorian England' (1990) 34(1) *Victorian Studies* 35, 36.
52 *Mordaunt v Moncreiffe (as Lady Mordaunt's guardian ad litem)* (1874) LR 2 Sc & Div 374.

back to the Divorce Court. Charles eventually was granted a divorce in 1875 on the ground of Harriet's adultery with Lord Cole, while Lady Mordaunt spent the rest of her life in a mental asylum.[53]

Wilde also decided a number of other influential cases on divorce law and helped to clarify ambiguity. This usually had the effect of limiting the scope of the bars to divorce. For example, Wilde limited the legal definition of condonation to only include acts of forgiveness in cases where the evidence proved that the petitioner had restored the marital status of the offending spouse.[54] Furthermore, Wilde recognised the principle of clean hands as a decisive element in determining connivance.[55] The majority of the House of Lords upheld Wilde's ruling, but rejected his reasoning by finding the test of *volenti not fit injuria* (to the consenting, no injury is done) rather than unclean hands should prevail.[56] In relation to the bar of collusion, Wilde found that the suppression of information did not constitute collusion in itself.[57] However, this was later overturned in *Butler v Butler and Burnham (The Queen's Proctor Intervening)*.[58]

Wilde was ennobled Lord Penzance on 6 April 1869. He used his position in the House of Lords to unsuccessfully introduce a bill for what was then perceived as a rather socially radical policy of legalising marriage with a deceased wife's sister.[59] In November 1872, Penzance resigned his position of judge ordinary due to poor health. In 1874, Penzance was appointed as a judge under the Public Worship Regulation Act 1874.[60] The Act was aimed at curtailing the rise in ritualism in the Church of England. Penzance was then appointed Dean of Arches in 1875 and served in this role until his retirement from the bench in 1899. He passed away in the same year. Penzance left the Court for Divorce and Matrimonial Causes in a salutary condition for his successor.

The creation of the Probate, Divorce and Admiralty Division

Sir James Hannen, the last judge ordinary of the Court for Divorce and Matrimonial Causes, was appointed on 20 November 1872.[61] During his three years on the Court, the judicial system of England was undergoing significant change, which resulted in the creation of a new family justice system. *The Times* characterised Hannen as man of stoic demeanour: 'Nature had given him a fierce temper; a strong will and powerful intelligence had so mastered it that on his almost impassive countenance no trace could be seen of the struggle going on

---

53 See Elizabeth Hamilton, *The Warwickshire Scandal* (Michael Russell 1999).
54 *Dent v Dent* (1865) 4 Sw&Tr 105.
55 *Gipps v Gipps and Hume* (1863) 3 Sw&Tr 116.
56 *Gipps v Gipps and Hume* (1864) 11 HLC 1.
57 *Alexandre v. Alexandre* (1870) LR 2 P&D 164.
58 (1890) 15 PD 66.
59 HL Deb 27 March 1871, vol 205, cols 639–55.
60 (37 & 38 Vict c 85).
61 Patrick Polden, 'Hannen, James, Baron Hannen (1821–1894),' *Oxford Dictionary of National Biography* (2004) <https://doi.org/10.1093/ref:odnb/12216>.

within.'[62] Hannen's appointment was warmly received, with *The Times* describing him as one 'who bears the highest character for sound legal knowledge and a conscientious and able discharge of his judicial duties.'[63]

For decades, there was a concerted effort among some members of the legal profession to reform the administration of civil justice through a fusion of common law and equity. The origins of the call for judicial and legal reform can be traced to the renowned speech of Henry Brougham in 1828.[64] Michael Lobban describes Brougham's law reform efforts as important, but his legacy was ambivalent as attempts at law reform were often met with political frustrations.[65] The Law Amendment Society founded by Brougham played an important role throughout the mid-nineteenth century in lobbying for the fusion of common law and equity. It saw the division of common law and equity as unnecessarily obfuscating the operation and administration of the law.[66] Indeed, a common law judge could only give a common law remedy. Likewise, an equity judge could only give an equitable remedy. This proved to be increasingly impractical, timely, and expensive for a plaintiff seeking a legal remedy. The Court for Divorce and Matrimonial Causes evolved without any devised strategy. The introduction of the Matrimonial Causes Act 1860 arose from circumstances rather than any careful planning. The lawmakers in 1857 never envisaged that there would be so many divorce petitions immediately after the enactment of the Matrimonial Causes Act 1857. The need for the Court to keep up with demand led to judicial reform, particularly allowing the judge ordinary to sit alone and issue divorce decrees under the 1860 Act. The annual average number of divorce decrees *nisi* in 1862–6 was 154.4.[67] In a letter addressed to the editor of *The Times*, there was even a suggestion that there should be an appointment of a separate judge ordinary to preside over the Court of Probate.[68] This was argued in order to allow the judge ordinary of the Court for Divorce and Matrimonial Causes to keep up with his own court business.[69]

The Judicature Commission was established in 1867 and chaired by Lord Cairns with the responsibility to inquire into judicial reform.[70] This royal commission came into being at the behest of Sir Roundell Palmer (later Lord Selborne), who called for an inquiry into judicial reform in the House of Commons.[71] The first report was published on 25 March 1869, and recommended the creation of a

62 'Death of Lord Hannen' *The Times* (London, 30 March 1894) 12.
63 'The New Judge of The Divorce Court' *The Times* (London, 12 November 1872) 11.
64 HC Deb 7 February 1828, vol 18, cols 127–258.
65 Michael Lobban, 'Henry Brougham and Law Reform' (2000) 115 *The English Historical Review* 1184–5.
66 Law Amendment Society, 'Fusion of Law and Equity' (1852) 16(1) *The Law Review* 184.
67 *Report of the Royal Commission on Divorce and Matrimonial Causes* (Cmd 6478, 1912) 54.
68 'To the Editor of the Times' *The Times* (London, 18 August 1863) 9.
69 *Ibid*.
70 Brian Abel-Smith and Robert Stevens, *Lawyers and the Courts: A Sociological Study of the English Legal System 1750–1965* (Heinemann 1967) 48.
71 HC Deb 30 July 1867, vol 189, cols 474–5.

single, unified Supreme Court that would be comprised of a Court of Appeal and a High Court.[72] The High Court would be composed of divisions from the jurisdictions of common law, equity, and civilians, where cases from the High Court could be appealed to the Court of Appeal.[73] It was envisaged that a High Court judge would be able to give whatever remedy was necessary in the delivery of justice.[74]

The lord chancellor, Lord Hatherley, proposed a bill that would enable all judges of the Supreme Court to sit in any other Division of the Court, and to split the Court into five divisions: Chancery, Queen's Bench, Common Pleas, Exchequer, and PDA.[75] In September 1872, Lord Selborne replaced Hatherley as lord chancellor and made some notable changes to Hatherley's bill. Selborne attempted to rename the divisions in ordinal numbers (i.e., first division, second division, etc), but the House of Commons voted in favour by 55 votes to 20 of keeping the original names.[76] Initially, Selborne proposed four divisions with the omission of PDA.[77] A later amendment restored the PDA as a fifth division unifying the civilian jurisdictions.[78] Hence, the PDA Division was humorously described as the court of 'wills, wives and wrecks' in A.P. Herbert's *Holy Deadlock*.[79] Selborne's bill eventually became the Supreme Court of Judicature Act 1873.[80] The inclusion of the PDA as the fifth division secured the place of the Divorce Court in the mainstream judiciary, where it had almost been left on the margins.

The fusion of common law and equity under the Judicature Act 1873 turned out to be institutional rather than doctrinal. The courts were merged into the High Court of Justice, but common law and equity remained conceptually distinct as a matter of law. Walter Ashburner sums the fusion in a rather imaginative metaphor: 'But the two streams of jurisdiction, though they run in the same channel, run side by side and do not mingle their waters.'[81] Although it is inconceivable to imagine streams of water parting within the same channel, the metaphor is a creative illustration of the fusion that took place under the Judicature Act 1873. The judges of the PDA Division were initially expected to go on circuit on behalf of the High Court 'so far as the state of business in the said division will admit.'[82] However, the question of who was responsible for deciding when business was such to allow a judge to go on circuit was not specified. In

---

72 *Judicature Commission: First Report of the Commissioners* (1868–9) BPP vol 25, 1–26.
73 *Ibid*. 9–10.
74 *Ibid*. 5–8.
75 HL Deb 18 March 1870, vol 200, col 171.
76 HC Deb 7 July 1873, vol 217, col 1878.
77 Patrick Polden, 'Mingling the Waters: Personalities, Politics and the Making of the Supreme Court of Judicature' (2002) 61(3) *Cambridge Law Journal* 575, 583.
78 Supreme Court of Judicature Act 1873, s 31.
79 A.P. Herbert, *Holy Deadlock* (Methuen 1934) 109.
80 (36 & 37 Vict c 66).
81 Walter Ashburner, *Principles of Equity* (Butterworth 1902) 23.
82 Supreme Court of Judicature Act 1875 (38 & 39 Vict c 77) s 8.

120 *The divorce courts*

1883, Sir Charles Butt was appointed as the second judge of the PDA Division to assist Hannen. Butt was the first judge of the PDA Division to go on circuit and did so twice. However, he refused to go on circuit for a third time, arguing it was incumbent on the division to exercise its discretion after Hannen raised his displeasure.[83] This ended the practice of sending PDA judges on circuit.[84] The creation of the PDA Division in the High Court helped to transition the Court for Divorce and Matrimonial Causes from a fringe tribunal into a mainstream court, albeit the smallest, and often seen as the lesser division of the High Court.

Reform of the Queen's Proctor

There were wider administrative reforms that extended beyond the judiciary as part of the broader push for utilitarian law reform. The Treasury Solicitor Act 1876[85] formally transferred the position of Queen's Proctor to the Department of the Solicitor to the Treasury.[86] This had been recommended to improve government efficiency after a departmental committee report.[87] The Queen's Proctor was an office of the Ecclesiastical Courts until their civilian jurisdiction was abolished.[88] Thereafter, it became a separate office managed by the Treasury solicitor and administered by civil servants.[89] The first Queen's Proctor was Francis Hart Dyke, who was a practising civilian in Doctors' Commons and continued to follow the principles and procedures of the Ecclesiastical Courts.[90] He was appointed Queen's Proctor in 1851, but held this office in relation to divorce for 16 years between 1860 and 1876.[91] Dyke's successor was a barrister, Augustus Keppel Stephenson, who was the first Treasury solicitor appointed Queen's Proctor, and served between 1876 and 1894.[92] The appointment of Stephenson marked the beginning of a radical departure from his predecessor, who shifted most interventions away from the difficult to prove cases of collusion to incontrovertible adultery trials. Wendie Ellen Schneider states:

> By the late 1870s and 1880s, the Queen's Proctor under Stephenson had clearly become skilled at preparing an incontrovertible case of adultery, judging by the number of cases in which the petitioner declined to defend himself or herself against the Queen's Proctor's charges.[93]

---

83 Polden (n 77) 607.
84 Lord Halsbury (ed), *The Laws of England: Volume XVI* (Butterworth 1911) 463.
85 (39 & 40 Vict c 18).
86 HC Deb 14 June 1877, vol 234, col 1760.
87 *Report of the Departmental Committee on the System upon which the Legal Business of the Government is Conducted* (1877) BPP vol 27, 70.
88 Ibid.
89 Ibid. 23.
90 Wendie Ellen Schneider, 'Secrets and Lies: The Queen's Proctor and Judicial Investigation of Party Controlled Narratives' (2002) 27(3) *Law & Social Inquiry* 449, 463.
91 Ibid.
92 'Legal News' *Solicitors' Journal* (London, 19 August 1876) 824.
93 Schneider (n 90) 471.

The Treasury solicitor held the position of procurator-general and thus Queen's Proctor by royal warrant.[94] Stephenson's successor, the Earl of Desart, was the Treasury solicitor and the Queen's Proctor between 1894 and 1909. He informed the Gorell Commission of 1909–12 that the Queen's Proctor inquired into 306 to 631 cases per year, but actually intervened in 11 to 34 cases per year.[95] According to Savage's sample data, the Queen's Proctor intervened in one-third of wife petitions and two-thirds of husband petitions.[96] Therefore, petitions initiated by husbands were twice as likely to attract the attention of the Queen's Proctor as petitions initiated by wives. The Queen's Proctor fulfilled the Divorce Court's inquisitorial duties, but by the early twentieth century it was publicly criticised for its intrusiveness and was often cited as a reason for the need to push for divorce law reform.

The Hannen court: A steady approach

The PDA Division still exercised a conservative jurisprudence at least in its first decade under Hannen's presidency. However, Sir Charles Butt and Lord St Helier began a palpable liberal shift in the PDA Division. Although the late Victorian court remained widely conservative in its application of legal principles, there were some noteworthy attempts at broadening the definition of the grounds to divorce and limiting the application of bars to divorce. It was clear that Butt and Lord St Helier represented a generational change that was more willing to push the boundaries and reflect the zeitgeist of the final decades of the nineteenth century.

On 1 November 1875, Sir James Hannen became the inaugural president of the PDA Division by virtue of being the incumbent judge ordinary for the Court for Divorce and Matrimonial Causes. Prime Minister William Gladstone personally sent a letter to Hannen offering this new appointment.[97] Sir Robert Phillimore was also appointed as a judge of the PDA Division as he was the incumbent judge of the Court of Admiralty. He retained his former rank and salary, which placed him below that of other High Court puisne judges.[98] The appointment of a second judge was a sign that the number of divorce cases had significantly increased.[99] Moreover, the three civilian jurisdictions were concentrated into a single division. This increased the overall workload of the Division, which demanded the appointment of a second judge. Phillimore was the only advocate

---

94 Stephen Cretney, 'The King and the King's Proctor: The Abdication Crisis and the Divorce Laws 1936–1937' (2000) 116 *Law Quarterly Review* 583, 593.
95 *Royal Commission on Divorce and Matrimonial Causes, Volume 2* (Cmd 6480, 1912) 145.
96 Savage (n 17) 223.
97 Edward Manson, *Builders of Our Law During the Reign of Queen Victoria* (2nd edn, Horace Cox 1904) 335.
98 Supreme Court of Judicature Act 1873, ss 5 and 11; Supreme Court of Judicature Act 1875, s 8.
99 The number of divorces granted increased from 161 in 1871 to 208 in 1876. By the end of Hannen's presidency, there were 369 divorce decrees in 1891. Lawrence Stone, *Road to Divorce* (Oxford University Press 1995) 435.

of Doctors' Commons appointed to the High Court and was renowned for his expertise in civilian law.[100] Therefore, he continued to practise almost exclusively in Admiralty cases on the new Division until he retired and was succeeded by Butt in 1883.

Hannen attempted to use Butt's appointment as an opportunity to introduce alternate sittings between Butt and himself to hear Admiralty cases in order to promote greater cohesion within the Division.[101] However, this was not welcomed by Admiralty practitioners who were accustomed to sittings by a single judge. Consequently, the idea was not introduced and Hannen allocated most of the Admiralty cases to Butt, who was an expert in Admiralty law. Although Hannen took evening classes with the Admiralty Court usher in an attempt to master an area of law of which he knew little, he rarely took part in Admiralty cases.[102] Despite the fusion of the civilian jurisdictions, Admiralty continued to be treated as a distinct practice from probate and divorce within the PDA Division. On 29 March 1894, Hannen died in his home in London at the age of 73. Hannen's name became synonymous with the Divorce Court in which he served for almost two decades.[103] *The Times* believed that Hannen did not reach his full potential, and could have gone onto greater things had he not held his post in the Divorce Court for so long.[104]

Hannen filled gaps in the law and clarified the definition on nullity of marriage. In *Durham v Durham*, Hannen denied the Earl of Durham a nullity of marriage, who claimed that his wife was insane at the time of contracting the marriage.[105] He held that the burden of proving insanity was high, since 'the contract of marriage is a very simple one, which does not require a high degree of intelligence to comprehend.'[106] However, this case was the exception. Hannen typically followed ecclesiastical precedents and continued the conservative legacy left by his predecessors. For example, Hannen found that an irregular marriage contracted in Scotland was not valid unless it could be proven that the couple were legitimately domiciled in that foreign jurisdiction.[107] This respected the earlier precedents on the legal status of foreign divorces.[108] Moreover, Hannen was known for applying precedents strictly. For example, he once refused to grant a divorce in a case involving the respondent's physical abuse of the child of the marriage. He held that it did not constitute cruelty as there was no direct harm

---

100 See J.H. Baker, 'Famous English Canon Lawyers: X Sir Robert Phillimore, QC, DCL († 1885) and the Last Practising Doctors of Law' (1997) 4(21) *Ecclesiastical Law Journal* 709; Norman Doe, 'Phillimore, Sir Robert Joseph, Baronet (1810–1885),' *Oxford Dictionary of National Biography* (2004) <https://doi.org/10.1093/ref:odnb/22138>.
101 Polden (n 61).
102 Henry Edwin Fenn, *Thirty-Five Years in the Divorce Court* (T Werner Laurie 1910) 20.
103 *Ibid*. 16.
104 'Death of Lord Hannen,' *The Times* (London, 30 March 1894) 12.
105 (1885) 10 PD 80.
106 *Ibid*. 82.
107 *Lawford (Otherwise Davies) v Davies* (1878) 4 PD 61.
108 *R v Lolley* (1812) Russ & Ry 237; *M'Carthy v DeCaix* (1831) 2 Russ & My 614.

to the petitioner.[109] Therefore, Hannen held a doctrinal view of the law that is reflected in his strict adherence to the ecclesiastical principles and precedents.

Matrimonial Causes Act 1878

Towards the end of the nineteenth century, a number of bills were successfully introduced that amended the Matrimonial Causes Act 1857. These bills were particularly aimed at protecting the welfare and financial status of separated married women. These piecemeal reforms helped to ameliorate some concerns and delay the wider campaign for divorce law reform until the early twentieth century. Although there was heated argument during the parliamentary debates of the 1850s over the introduction of the Divorce Court, there was no discussion on the creation of a parallel family justice system administered by local courts in the late nineteenth century. Divorce law was still seen as a jurisdiction that required the expertise of the High Court rather than the summary courts.[110] It soon became apparent that the family justice system was out of reach for many of those in the working class, where the only legal remedy for a matrimonial dispute was found in London. The cost of divorce was estimated to range from £100 to £200 in 1861,[111] and from £30 to £150 in 1912.[112] Although this was significantly less expensive than the costs of the tripartite divorce process, the expense was still too high for many working-class individuals.[113] The law offered almost no protection for married women from physical harm or financial loss following separation unless they were able to afford the costs of the Divorce Court.[114]

The leading feminist Frances Power Cobbe published a pamphlet, *Wife-Torture in England*, that drew attention to the suffering of working-class married women and advocated for the expansion of legal remedies available to wives suffering domestic violence.[115] Parliament adopted Cobbe's proposals after Lord Penzance added amendments to an existing bill on the costs of the Queen's Proctor.[116]

---

109 *Birch v Birch* (1873) 42 LJ(P&M) 23.
110 Patrick Polden, *A History of the County Court 1846–1971* (Cambridge University Press 1999) 107.
111 Penelope Russell, 'Matrimonial Causes Act 1857' in Erika Rackley and Rosemary Auchmuty (eds), *Women's Legal Landmarks: Celebrating the History of Women and Law in the UK and Ireland* (Hart Publishing 2018) 67.
112 Earl Russell, *Divorce* (Heinemann 1912) 132.
113 A party who had less than £25 in assets or an income not exceeding 30s per week could receive gratuitous legal representation to petition for divorce *in forma pauperis*, but even then the party would still have had to pay for the out-of-pocket expenses of the counsel or agent, travelling expenses, and witness fees. From 1883 to 1907, there were only 812 petitions for leave to sue or defend *in forma pauperis*. In the same period, there were 15,505 petitions for dissolution and 2,626 petitions for judicial separation. Therefore, very few had access to legal aid and would have had to bear the expense of litigation themselves. Matrimonial Causes Act 1857, s 54; *Report of the Royal Commission on Divorce and Matrimonial Causes* (Cmd 6478, 1912) 129–32.
114 Maeve Doggett, *Marriage, Wife-Beating and the Law in Victorian England* (Weidenfeld & Nicholson 1992) 126–33.
115 Frances Power Cobbe, 'Wife-Torture in England' (1878) 32 *The Contemporary Review* 55.
116 HL Deb 29 March 1878, vol 239, col 191.

124 *The divorce courts*

The bill became the Matrimonial Causes Act 1878.[117] This enabled magistrates to issue separation orders for a wife.[118] This allowed a wife to live separately from a husband convicted of assaulting her. For a separation order to be granted, the magistrate had to ensure the objective of providing for the wife's safety was satisfied.[119] The effect of the Act was akin to a judicial separation: 'such order shall have the force and effect in all respects of a decree of judicial separation on the ground of cruelty.'[120]

It is important to distinguish the difference between a judicial separation and a separation order. A judicial separation was only granted by the Court for Divorce and Matrimonial Causes and the High Court. It would be issued in the case of a wife who successfully proved at least one of the grounds for divorce, but usually after failing to prove another ground necessary to be granted a divorce. On the other hand, a separation order was granted by courts of summary jurisdiction, such as by magistrates in local courts. It was aimed at those who could not afford relief in the High Court. A separation order allowed the parties to live separately with the aim of protecting the wife from the cruelty of the husband. Both orders allowed the parties to live separately, and it was necessary in order for married women to be granted the rights of *feme sole* prior to 1882. The Court could also order the husband to pay the wife on making a non-cohabitation order under the Act.[121] This expanded the scope of divorce law in England and made it easier for the working class to access the family justice system.

Matrimonial Causes Act 1884

Another issue that soon became apparent to judges was the problem of enforcing a restitution of conjugal rights order. There were only an average of four decrees *per annum* granted between 1868 and 1878.[122] Such an order could be made to compel the offending spouse to return to the matrimonial home, but it was often used 'for the payment by the husband of alimony to the wife.'[123] In fact, Hannen noted that he had only known of petitioners applying for a restitution of conjugal rights order to enforce a money demand.[124] However, an unusual case swiftly brought about changes to the restitution of conjugal rights. In *Weldon v Weldon*,[125] the husband, Sir William Henry Weldon, provided his separated wife,

---

117 (41 & 42 Vict c 19).
118 The marginal notes state, 'If husband convicted of aggravated assault, Court may order that wife be not bound to cohabit.' See Matrimonial Causes Act 1878, s 4; Cretney (n 18) 444.
119 *Dodd v Dodd* [1906] P 189, 200.
120 Matrimonial Causes Act 1878, s 4.
121 Matrimonial Causes Act 1878, s 4(1).
122 *Report of the Royal Commission on Marriage and Divorce* (Cmd 9678, 1956) 363 (Appendix II, Table 2(iv)).
123 Matrimonial Causes Act 1857, s 17.
124 *Marshall v Marshall* (1879) 5 PD 19, 23.
125 (1883) 9 PD 52.

Georgina Weldon, a house, servants, and an income of £500 per year.[126] Despite the husband's financial support, the wife initiated a suit for non-obedience of a decree for restitution of conjugal rights against her husband. Hannen, bound by precedent,[127] found that he had no choice but to enforce the decree for restitution of conjugal rights by issuing a writ of attachment sentencing the husband to imprisonment.[128] The writ was issued despite his feelings that it was an inappropriate sanction. He preferred the Scottish law of the restitution of conjugal rights which could only be enforced by a decree for alimony rather than imprisonment.[129]

The government quickly responded and nine months later the Matrimonial Causes Act 1884[130] was passed.[131] There was very little debate during its passage as a bill. Solicitor-General Sir Farrer Herschell (later Lord Herschell), most likely alluding to *Weldon*, said, 'The Bill was dictated by practical experience, and would meet a very serious evil.'[132] This was a rare example of judicial activism pushing the government into piecemeal *ad hoc* reform. The Act abolished the penalty of imprisonment for failure to comply with a restitution of conjugal rights decree and empowered the courts to make financial orders instead.[133] Hannen found that the Matrimonial Causes Act 1884 applied retrospectively and rejected the wife's writ of attachment when the matter was heard again in 1885.[134] More significantly, instead of waiting for a period of two years to elapse in order to prove desertion, the Act gave married women the right to petition for divorce immediately after proving the husband's adultery and failure to comply with a restitution decree.[135] Hence, it became known as the 'Weldon Relief Act' and provided a way for married women to circumvent the Matrimonial Causes Act 1857.[136]

---

126 Sir William was a lieutenant in the Eighteenth Hussars and Mrs Weldon was a notable spiritualist and campaigner against lunacy laws. See John Martin, 'Weldon, Georgina (1837–1914),' *Oxford Dictionary of National Biography* (2004) <https://doi.org/10.1093/ref:odnb/53148>; Roy Porter, Helen Nicholson, and Bridget Bennett (eds), *Women, Madness, and Spiritualism: Georgina Weldon and Louisa Lowe, Volume 1* (Routledge 2003); Storm Bird, *The Strange Life of Georgina Weldon* (Chatto and Windus 1959).
127 *Lakin v Lakin* (1854) 1 Spinks Ecc Ad Rep 274; *Alexander v Alexander* (1861) 30 LJ(PM&A) 173; *Scott v Scott* (1865) 4 Sw&Tr 113.
128 *Weldon v Weldon* (1883) 9 PD 52, 57.
129 *Ibid.* 56.
130 (47 & 48 Vict c 68).
131 Judgment was handed down in *Weldon* on 27 November 1883. The Matrimonial Causes Act 1884 was given Royal Assent on 14 August 1884; HL Deb 14 August 1884, vol 292, col 651.
132 HC Deb 8 August 1884, vol 292, col 356.
133 Matrimonial Causes Act 1884, s 2.
134 *Weldon v Weldon* (1885) 10 PD 72.
135 Matrimonial Causes Act 1884, s 5.
136 Alfred Fellows, 'Changes in the Law of Husband and Wife' (1906) 22 *Law Quarterly Review* 64, 66; Philip Treherne, *A Plaintiff in Person: The Life of Mrs Weldon* (William Heinemann 1923) vii.

The Butt court: A brief presidency

Butt succeeded Sir Robert Phillimore as judge of the PDA Division on 31 March 1883 and was knighted on 20 April 1883. *The Times* reflected on the merits of Butt's judicial appointment at the time of his death.

> His forensic position fully justified his elevation, though it cannot be said that the appointment was wholly apart from political considerations. He was not an exceptionally great lawyer, but he was completely master of the limited field of jurisprudence in which his duties lay, and he was thoroughly versed in Admiralty law.[137]

Butt was a competent judge, but he did not share the judicial flair of his predecessors. In *Otway v Otway and Hoffer*, the husband and the wife were both found to have committed adultery, and the husband was also found to have committed cruelty.[138] Butt granted the wife a judicial separation, despite the fact that her adultery barred her from both divorce and judicial separation. Perhaps he was emotionally moved to act as a result of the aggravated nature of the husband's cruelty, which included acts of violence towards the wife and indecent assaults on the daughter of the marriage. However, Butt was overturned by the Court of Appeal, where they ruled that he had no jurisdiction to grant a decree of judicial separation in a case where the petitioner was barred from relief.[139] This case may demonstrate Butt's willingness to depart from settled principles and grant divorce on wider grounds.

He was an innovator to greater effect on other occasions too. In *Lister v Lister*, Butt granted a divorced wife alimony of one-third of the husband's income for the absolute duration of her life, regardless whether she remarried, based on the Court's absolute discretion under section 32 of the Matrimonial Causes Act 1857.[140] The judgment was upheld in the Court of Appeal.[141] This was an early articulation of the one-third rule, which was later applied as a guiding principle in determining ancillary relief.[142] In the case of *Scott v Sebright*, Butt granted a nullity of marriage after finding that there was a lack of consent.[143] The petitioner was a 22-year-old woman who was compelled to pay the respondent's debts and coerced into marriage on the threat of being shot by the respondent.

---

137 'Death Of Sir C Butt' *The Times* (London, 27 May 1892) 3.
138 (1887) 13 PD 12.
139 *Otway v Otway and Hoffer* (1887) 13 PD 141.
140 (1889) 14 PD 175.
141 (1889) 15 PD 4.
142 *Wachtel v Wachtel* [1973] Fam 72, per Lord Denning. See also Gillian Douglas, 'Beginning an End to the Matrimonial Post Mortem: Wachtel v Wachtel and its Enduring Significance for Ancillary Relief' in Stephen Gilmore, Jonathan Herring, and Rebecca Probert (eds), *Landmark Cases in Family Law* (Hart Publishing 2011) 135–54.
143 (1886) 12 PD 21.

In 1886, Butt also heard the sensational divorce case of Donald Crawford at trial without jury in which his friend and Liberal leader Sir Charles Dilke was the co-respondent accused of adultery.[144] Although this case may have been personally difficult for him to hear, he discharged his duties in accordance with the letter of the law. On 29 January 1891, he was appointed president of the PDA Division, succeeding Hannen on his retirement. However, his presidential term was short-lived as his health began to rapidly deteriorate. He succumbed to a cardiac paralysis and died on 25 May 1892 at the age of 61. History may have been kinder in its assessment of Butt's judicial career had he lived longer, but for his brief and unremarkable spell as president of the PDA Division.

The Jeune court: The road to reform

Sir Francis Jeune replaced Butt as judge of the PDA Division in 1891, after Butt was appointed president of the PDA.[145] Although Jeune was recognised as an able lawyer, the decision came as a surprise to the legal profession for he seldom appeared in the PDA Division.[146] Jeune was a friend of the English novelist and poet Thomas Hardy. They used to meet at Jeune's home in London and discussed all manner of topics, particularly the law of divorce.[147] This may have influenced the plot in Hardy's *Jude the Obscure*.[148] Jude divorces his wife Arabella for committing adultery after she left him, moved to Australia, and entered into a bigamous relationship. Jude assents to Arabella's request that he petition for divorce, so that she may marry her bigamous partner. This means that both parties had committed collusion. Thus, if this fact was known to the Court, it would have been an absolute bar to divorce. Jude's love interest Sue is granted a divorce after her husband Phillotson successfully petitions for divorce by pleading that Sue had committed adultery with Jude. However, Sue at that stage of the novel had not had sexual relations with Jude. Moreover, Sue's request to Phillotson for a divorce would have also constituted collusion.[149] Collusion was a practice that occurred at the commencement of the Matrimonial Causes Act 1857, but became more popularly depicted from the late nineteenth century onwards.

George Moore's *Esther Waters* is another popular depiction of divorce that was published in 1894.[150] The protagonist Esther Waters, a young working-class woman, becomes pregnant after having a premarital relationship with a colleague,

---

144 *Crawford v Crawford and Dilke (The Queen's Proctor Intervening)* (1886) 11 PD 150.
145 Herbert Stephen, 'Jeune, Francis Henry, Baron St Helier (1843–1905)' (2004) *Oxford Dictionary of National Biography* <https://doi.org/10.1093/ref:odnb/34188>.
146 'Death of Lord St Helier' *The Times* (London, 10 April 1905) 6.
147 Lady Mary St Helier, *Memories of Fifty Years* (Edward Arnold 1909) 240.
148 Thomas Hardy, *Jude the Obscure* (first published 1895, Penguin 2019).
149 William Davis, 'Hardy and the Law: Sexual Relations and "Matrimonial Divergence"' in Rosemarie Morgan (ed), *The Ashgate Research Companion to Thomas Hardy* (Ashgate 2010) 113–50; Melanie Williams, *Secrets and Laws: Collected Essays in Law, Lives, and Literature* (UCL Press 2005) 103–21.
150 George Moore, *Esther Waters* (first published 1894, Oxford University Press 2012).

William Latch, while they are both performing domestic work for the Barfields. William abandons Esther for Peggy, a young niece of Mrs Barfield, with whom he is having an affair, and the two later elope. Esther then gives birth to a son named Jackie. Nine years later, Esther meets William again, who has since separated from Peggy after she was caught having an adulterous relationship with another man. Peggy lets William get a divorce at any time. The two of them agree that Peggy will petition for divorce against William for adultery and desertion based on the advice of their solicitors. Peggy's plea of William's desertion is rather ironic given the fact that he had initially deserted Esther for Peggy and now wants to marry Esther. William's solicitor advises that it would be too difficult for William to prove Peggy's adultery, because he had not obtained evidence of adultery at the time it had occurred and Peggy had thereafter lived an outwardly circumspect life. Peggy then agrees to bear all the legal expenses in exchange for William acting as the guilty party by living with Esther. If their agreement was to be discovered by the Court, it would constitute collusion and bar them from divorce. William professes his love for Esther, who is coaxed into living with him. The divorce petition is eventually successful and Esther subsequently accepts William's marriage proposal for the sake of their son. The novel illustrates the evidentiary challenges of proving adultery and the growing acceptance of divorce by mutual consent among some people. However, this idea was still outside of mainstream thinking in the 1890s.[151]

For most of Butt's presidency, the Division's work fell predominantly onto Jeune as a result of Butt's deteriorating health. On 31 May 1892, Jeune succeeded as the president of the PDA Division after the death of Butt.[152] John Gorell Barnes (later Lord Gorell) replaced Jeune as judge of the PDA Division.[153] In the same year, Jeune was also appointed as a privy councillor and judge advocate general. Jeune presided over a court that was experiencing a visible rise in divorce, and a society increasingly tolerant of divorce. The divorce rate sharply increased from 369 decrees in 1891 to 546 decrees in 1906.[154] Despite the increase in divorce petitions, the Division did not fall into arrears.

Jeune presided over a number of important divorce law cases during a total of 14 years on the PDA Division. It was clear in some of his decisions that he was demonstrating a subtle degree of judicial activism in promoting a more liberal interpretation of divorce law. In *Jeapes v Jeapes*, Jeune delivered a noticeably more creative interpretation of the definition of cruelty.[155] In this case, the husband neglected his pregnant wife and her two children by leaving them penniless after making false claims that the child soon to be born was not biologically his and consequently that the wife had committed adultery. The wife petitioned for divorce on the grounds of adultery and cruelty. Jeune held that the husband's

---

151 The novel faced a significant degree of hostility for its portrayal of sexual immorality. George Watt, *The Fallen Woman in the Nineteenth-Century English Novel* (Croom Helm 1984) 177.
152 'Court Circular' *The Times* (London, 31 May 1892) 9.
153 *Ibid*.
154 Stone (n 99) 435.
155 (1903) 89 LT 74.

neglect of his wife constituted cruelty. This case was decided after the landmark House of Lords ruling in *Russell v Russell*, which held that only acts directly harming or endangering another spouse constituted cruelty.[156]

The *Jeapes* case bore a close resemblance to the material facts of *Russell*. Both cases featured an unsubstantiated accusation of a sexual offence that arguably made conjugal residency impossible. However, cruelty was not found in *Russell*, because the respondent's unfounded accusations of homosexuality against the petitioner did not fit the House of Lord's strict definition of cruelty. Jeune distinguished his judgment in *Jeapes* from *Russell* by arguing that there was evidence of direct harm to the wife that constituted cruelty, namely that the husband's abandonment led to the wife being left in an impecunious position causing her to starve.[157] Adultery was also proven; therefore, the wife was granted a divorce. Jeune's judgment was within the definition of cruelty set in *Russell*. However, he took the initiative to find a way to grant the wife a divorce in order to deliver a just outcome. This was a clever judgment that could be viewed both as a strict application of the existing law and judicial activism with the aim of extending the scope of cruelty as a matrimonial cause.

Summary Jurisdiction (Married Women) Act 1895

During Jeune's presidency, Parliament introduced further legislation protecting the financial rights and safety of married women, particularly those from the working class. The Married Women (Maintenance in Cases of Desertion) Act 1886 enabled a deserted wife to apply for a court order from a magistrate to seek a financial remedy against the husband of a sum not exceeding £2.[158] This measure ended the practice of compelling deserted wives to enter workhouses under the Poor Law.[159] The Summary Jurisdiction (Married Women) Act 1895 was another important piece of legislation that enabled magistrates to deliver separation orders that could provide maintenance and protection for married women.[160] The Act consolidated the Matrimonial Causes Act 1878 and the Married Women (Maintenance in Cases of Desertion) Act 1886. The aim of the Act was to protect any married woman whose husband was found to have been convicted of assault, desertion, cruelty, or wilful neglect to provide reasonable maintenance to the wife or infant child of the marriage.[161] During the parliamentary debates, the bill's promoter Edmund Byrne said:

> [The bill] was intended to get rid of some anomalies which existed in the civil law and the criminal law in cases of aggravated assaults on wives by husbands,

---

156 [1897] AC 395.
157 *Jeapes v Jeapes* (1903) 89 LT 74, 75.
158 (49 & 50 Vict c 52).
159 *Report of the Committee on One-Parent Families* (Cmd 5269, 1974) 122–3 (Appendix 5).
160 (58 & 59 Vict c 39).
161 Summary Jurisdiction (Married Women) Act 1895, s 4.

and, further, to give similar relief in cases of persistent cruelty by a husband towards a wife as now existed in cases of aggravated assault.[162]

The government supported the bill in the belief that it would improve legal procedure, and it passed both houses with little debate.[163] Ann Sumner Holmes states, 'The laws of England no longer required women to maintain absolutely the ideal of self-sacrifice.'[164] Indeed, the Act extended the power of summary courts to make orders for separation (i.e., non-cohabitation orders with the effect of judicial separation), custody of children under the age of 16, spousal maintenance, and legal costs.[165] A wife was entitled to petition for a separation order with spousal maintenance, where the husband was found to have been guilty of assaulting the wife and convicted to a term of imprisonment exceeding two months or sentenced to pay a fine of more than £5.[166] However, a major problem was that a wife who was granted a separation order could not subsequently claim that the husband committed desertion as a matrimonial cause for divorce after two years of separation had expired.[167] The Act remained in force for 70 years. It helped to shift a majority of matrimonial cases onto the summary courts.

Within a few decades after civil divorce was introduced, amendments were passed to rectify some of the impracticalities surrounding the operation of the Matrimonial Causes Act 1857. Nevertheless, the amendments failed to comprehensively address the critical issue of sex discrimination against married women and the social inequality of access to the family justice system that inherently existed within the Matrimonial Causes Act 1857. The Summary Jurisdiction (Married Women) Act 1895 also resulted in magistrates prioritising the bond of marriage and the headship of the husband over the wife.[168] This was clearly at the expense of the principal aim of the legislation to protect married women from their abusive husbands. There was no coherent organised campaign for divorce law reform until the early 1900s, which limited debate on these issues in the late nineteenth century.

Granting divorce in spite of the petitioner's adultery

The Court from the late nineteenth century was becoming increasingly willing to grant divorce, even if the discretionary bars of condoned, innocent, or unwilling

---

162 HC Deb 22 May 1895, vol 34, col 62.
163 *Ibid*.
164 Ann Sumner Holmes, 'The Double Standard in the English Divorce Laws, 1857–1923' (1995) 20(2) *Law and Social Inquiry* 601, 608.
165 Summary Jurisdiction (Married Women) Act 1895, s 5.
166 Summary Jurisdiction (Married Women) Act 1895, s 4.
167 *Dodd v Dodd* [1906] P 189.
168 Gail Savage, '"The Magistrates are Men": Working-Class Marital Conflict and Appeals from the Magistrates' Court to the Divorce Court after 1895' in George Robb and Nancy Erber (eds), *Disorder in the Court: Trials and Sexual Conflict at the Turn of the Century* (New York University Press 1999).

adultery were found. There were three established excuses for the petitioner's adultery. Condoned adultery referred to the adultery of the petitioner that was forgiven by the respondent.[169] In the late nineteenth century, relief would only be granted if the petitioner's condoned adultery was not the cause of the respondent's matrimonial offence. This was known as the doctrine of causal responsibility.[170] This doctrine was not strictly followed in the early twentieth century, because the Court exercised its discretion based on a more contemporary interpretation of public interest.[171] Public morality had shifted at the turn of the century, with judges more willing to grant divorce despite the adultery of the petitioner, so long as their decisions did not elicit moral outrage. Some judges were more willing to exercise their discretion in favour of the wife's petition for divorce based on the perceived sexual weakness of women.[172] Even if the petitioner's adultery was condoned, the Court could still refuse to grant divorce unless there were special circumstances suggesting that the petitioner's adultery was more venial than that of the respondent.[173]

Innocent adultery involved a mistake where the petitioner had committed adultery after honestly and reasonably believing that the respondent was deceased[174] or the marriage was already legally dissolved.[175] If the petitioner continued to commit adultery after discovering that the respondent was actually alive, then the petitioner would be barred from divorce.[176] Unwilling adultery involved the husband forcing the wife into prostitution. The wife would not have her petition denied if she could prove that her husband coerced her into prostitution against her will.[177] These three excuses were accepted, since they mitigated or absolved the petitioner's moral culpability for committing adultery.

169 *Goode v Goode and Hamson* (1861) 2 Sw&Tr 253.
170 *Clarke v Clarke and Clarke* (1865) 34 LJ(PA&M) 94; *McCord v McCord* (1875) LR 3 P&D 237; *Symons v Symons (The Queen's Proctor Intervening)* [1897] P 167.
171 *Evans v Evans and Alford* [1906] P 125, 130; *Apted v Apted and Bliss* [1930] P 246.
172 In *Pretty v Pretty* [1911] P 83, 87, Bargrave Deane J states,

> Some people think that, in such matters, you must treat men and women on the same footing. But this Court has not taken, and, I hope, never will take, that view. I trust that, in dealing with these cases, it will ever be remembered that the woman is the weaker vessel: that her habits of thought and feminine weaknesses are different from those of the man: and that what may perhaps be excusable in the case of the woman would not be excusable in the case of the man. Where you find that the woman has been guilty of adultery and that her adultery has resulted from her husband's conduct towards her, this Court does, and I hope always will, make allowances and treat her error with leniency.

173 *Clarke v Clarke and Clarke* (1865) 34 LJ(PA&M) 94; *McCord v McCord, Ogle and Coxon* (1875) LR 3 P&D 237; *Grosvenor v Grosvenor* (1885) 34 WR 140.
174 *Joseph v Joseph and Wenzell* (1865) LJ(PA&M) 96; *Freegard v Freegard, Cowper and Lucas* (1883) 8 PD 186; *Potter v Potter* (1893) 67 LT 721.
175 *Wickham v Wickham* (1880) 6 PD 11; *Snook v Snook and Woolacott (The Queen's Proctor Showing Cause)* (1892) 67 LT 389; *Moore v Moore (The Queen's Proctor Showing Cause)* [1892] P 382; *Whitworth v Whitworth and Thomasson* [1893] P 85.
176 *Pegg v Pegg and Gowing* (1904) 20 TLR 353; *Hynes v Hynes and Lake* (1904) 20 TLR 781.
177 *Coleman v Coleman* (1866) LR 1 P&D 81; *Barker v Barker* (1907) 24 TLR 31.

Where the husband was found to have raped a minor, the Court was willing to overlook the wife's own adultery and grant divorce in her favour.[178] In *Constantinidi v Constantinidi and Lance*, the wife was found guilty of committing adultery with the co-respondent.[179] The wife left the husband in 1897 for Ireland with the intention of never returning. In 1901, she moved to America and a year later she was granted a divorce by the State of South Dakota. Immediately afterwards, she married the co-respondent in Sioux Falls. During that same period, the husband committed adultery with a prostitute. He admitted this in his petition for divorce. Jeune concluded 'that the respondent conduced to the adultery committed by the petitioner.'[180] The wife's desertion was deemed to have been a relevant factor causing the adultery of the husband. Therefore, the husband was not barred from divorce. These exceptional cases demonstrate that the respondent's conduct was sometimes a relevant consideration in determining the exercise of the Court's discretion for cases involving the petitioner's adultery.

More of these cases emerged around the beginning of the twentieth century. This indicates that the Courts were becoming increasingly willing to exercise their discretion in expanding the circumstances in which divorce would be granted. In *Northover v Northover*, the adultery of the wife did not bar her from being granted a divorce for the husband's cruelty.[181] In this case, the husband violently beat the wife until she submitted to his demand to act as a paramour for male clients that he invited to the matrimonial home. The husband sought to extort them for money, even though no sexual intercourse took place. The moral turpitude of the respondent was an important consideration in the Court's exercise of its discretion.

Legacy of Lord St Helier

It is important to recognise that Jeune still often followed the overall conservativeness of the PDA Division. It would be inaccurate to describe Jeune as a liberal judge, especially when compared to his successor Lord Gorell. In *Hall v Hall and Kay*, Jeune coined the expression 'blow hot and cold' to describe how a petitioner could not claim a divorce after reprobating and approbating the other spouse's matrimonial offences.[182] This re-enforced the existing understanding of the bars to divorce. In *Churchward v Churchward and Holliday (The Queen's Proctor Intervening)*, Jeune extended the definition of collusion to also include in its definition a compact between the parties to conceal relevant information

---

178 *Collins v Collins* (1884) 9 PD 231; *Symons v Symons (The Queen's Proctor Intervening)* [1897] P 167.
179 [1903] P 246.
180 *Ibid*. 261.
181 (1910) 26 TLR 224.
182 (1891) 64 LT 837, 838.

or an agreement for the respondent not to defend.[183] It seems that collusion became an increasing concern and efforts were made to expand its definition in order to make it more difficult for parties to manipulate the law of divorce. In January 1905, Jeune resigned as president of the PDA Division due to poor health and was ennobled Lord St Helier.[184] However, his health further declined after the death of his only son. Soon afterwards he died, on 9 April 1905 in his home in London. Jeune continued the steady course established by the previous presidents of the PDA Division. Although his legal strength lay in other areas of law, he rose to the occasion and was a consummate judge in the PDA Division.

Lord St Helier set a tone of greater openness in the PDA Division that paved the way for more radical judicial activism in the early twentieth century. The early judges of the Divorce Court were more comfortable with following the ecclesiastical precedents. However, as the nineteenth century wore on there was greater willingness to establish new precedent independent of ecclesiastical jurisprudence. The Victorian era was over and the Divorce Court would soon experience a significant shift from its overall conservative tone. The Divorce Court was already further recognising the legal rights of women, particularly after the introduction of protection orders under the Matrimonial Causes Act 1878 and the introduction of the right of married women to own separate legal property under the Married Women's Property Act 1882.[185] Alfred Fellows stated, 'During the progress of the wife's independence and emancipation, the practice of the Divorce Court exhibits an almost similar spirit of chivalry…'[186] Jeune's successor as president was his colleague Gorell Barnes, who later became known for his outspoken advocacy of divorce law reform.

---

183 [1895] P 7.
184 'Resignation of Sir Francis Jeune' *The Times* (London, 30 January 1905) 6.
185 (45 & 46 Vict c 75).
186 Alfred Fellows, 'Changes in the Law of Husband and Wife' (1906) 22 *Law Quarterly Review* 64, 68.

6 Divorce law reform in the early twentieth century

Hunter bill

In 1892, Dr William Alexander Hunter, a Scottish Liberal MP for Aberdeen North and a professor of Roman law at University College London,[1] introduced a bill to extend the grounds for divorce.[2] This was the first significant attempt to fundamentally change the Matrimonial Causes Act 1857. When the bill was first introduced in 1889, it was initially described as a 'Bill to assimilate the Law of Divorce in England and Scotland.'[3] Although Hunter supported the bill in order to eliminate the double standard between genders in accessing the grounds for divorce, he framed the debate as a conflict of law issue rather than as a matter of equality and justice.[4] This did not necessarily mean that there was an absence of support from groups advocating for the latter.

The Women's Liberal Federation, a women's rights organisation within the Liberal Party, supported Hunter's bill based on its belief that the grounds for divorce should be equalised between genders.[5] Elizabeth Wolstenholme Elmy was one of the leading feminists of the time. She was actively involved in the Married Women's Property Committee that successfully campaigned for the right of married women to own property *feme sole* under the Married Women's Property Act 1882.[6] After legislative success, she turned her attention by advocating for equal rights for women in other areas of the law, including the abolition of the sexual double standard in Hunter's bill.[7] Elmy played a role in establishing the Women's Franchise League in 1889 and soon after formed her own organisation, the Women's Emancipation Union, in 1892. This group was dedicated to

---

1 Eliza Orme, 'Hunter, William Alexander (1844–1898),' *Oxford Dictionary of National Biography* (2004) <https://doi.org/10.1093/ref:odnb/14236>.
2 HC Deb 26 April 1892, vol 3, col 1437.
3 HC Deb 22 February 1889, vol 333, col 128.
4 HC Deb 26 April 1892, vol 3, col 1437.
5 Rebecca Probert, 'The Controversy of Equality and the Matrimonial Causes Act 1923' (1999) 11 *Child and Family Law Quarterly* 33, 35.
6 Lee Holcombe, *Wives and Property: Reform of the Married Women's Property Law in Nineteenth-Century England* (University of Toronto Press 1983) 118–47.
7 Maureen Wright, *Elizabeth Wolstenholme Elmy and the Victorian Feminist Movement: The Biography of an Insurgent Woman* (Manchester University Press 2011) 122.

the promotion of women's rights, particularly campaigning against the injustice of marital rape.[8] The Moral Reform Union, a society founded in 1882 with the aim of promoting 'pure family life,'[9] also lent its support to Hunter's bill.[10] Although it harboured reservations about supporting desertion as a sole ground for divorce, it nevertheless came to the conclusion that the law should provide equal grounds to divorce between genders.[11] Women comprised three-fourths of the Moral Reform Union.[12] This may help to explain its support for the removal of the double standard through the Hunter bill.

During the parliamentary debates of 1892, Hunter proposed that the English adopt the Scottish laws of divorce. He argued that intermarriage between the English and the Scots was such a common occurrence that the laws ought to be unified.[13] The proposed change would mean that either spouse under English law would be able to divorce on the grounds of desertion or adultery alone. Hunter argued that the experience of three centuries of the law's operation in Scotland was that such a measure would not lead to a sharp increase in the divorce rate.[14]

Attorney-General Sir Richard Webster, however, was not convinced. He expressed concern that taking this course of action would lead to an increase in collusive divorce and lower the standard of morality.[15] The Hunter bill was comfortably defeated by 71 votes to 40 during its Second Reading.[16] Stephen Cretney notes that the double standard of divorce created a wide sense of injustice, 'And yet the nineteenth century saw little institutional campaigning for change.'[17] Similarly, Rebecca Probert states, 'Even those groups who were in favour of reform did not play an active role in promoting changes to the law.'[18] Although there were no societies dedicated to the promotion of divorce reform at the time, women and civic groups were already beginning to voice concern about the operation of the Matrimonial Causes Act 1857. However, the late nineteenth century was not the time for the widespread campaign for divorce reform. At the turn of the century, a more active and organised movement began to emerge.

First Russell bills

The political conservatism of the Victorian era on the issue of divorce law was about to change. The Edwardian period was known for its political upheavals.

---

8 Sandra Stanley Holton, 'Elmy, Elizabeth Clarke Wolstenholme (1833–1918),' *Oxford Dictionary of National Biography* (2004) <https://doi.org/10.1093/ref:odnb/38638>.
9 F.K. Prochaska, *Women and Philanthropy in Nineteenth-Century England* (Oxford University Press 1980) 217.
10 Probert (n 5) 35.
11 *Ibid.*
12 Prochaska (n 9) 217.
13 HC Deb 26 April 1892, vol 3, col 1437.
14 *Ibid.* col 1438.
15 *Ibid.* cols 1439–43.
16 *Ibid.* col 1449.
17 Stephen Cretney, *Family Law in the Twentieth Century* (Oxford University Press 2003) 202.
18 Probert (n 5) 35.

David Brooks states, 'Traditional values and constraints on behaviour appeared to be breaking down under the impact in particular of militant feminism and trade unionism.'[19] The issue of divorce reform was no exception. The divorce reform campaign began to effectively mobilise during the Edwardian period. Yet despite the concerted attempts for political reform on this issue, there would be no significant changes to the law until the 1920s. The introduction of the Russell bill in 1902 was the next unsuccessful attempt at divorce law reform. The promoter of the bill was the Second Earl Russell (born John Francis 'Frank' Stanley Russell), the grandson of Lord John Russell, who had convened the Campbell Commission. Russell was convicted of bigamy after absconding to America, where he obtained a divorce and married his mistress in the State of Nevada.[20]

Unlike Dr Hunter, who dispassionately presented his bill as a panacea to remedy the conflict of matrimonial laws between England and Scotland, Russell was motivated by his personal acrimonious experience with the English family justice system involving his own divorce proceedings.[21] His personal background in the matter would prove to be a disservice to his cause.[22] On 1 May 1902, Russell introduced the divorce bill into the House of Lords for debate after taking three years to draft.[23] The Russell bill proposed that adultery remain a ground of divorce, but sought to abolish the double standard against married women.[24] The bill also proposed to introduce five additional sole grounds for divorce applied equally to the husband or the wife, including 'cruelty, penal servitude for a term of not less than three years, lunacy, living apart for three years, and living apart for one year provided the other party concurs in the petition.'[25] Furthermore, the bill also contained clauses to allow the wife to sue for damages against the co-respondent, and proposed the abolition of petitions for judicial separation, restitution of conjugal rights, and jactitation of marriage.[26]

In relation to the family justice system, the bill sought to abolish the ecclesiastical procedures of the PDA Division and replace them with the common law procedures of the King's Bench Division.[27] Moreover, the bill proposed to grant the County Court the jurisdiction to hear divorce suits for parties where their total joint annual income did not exceed £500.[28] This was an attempt to improve

---

19 David Brooks, *The Age of Upheaval: Edwardian Politics, 1899–1914* (Manchester University Press 1995) 1.
20 See Ann Sumner Holmes, '"Don't Frighten the Horses": the Russell Divorce Case" in George Robb and Nancy Erber (eds), *Disorder in the Court: Trials and Sexual Conflict at the Turn of the Century* (New York University Press 1999) 140–63.
21 *Russell v Russell* [1897] AC 395.
22 Lord Halsbury accused Russell of bringing the bill forward because of his personal interests in the matter, though Russell denied it. HL Deb 1 August 1905, vol 150, cols 1068–9.
23 HL Deb 1 May 1902, vol 107, col 389.
24 *Ibid.* cols 389–90.
25 *Ibid.* col 390.
26 *Ibid.*
27 *Ibid.*
28 *Ibid.*

access to justice for the working class. The Gorell Royal Commission of 1909–12 adopted many of the proposals in the Hunter bill, which would eventually find its way into the Matrimonial Causes Act 1937.[29] The proposal for divorce after 12 months' separation with both parties consenting was rather radical for its time. A similar proposal was only recommended in 1990.[30] The Conservative lord chancellor, Lord Halsbury, found that this particular clause showed 'that practically this Bill is one for the abolition of the institution of marriage.'[31]

The bill would have made divorce more accessible to those on more modest incomes, simplified the legal procedure for obtaining a divorce, and significantly broadened the grounds for divorce had it passed. However, it was overwhelmingly rejected without a call for division in its Second Reading.[32] Lord Halsbury delivered a stinging condemnation.

> I say that the introduction of such a provision as that is an outrage upon your Lordships' House, something in the nature of an insult to your Lordships, and it is a thing which I, for one, deprecate most strongly.[33]

Russell attempted to introduce his bill again the following year, but it was once again rejected. Lord Halsbury repeated his concerns about such a bill.[34] In 1905, Russell tried for the third time to introduce a bill. This time he cut back on his previous demands. He only sought that desertion without cause for two years and upwards should be included as an additional ground of divorce.[35] Desertion was already a ground for judicial separation under section 16 of the Matrimonial Causes Act 1857. The proposed amendment to section 27 of the Matrimonial Causes Act 1857 was similar to the failed Hunter bill. The House of Lords declined to further debate the bill for a Second Reading by an overwhelming margin of 44 votes to 4.[36] The Russell bills were strongly opposed by the government and attracted little support in Parliament. In order to reach the statute books, all earlier legislation concerned with divorce and matrimonial property had required government support. Government support was a recurring theme of successful divorce law reforms from the enactment of the Matrimonial Causes Act 1857 to the Interwar period.

Russell's more important legacy was his establishment of the 'Society for Promoting Reforms in Marriage and Divorce Laws in England' in 1902. The Society later merged with the Divorce Law Reform Association to become the

---

29 (1 Ed VIII & 1 Geo VI c 57).
30 The Law Commission recommended allowing divorce 12 months after notice of intent is filed irrespective of whether the parties have consented. The Law Commission, *Family Law The Ground for Divorce*, No 192 (1990) 20 [3.48].
31 HL Deb 1 May 1902, vol 107, col 408.
32 *Ibid*. col 409.
33 *Ibid*. cols 408–9.
34 HL Deb 23 June 1903, vol 124, cols 212–13.
35 HL Deb 1 August 1905, vol 150, col 1065.
36 *Ibid*.

Divorce Law Reform Union (DLRU) after E.S.P. (Edmund Sidney Pollock) Haynes orchestrated their union in 1906.[37] The DLRU was comprised of both men and women during this period, mostly from the middle class.[38] The DLRU had rather humble ambitions. Its aim was simply to call for the government to appoint a royal commission to investigate reform of the divorce law.[39] One of its supporters was John Gorell Barnes, the president of the PDA Division (1905–9). The DLRU played an active role in the campaign for divorce reform, but ultimately Barnes was responsible for the establishment of a royal commission.

The Mothers' Union was the antithesis of the DLRU and was ideologically opposed to the expansion of the grounds of divorce based on Christian moral teaching.[40] The organisation was founded in 1876 and affiliated with the Church of England. The aim of the society was to promote Christian family life and support women for the vocation of motherhood.[41] Both the DLRU and Mothers' Union were initially influential at the beginning of the twentieth century, finding support from progressive reformers and the Church of England respectively. However, their influence waned in the 1930s with the changing political atmosphere as the DLRU was no longer the dominant force it once was in shaping policy and the Mothers' Union's conservative stance was beginning to diverge with the Church of England, which became increasingly more open to the expansion of the grounds for divorce.[42]

The Gorell court: Call for reform

Barnes was appointed as judge of the PDA Division in 1892. It was expected that he would become president of the PDA Division upon the position becoming vacant, as was the pattern of replacing the president with the judge from the same Division. This tradition continued with the appointment of Barnes as president of the PDA Division in 1905. He served in this role for four years until he resigned in 1909 upon receiving a peerage, becoming Baron Gorell of Brampton. He was an active member of the House of Lords and served as a Law Lord and chair on a number of committees. This included the County Courts Committee and the Copyright Committee.[43]

---

37 E.S.P. Haynes was a lawyer and writer. He is most well-known for his decades of campaigning for divorce law reform. See E.S.P. Haynes, *The Lawyer: A Conversation Piece* (Eyre and Spottiswoode 1951); Stephen Cretney, 'Haynes, Edmund Sidney Pollock (1877–1949),' *Oxford Dictionary of National Biography* (2004) <https://doi.org/10.1093/ref:odnb/38874>.
38 *Minutes of Evidence Taken Before the Royal Commission on Divorce and Matrimonial Causes* (Cd 6481, 1912) vol 3, 453.
39 *Ibid*.
40 Cordelia Ann Moyse, 'Reform of Marriage and Divorce Law in England and Wales 1909–1937' (DPhil thesis, University of Cambridge 1996) 103.
41 Sue Anderson-Faithful, 'Aspects of Agency: Change and Constraint in the Activism of Mary Sumner, Founder of the Anglican Mothers' Union' (2019) 28(6) *Women's History Review* 835, 846.
42 Moyse (n 40) 132.
43 This committee's report led to the enactment of the Copyright Act 1911 (1 & 2 Geo V c 46).

Over the course of Barnes' legal career, he showed liberal reforming instincts, especially in the area of divorce law. An example of Barnes' legal progressivism is illustrated in his broad interpretation of statutory damages. In *Lord v Lord and Lambert*, Barnes held that awarding statutory damages was discretionary, even in cases where the co-respondent paramour was ignorant of the wife's marital status.[44] This was later confirmed in *Smith v Smith and Reed*, when Duke J (later Lord Merrivale) ruled:

> As regards damages I am glad to say that it is well established now that a plea of ignorance is no bar to an award of damages. The fact of knowledge is an aggravation, but absence of knowledge is not a bar.[45]

However, Barnes was also constrained by the law and was compelled to deny divorce in a case involving recrimination. In *Hodgson v Hodgson and Turner*, the husband had violently assaulted his wife and then deserted her for America knowing that she was pregnant in 1890.[46] Ten years later, the wife, not knowing whether her husband was dead or alive, unwittingly entered into an adulterous relationship. The husband returned to England and petitioned for divorce on the wife's adultery. Barnes denied the husband a divorce on the bar of recrimination.[47] Expressed statutory provisions were enforced, but Gorell exercised more liberal discretion if he was not constrained by the Matrimonial Causes Act 1857.

During Gorell's time as the president of the PDA Division, he delivered a scathing rebuke of the existing divorce law and called for reform to the Matrimonial Causes Act 1857 in *Dodd v Dodd*.[48] The case concerned a couple who married in 1891 and separated in 1896. The husband was neglectful of his wife and child after failing to provide them reasonable maintenance as a result of his alcoholism that contributed to the loss of his Manchester provision merchant business.[49] The wife left the matrimonial home to live with her mother. She petitioned for a judicial separation a few weeks later under the provisions of the Summary Jurisdiction (Married Women) Act 1895.[50] In particular, she claimed that the husband was guilty of wilful neglect to provide reasonable maintenance to her and their infant child. The stipendiary magistrate found in favour of the wife. He granted judicial separation, gave legal custody of the child to the wife, and made alimony orders directing the husband to pay the wife weekly maintenance. The husband failed to pay his wife.

---

44 [1900] P 297, 301. Followed in *Norris v Norris and Smith* [1918] P 129, 130; *Butterworth v Butterworth and Englefield* [1920] P 126, 155.
45 [1922] P 1, 2. The Court was given comprehensive power over costs under s 5 of the Judicature Act 1890 (53 & 54 Vict c 44). This expanded the judicial discretion of costs found in the Matrimonial Causes Act 1857, s 51.
46 [1905] P 233.
47 Matrimonial Causes Act 1857, s 31.
48 [1906] P 189.
49 *Ibid.* 191–2.
50 (58 & 59 Vict c 39).

In 1905, the wife was finally able to file a petition for divorce after proving that the husband committed adultery. The case was heard before Barnes in 1906. Adultery was proven, so the wife attempted to demonstrate the ground of desertion in order to succeed in her petition for divorce. Barnes found that desertion was not proven, thus the wife's petition for divorce was dismissed.[51] The *ratio decidendi* was that the matrimonial cause of desertion could not exist at all in a case where judicial separation was obtained on the ground of wilful neglect rather than desertion under the Summary Jurisdiction (Married Women) Act 1895.[52] The wife was expected to resume cohabitation with the husband once his offending behaviour ceased, who in this case wanted to remain with her. Therefore, the period of separation was not an act of desertion.

Although Barnes felt he had no choice but to apply the law and deny the wife's petition for divorce, he used his judgment as an opportunity to criticise the injustices of the divorce law. Barnes said, 'The law is full of inconsistencies, anomalies, and inequalities amounting almost to absurdities; and it does not produce desirable results in certain important respects.'[53] He pointed out that magistrates' orders were often ignored as 'the man goes elsewhere, either to another town, or to America, or to the Colonies, and forms other ties almost as a matter of course.'[54] In relation to decrees of judicial separation, Barnes explained that their application bore unequal consequences to the parties. The decrees were usually made by magistrates without considering the long-term implications that could effectively bar the wife from a divorce for life, as happened to Mrs Dodd.[55] Moreover, he believed judicial separations were conducive to immorality as he was convinced that they had caused many married women to rush off at the slightest provocation to obtain a divorce.[56]

The concerns of Barnes were also echoed by Arnold Bennett in his novel *Whom God Hath Joined*, published in 1906, the same year as the *Dodd* judgment.[57] The book features two fictional divorce cases. The first involves Lawrence Ridware, a law clerk, petitioning to divorce his wife, Phyllis Ridware, for adultery. The second involves Charles Fearns, Lawrence's employer, being petitioned by his wife, Alma Fearns, for divorce on the ground of his adultery. Lawrence fails to obtain a divorce in England, because to his surprise he is deemed to be domiciled in Scotland rather than England. He subsequently divorces in Scotland. The divorce suit against Charles is aborted, as Alma does not want to continue the ordeal of the divorce trial. Bennett uses Ridware's younger brother, Mark Ridware, in the novel as a mouthpiece to express his own personal view of divorce.

---

51 *Dodd v Dodd* [1906] P 189, 208.
52 *Ibid.* 193.
53 *Ibid.* 207.
54 *Ibid.* 206.
55 *Ibid.* 203.
56 *Ibid.*
57 Arnold Bennett, *Whom God Hath Joined* (David Nutt 1906).

> In England, what with the sickening curiosity of idlers … and what with the newspapers waiting to give names and addresses and everything that's really tasty, a witness in a divorce case is likely to be frightened out of his life. And that doesn't help justice, does it? The truth is that justice is sacrificed to the lascivious tastes of the great enlightened British public.[58]

Barnes was also critical of the double standard of divorce, emphasising that it was harder for a wife to obtain a divorce.[59] On the other hand, the husband could not obtain a judicial separation but only divorce on the ground of adultery, 'however unbearable his life may have become from his wife's drunkenness (short of her becoming a habitual drunkard within the meaning of the aforesaid Act), violence, desertion or other cause.'[60] Barnes concluded by stating that had Mrs Dodd gone to Scotland, she would have succeeded in her petition.[61] This fact would have been little comfort to her, but it highlighted how strict the grounds for divorce were in England. The *Dodd* judgment was well timed. The Liberal Party, which was intent on social welfare reform, was swept into office in a landslide victory after the general election of 1906. J.R. Hay states:

> In the history of social policy in Britain, the years between 1906 and 1914 stand out as one of the periods of major reform. Old age pensions, insurance against ill-health and unemployment, school meals, and medical services for children were introduced.[62]

The Liberals won 399 seats in the House of Commons, while the Conservatives gained 156 seats and Labour secured 29 seats.[63] Haynes believed Barnes played a significant role in putting divorce law reform back on top of the government's agenda. He described Barnes' judgment in *Dodd* as 'fearless utterances at a period of life when most men are only too ready to acquiesce in things as they are.'[64]

Second Russell and Gorell bills

In 1908, Russell, buoyed by the criticism of the existing divorce law in *Dodd*, sought to introduce a bill to amend the Matrimonial Causes Act 1857 once again.[65] The bill was the same one that Russell had presented in 1905, and as such sought to expand the grounds of divorce to encompass desertion without cause for two years and upwards.[66] The Lambeth Conference of 1908 was also being

---

58 *Ibid.* 410.
59 *Dodd v Dodd* [1906] P 189, 205.
60 *Ibid.* 206.
61 *Ibid.* 208.
62 J.R. Hay, *The Origins of the Liberal Welfare Reforms 1906–1914* (Macmillan 1975) 11.
63 F.W.S. Craig, *British Electoral Facts: 1832–1987* (Parliamentary Research Services 1989) 18.
64 E.S.P. Haynes, *Divorce Problems of Today* (W Heffer and Sons 1912) v.
65 HL Deb 22 July 1908, vol 193, cols 4–13.
66 *Ibid.* col 9.

held close to the time of the parliamentary debate. Russell criticised the Church's stance that marriage is strictly indissoluble.[67] He posed the rhetorical question of why non-believers, such as him, should be bound by the views of others.[68] Although Russell accepted that divorce reform should be taken up by the government and considered by a royal commission, he presented the bill for the fourth time in order to draw political attention to the inadequacies of the divorce law, 'meanwhile many thousands of people every year suffer great hardship from the existing law.'[69] He used his House of Lords speech to repeat the many concerns Barnes had expressed in *Dodd*. Although Russell was again unsuccessful, his bill helped to put pressure on the government to create a royal commission into divorce the following year.

The bill was met with disapprobation from the Church of England and the Liberal government. George Forrest Browne, the Bishop of Bristol, who was only present to read prayers, decided to stay upon hearing Russell explain his proposals in his bill. Browne just so happened to be the chairman of a bishops' committee on marriage and divorce during the Pan-Anglican Conference.[70] He described the bill as a 'miserable piece of piecemeal legislation' and called for a royal commission to investigate the laws of divorce.[71] Browne boldly proclaimed, 'When that Royal Commission sits they will have before them, I believe, evidence which will tend rather to stringency than to leniency with regard to the marriage laws.'[72] The Liberal lord chancellor, Lord Loreburn, expressed his view that the bill would be 'absolutely impossible' for him to support.[73] In particular, he expressed concern that it would leave married women vulnerable: 'The woman being the weaker of the two, the man might very easily by his conduct cause his wife to desert him for two years and then get rid of her.'[74] In the eyes of Loreburn, the proposal was akin to legislating for divorce by discretion. The bill was once more defeated during the Second Reading by 61 votes to 2.[75]

Gorell, who was by this stage a member of the House of Lords, used his position as an opportunity to introduce a motion calling for poor persons' divorce cases to be heard under the jurisdiction of the County Court. During the course of parliamentary debate, Lord President Viscount Wolverhampton[76] and Loreburn[77] expressed their willingness to appoint a royal commission to investigate the law of divorce, despite moral protest from Archbishop of Canterbury

---

67 The Lambeth Conference of 1908 reaffirmed the Church's teaching that divorce is forbidden except in the case of fornication or adultery. *The Lambeth Conference: Resolutions Archive from 1908* (Anglican Communion Office 2005) 10 (Resolution 39).
68 HL Deb 22 July 1908, vol 193, cols 4–5.
69 *Ibid*. col 9.
70 *Ibid*. col 10.
71 *Ibid*. col 11.
72 *Ibid*.
73 *Ibid*. col 12.
74 *Ibid*.
75 *Ibid*. cols 12–13.
76 HL Deb 14 July 1909, vol 2, cols 498–500.
77 *Ibid*. cols 503–6.

Randall Davidson.[78] Consequently, Gorell withdrew his bill after being satisfied that a royal commission would be called. The Liberal government set up the Royal Commission on Divorce and Matrimonial Causes a few months later, in October 1909. Loreburn informed Prime Minister H.H. (Herbert Henry) Asquith that Gorell was 'a very liberal minded man, whatever his party may be.'[79] Without a doubt this was a contributing factor to Gorell receiving peerage and being appointed chairman of the Gorell Commission by the Liberal government. Within three years, Gorell accomplished more for the cause of divorce reform than the decades of agitation by the likes of Dr Hunter and the Second Earl Russell.

The Gorell Commission

The Royal Commission on Divorce and Matrimonial Causes (Gorell Commission)[80] was appointed in 1909 and handed down its lengthy report in 1912 after sitting for a total of 71 times (of which 56 occasions were dedicated to ascertaining evidence).[81] A total of 246 witnesses appeared before the Gorell Commission.[82] Many of the witnesses were from the judiciary and legal profession. Other groups represented included theologians and religious groups (particularly the Church of England), the medical profession, and various lobby groups.

The Law Society of England and Wales represented the entire legal profession in England and Wales and was an influential body in the area of law reform. The president of the Society, William Howard Winterbotham, appeared as a witness and stated, 'If divorce is to be given at all—if it is a remedy that is desirable—then it should be made easy.'[83] The views expressed by Winterbotham represented the opinion of many lawyers that saw the existing system of divorce law as costly and time-consuming, with the grounds of divorce being too narrow. However, the expansion of the grounds for divorce was not universally supported by all lawyers and depended on individual views. For example, Walter Charles Williams was a poor man's lawyer who handled divorce cases in the London district of Walworth.[84] He was not supportive of making drunkenness a ground of divorce on its own, unless the drunkenness could be interpreted as legally constituting insanity or cruelty.[85] Williams explained, 'A man married for better or worse, and some of them get the "worse," and have to put up with it.'[86] This is an allusion to the exchange of marriage vows in the form of solemnisation of matrimony in the

78 *Ibid.* cols 485–94.
79 R.F.V. Heuston, *Lives of the Lord Chancellor 1885–1940* (Oxford University Press 1964) 149.
80 *Report of the Royal Commission on Divorce and Matrimonial Causes* (Cd 6478, 1912).
81 *Ibid.* 3.
82 *Ibid.*
83 *Royal Commission on Divorce and Matrimonial Causes* (Cd 6479, 1912) vol 1, 461.
84 *Royal Commission on Divorce and Matrimonial Causes* (Cd 6480, 1912) vol 2, 63.
85 *Ibid.* 65.
86 *Ibid.*

Book of Common Prayer.[87] Christian moral teaching was still influential in English society, even for some divorce lawyers.

The appointment of the Commission was something that the DLRU and Gorell had longed for. It was greeted with optimism. The *Solicitor's Journal* notes, 'The Government have therefore taken a wise step in referring the matter to a Royal Commission, the personnel of which ensures that the matter will have complete consideration.'[88] In 1911 there were 580 divorce decrees, an increase of more than half compared to two decades prior.[89] Even so, divorce was still denied to many people due to a lack of means of accessing the courts. This was highlighted in the Commission's terms of reference.

> We have deemed it expedient that a Commission should forthwith issue to inquire into the present state of the law and the administration thereof in divorce and matrimonial causes and applications for separation orders, especially with regard to the position of the poorer classes in relation thereto ...[90]

The Commission was originally comprised of 15 members (though only 13 commissioners remained by the end) that included most notably, among others, Lord Gorell as chairman and Archbishop of York Cosmo Gordon Lang. Gorell and Lang held opposing views on the question of divorce law. The Committee comprised of just two women, who supported reform: Lady Frances Balfour[91] and May Edith Tennant.[92] The other commissioners who supported reform were mainly comprised of judges and politicians that included many Liberal-sympathising commissioners.[93] The appointment of Gorell as chairman alongside the chosen commissioners skewed the Commission in favour of recommending reform of divorce law.

The Gorell Commission failed to reach a unanimous agreement, thus two reports were prepared. The majority report recommended the expansion of the grounds for divorce to not only include adultery, but also wilful desertion for three years and upwards, cruelty, incurable insanity after five years' confinement,

---

87 *The Book of Common Prayer* (Cambridge University Press 2004) 304.
88 'November 6, 1909' (1909) 54 *Solicitors' Journal* 23–24.
89 Lawrence Stone, *Road to Divorce* (Oxford University Press 1995) 435.
90 *Report of the Royal Commission on Divorce and Matrimonial Causes* (Cd 6478, 1912) iii.
91 Balfour was the president of the National Society for Women's Suffrage, a non-violent suffragist organisation, and the daughter of the Liberal politician the Eighth Duke of Argyll.
92 Tennant was the wife of the Scottish Liberal MP Harold John Tennant.
93 The other commissioners who supported Lord Gorell's reform agenda included the trade unionist Thomas Burt, Edward George Villiers (the Liberal Earl of Derby), Scottish judge Charles John Guthrie (Lord Guthrie), the Liberal MP Sir George White, County Court judge Henry Tindal Atkinson, Liberal MP Rufus Daniel Isaacs (later the Marquess of Reading), Manchester magistrate Edgar Brierley, and John Alfred Spender. The surgeon Sir Frederick Treeves, who also supported Gorell, replaced Isaacs after he was made solicitor-general in 1910. The Earl of Derby resigned in 1911 prior to the Commission's conclusion due to other political responsibilities. White died in 1912 before the Commission finished.

habitual drunkenness found incurable after three years, and life imprisonment under commuted death sentence.[94] It also argued that the grounds for divorce should be placed on an equal footing for both genders.[95] Concern was expressed that the existing law denied access to divorce to the poor, as was alluded to in *Dodd v Dodd*.[96] The majority report suggested one way of dealing with this problem was to recommend that the High Court should go on circuit exercising jurisdiction locally and sitting in cases where the joint income of the parties did not exceed £300, with assets of no more than £200.[97] This was suggested as an alternative to transferring any jurisdiction of the Matrimonial Causes Act 1857 to the County Courts. Patrick Polden states:

> Permeating the Report is the conviction that the only real form of justice is high court justice and that people should not be encouraged to seek redress outside the high court except where it is plainly impracticable to make the high court available to them.[98]

Indeed, the commissioners expressed admiration for the High Court and held a low view of the County Courts.[99] Although the majority report did not push for a radical change to the jurisdiction of courts over divorce law, the recommendations for the grounds for divorce provoked some opposition.

The minority report was prepared by three dissenters: the Archbishop of York, the Liberal Unionist MP Sir William Reynell Anson, and Dean of Arches Sir Lewis Tonna Dibdin. These men were conservative in political ideology and represented the views of the Church of England. The minority report argued against any expansion to the grounds of divorce and upheld the legal principle of the Matrimonial Causes Act 1857 that marriage is indissoluble except in cases of adultery. The dissenters argued that there was no widespread demand for extending the grounds of divorce.[100] They believed that expanding the grounds for divorce as proposed in the majority report would open the floodgates to collusive divorces for mere incompatibility.[101] In their view, the relaxing of divorce law would lead to moral decline in England, as they claimed had happened in the United States and other Western nations.[102] The main reason for their opposition to the majority report was their conservative Christian beliefs: 'All are agreed that Christ intended to proclaim the great principle that marriage ought to be indissoluble.'[103] Since they believed that the Christian faith should form the foundation

---

94 *Report of the Royal Commission on Divorce and Matrimonial Causes* (Cd 6478, 1912) 113.
95 *Ibid.* 89.
96 *Ibid.* 46.
97 *Ibid.* 162.
98 Patrick Polden, *A History of the County Court 1846–1971* (Cambridge University Press 1999) 107.
99 *Report of the Royal Commission on Divorce and Matrimonial Causes* (Cd 6478, 1912) 56.
100 *Ibid.* 179.
101 *Ibid.* 185.
102 *Ibid.* 173–5.
103 *Ibid.* 186.

of English society, they came to the conclusion that there should be no expansion to the grounds for divorce in the law. Although there was division on the grounds for divorce, both reports did reach some consensus. There was agreement on the abolition of the double standard between genders in the grounds for divorce, the extension of the High Court's jurisdiction to local courts, the recognition of divorce on the presumption of death, and the expansion of the grounds of nullity of marriage.[104]

Criticism was expressed about the continued existence of the office of King's Proctor by those giving evidence to the Gorell Commission. W.G.R. Fairfax, the President of the DLRU, along with two experienced divorce law solicitors, Sir George Lewis and Frederick Palmer, recommended the abolition of the office of King's Proctor. Fairfax criticised the King's Proctor: 'Two or three stiff sentences for perjury would do all the good the King's Proctor could do in 20 years.'[105] Lewis believed that parties should not be barred to divorce if they both came to the Court with 'unclean hands,' and that divorce should be made absolute at first instance without the need for the petitioner to go through the intermediary stage of decree *nisi*.[106] He saw the King's Proctor as of little use except in investigating cases of collusion.[107] Furthermore, he thought the registrars and bailiffs of the County Courts would do a far better job in dealing with divorce cases than the perceived incompetence of the King's Proctor.[108] Lewis harboured a negative opinion of the King's Proctor for quite some time; as he remarked in 1885, 'The whole paraphernalia of the Queen's Proctor is a survival of the Ecclesiastical Beadleocracy of Doctors' Commons.'[109] Similarly, Palmer called for abolition and described the office as 'an extremely mischievous one.'[110] However, he went further than Fairfax and Lewis by supporting what was then a relatively radical suggestion of permitting divorce by mutual consent.[111] The perceived meddlesomeness and the overall low regard towards the reputation and professionalism of the King's Proctor were the main reasons presented to call for the abolition of the office.

Although there were vocal calls to get rid of the King's Proctor, there was also strong support for maintaining the office. Sir John Bigham, the president of the PDA Division, stated that in his experience most cases involving the intervention of the King's Proctor were due to the recriminations of the petitioners rather than cases of collusion.[112] Therefore, he had no difficulties with supporting

104 *Ibid*. 190–1. The proposed expansion of the grounds of nullity included unsound mind, epilepsy, insanity, venereal disease, pregnancy of the wife by a man other than the husband at the time of marriage, and wilful refusal to consummate the marriage
105 *Royal Commission on Divorce and Matrimonial Causes* (Cd 6479, 1912) vol 1, 211.
106 *Ibid*. 84.
107 *Ibid*.
108 *Ibid*. 77.
109 George Lewis, 'Marriage and Divorce' (May 1885) 37(221) *Fortnightly Review* 640, 649.
110 *Royal Commission on Divorce and Matrimonial Causes* (Cd 6480, 1912) vol 2, 98.
111 *Ibid*. 99.
112 *Royal Commission on Divorce and Matrimonial Causes* (Cd 6479, 1912) vol 1, 40.

the inquisitorial role of the King's Proctor.[113] Lord Alverstone, the lord chief justice of England, expressed his support for the King's Proctor more overtly. He believed that in order to 'prevent improper divorces' being formed as a result of collusion and tainted by the recriminations of the petitioner, it was absolutely necessary for the King's Proctor to continue to exist.[114] Likewise, the Earl of Desart vigorously defended the need to maintain his former post.

> I do not think the time has come myself when the law ought to say that a guilty person is entitled to the relief of divorce, and on the whole, although I admit there is great difficulty, I have come to the conclusion that the principle that the petitioner must show clean hands before he or she can obtain a divorce, should be maintained.[115]

He did concede that judges should be given more discretion to decide whether there should be an intervention based on the interests of the parties, their children, and public policy.[116] The views of those who supported the King's Proctor carried the day. Despite heavy criticism, it was thought that the King's Proctor continued to play an important role in preserving public morality and the sanctity of marriage.

Second Lord Gorell bill

The movement suffered a setback with the death of Lord Gorell in 1913. His son Henry Gorell Barnes, who was secretary to the Gorell Commission, succeeded him to the baronetcy. On the first day of World War I, the Second Lord Gorell attempted to introduce a bill to enact the agreed recommendations of both the majority and minority reports. These were the bill's main provisions: removing the double standard for divorce, making insanity an additional divorce ground, adding venereal disease as a nullity ground, allowing the High Court to issue a decree *nisi* on presumption of death, abolishing trial by jury for divorce cases, limiting the power of County Courts to issue orders of judicial separation to only cases that require the immediate protection or provision of the wife and children, and some restrictions on the publication of divorce proceedings.[117] The proposals were rather modest when compared with the recommendations of the majority report. Asquith indicated to Gorell that there was no prospect at the present time for the government to deal with the matter.[118] The introduction of the bill was untimely as the country was about to be embroiled in war. Matters of domestic reform would have to be put on hold.

113 *Ibid.* 52.
114 *Royal Commission on Divorce and Matrimonial Causes* (Cd 6480, 1912) vol 2, 124.
115 *Ibid.* 141.
116 *Ibid.*
117 HL Deb 28 July 1914, vol 17, col 190.
118 *Ibid.*

The Archbishop of York supported the legislation, albeit reluctantly. Although he wrote in opposition to the expansion of the grounds for divorce in the minority report and continually expressed those views during the parliamentary debates, he accepted that the bill would 'make good of our common life.'[119] In particular, the bill would remove the double standard between genders in the grounds for divorce that the prelate pointed out did not exist when the Ecclesiastical Courts held matrimonial jurisdiction over divorce *a mensa et thoro*.[120] The Archbishop of York came to support this compromise in order to protect Christian morality in the law rather than promoting the natural law of marriage.[121] This was a recognition of the Church of England's declining place in society, which began to see itself as an influencer of the law rather than an imposer of religious values.[122] Lord Braye, a Roman Catholic peer, opposed the bill and attempted to introduce an amendment delaying the Second Reading for six months.[123] His view that the existence of civil divorce was 'one of the greatest inciting causes to immorality' by then was seen as rather old-fashioned.[124] It was something that would have been more popularly accepted in the mid-nineteenth century.

By 1914, English society had become accustomed to the operation of civil divorce. Instead of calls to repeal civil divorce, there was strong agitation for further reform. The lord chancellor, Lord Haldane, supported the bill and described it as 'a very moderate and substantially non-controversial measure of reform.'[125] The Marquess of Salisbury representing the Conservative opposition called for Gorell to withdraw the bill as there was no prospect of it being passed by year's end as it was already too late in the parliamentary session.[126] Even those who were sympathetic with the bill, such as the Earl of Derby and Viscount Halifax, also called for Gorell to withdraw it on the same grounds. Gorell, sensing that he did not have enough support, withdrew the bill.[127] Tragically, the Second Lord Gorell was killed in action near Ypres on 16 January 1917. The hope for immediate legislative change following the Gorell Commission was dashed as the political climate shifted from domestic to international affairs. The success of any legislative changes in relation to divorce required the support of the incumbent government otherwise it was doomed to failure, as had occurred with the Hunter, Russell, and Gorell bills.

Post-war English society

England was a rather different society after World War I. Ann Sumner Holmes states, 'One of the most obvious differences in postwar society was the further legal

---

119 *Ibid.* col 214.
120 *Ibid.* col 209.
121 E.R. Norman, *Church and Society in England: 1770–1970* (Oxford University Press 1976) 268–9.
122 *Ibid.* 269.
123 HL Deb 28 July 1914, vol 17, 204.
124 *Ibid.* col 202.
125 *Ibid.* col 206.
126 *Ibid.* col 221.
127 *Ibid.* col 225.

emancipation of women ... women gained the right to vote, to serve on juries, and to sit in Parliament.'[128] Arthur Marwick explains that the contribution of women during the war years helped to advance women's rights and weaken male bigotry, particularly winning the right of suffrage.[129] Indeed, the growing recognition of the equal status of women in the law was a significant reason for the removal of the double standard in the grounds for divorce through the introduction of the Matrimonial Causes Act 1923.[130] However, it would be misguided to suggest that the reform was achieved as a result of feminist ideals.[131] The influential Church of England maintained the teaching that marriage is a lifelong union at the Lambeth Conference of 1920, but by this time the views of the Church and the state had begun to diverge.[132] Legal change was already under way after the unanimous support of the Gorell Commission for the removal of the double standard.

Post-war England also witnessed a surge in divorce. Many men coming back home from the battlefield discovered that their wives had committed adultery.[133] The annual rate of divorce decrees surpassed 1000 for the first time in 1918.[134] Lesley Hall argues that the Gorell Commission made divorce an acceptable remedy in the minds of many people.[135] Sexual morality was becoming more liberalised post-war. Marie Stopes' *Married Love* was published in 1918 and illustrates this change in sexual morality.[136] It advocated, among other things, for women to embrace their sexual desires, the use of birth control, and a belief in marital equality.

John Galsworthy's *The Forsyte Saga* was a collection of novels published between 1906 and 1922 portraying middle-class propriety.[137] In the novel *In Chancery*, published in 1920, Winifred Dartie on the legal advice of her brother and solicitor Soames Forsyte sues her husband Montague Dartie for a suit of restitution of conjugal rights after he leaves for Buenos Aries with another woman.[138] Soames gives Winifred the advice in order to allow her to get an expedited divorce by obtaining a restitution order against Montague in the hope he does not come back. This would then be deemed desertion and Winifred would be in a position to divorce without waiting the two-year period of separation for divorce. Although Montague's adultery could be established, Winifred would still not

---

128 Ann Sumner Holmes, 'The Double Standard in the English Divorce Laws, 1857–1923' (1995) 20(2) *Law and Social Inquiry* 601, 616.
129 Arthur Marwick, *The Deluge* (Bodley Head 1965) 96.
130 (13 & 14 Geo V c 19).
131 Rebecca Probert, 'The Controversy of Equality and the Matrimonial Causes Act 1923' (1999) 11 *Child and Family Law Quarterly* 33, 41.
132 Ann Sumner Holmes, *The Church of England and Divorce in the Twentieth Century: Legalism and Grace* (Routledge 2017) 39.
133 *Wilson v Wilson* [1920] P 20; Rebecca Probert, *The Changing Legal Regulation of Cohabitation: From Fornicators to Family, 1600–2010* (Cambridge University Press 2012) 131–3.
134 Stone (n 89) 435.
135 Lesley Hall, *Sex, Gender and Social Change in Britain Since 1880* (Macmillan Press 2000) 84.
136 See Marie Stopes, *Married Love* (first published 1918, Oxford University Press 2004).
137 Fred Shapiro and Jane Garry, *Trial and Error: An Oxford Anthology of Legal Stories* (Oxford University Press 1998) 126.
138 John Galsworthy, *In Chancery* (William Heinemann 1920).

be able to petition for divorce unless she could prove either cruelty or desertion. Cruelty is not pleaded. The judicial order is granted, but Montague returns to Winifred. Thus, the ground of desertion is not established. Eventually Soames himself successfully divorces his wife Irene after pleading that she committed adultery with his cousin Young Jolyon. It is evident that by the early twentieth century legal loopholes were regularly sought by parties and lawyers in order to exploit the law of divorce to their advantage

To deal with the surge in divorce petitions, the Administration of Justice Act 1920 was passed.[139] The 1920 Act granted Assize judges the jurisdiction to hear undefended divorce petitions,[140] and cases involving the special Poor Persons' Procedure for those with assets of no more than £50.[141] This helped to redress some of the Gorell Commission's demands, but it did not encompass contested divorce cases or comprehensively resolve the issue of divorce among poorer people. Furthermore, this undermined the expectation of the Matrimonial Causes Act 1857 for family law judicial experts to preside over divorce cases.

Decline of statutory damages

The use of statutory damages to remedy breach to the *consortium vitae* was in decline by 1920. The courts increasingly exercised their own discretion in decision making and often judges were reluctant to grant an application for statutory damages. When judges did grant statutory damages to the petitioner, the payments were far more moderate compared to cases in the mid-nineteenth century.[142] A good illustration of the discretion exercised by the Court is found in *Langrick v Langrick and Funnell*.[143] The petitioner was an army sergeant and successfully received damages and costs against the co-respondent who was a sub-lieutenant in the same regiment. It was held that the co-respondent had the fullest means of knowledge despite his plea of ignorance of the wife's marital status. The Court found that he was put on inquiry when he entered the matrimonial home, containing photographs of the married parties clearly displayed, yet persisted in taking the wife to a hotel and committing adultery. Even if the co-respondent was truly ignorant, the Court found that objectively speaking he should have known otherwise. Given the aggravating circumstances, he was ordered to pay both damages and costs to the petitioner.

The development of the common law of statutory damages and costs against co-respondents was applied inconsistently throughout its legal operation.

139 (10 & 11 Geo V c 81).
140 Administration of Justice Act 1920, s 1. Assize judges could exercise jurisdiction over any class or matter of matrimonial causes as prescribed by the lord chancellor.
141 Cretney (n 17) 306–8. The Poor Persons' Procedure was established in 1914 and managed by the High Court Poor Persons' Department for a decade. The procedure involved the Department referring an application onto a reporting solicitor. The lawyer was not allowed to profit for their work and the court would not charge fees or award costs either for or against the petitioner.
142 *Bell v Bell and Marquis of Anglesey* (1858) 1 Sw&Tr 565.
143 [1920] P 90.

McCardie J commented that 'the relevant authorities reveal a striking conflict of opinion as to the principles to be applied and the considerations to be regarded.'[144] Furthermore, he noted that in assessing damages it is important to maintain moderation rather than falling into the temptation of awarding excessive or punitive damages found in earlier precedents.[145] Judicial inconsistency and the reduction in the amount of damages awarded led to the decline in petitioners seeking statutory damages.

Moreover, the growing rejection of placing a monetary value on the wife to satisfy the husband's vanity also led to the decline of statutory damages. The Gorell Commission had recommended the abolition of statutory damages in favour of a system of the co-respondent providing a property settlement or payments to benefit the children of the marriage or the wife with whom he had committed adultery.[146] This was a natural progression, because statutory damages were aimed at compensating the family, replacing the old system of criminal conversation where the husband was awarded exemplary damages. After the Juries Act 1918, a majority of statutory damage cases were heard by a judge alone for both claim and cost of damages.[147] The right of parties to demand a jury for trials of statutory damage claims was abolished under section 99(1)(h) of the Supreme Court of Judicature (Consolidation Act) 1925.[148] This was formal legal recognition of the increasingly common practice of trials before a judge sitting alone. Despite ongoing criticism of the existence of statutory damages in the law and the decline of its use,[149] it was not until 1970 that the right to claim damages for adultery was finally abolished.[150] Victorian views of compensating the husband persisted for more than a century until the elimination of an exclusively fault-based divorce system under the Divorce Reform Act 1969.

Matrimonial Causes Act 1923

The former wartime Liberal lord chancellor Lord Buckmaster was a major proponent for divorce law reform. In a letter to *The Times*, he supported the proposition that the divorce laws were 'immoral and unjust.'[151] The campaign for

---

144 *Butterworth v Butterworth and Englefield* [1920] P 126, 128. Compounding the confusion, McCardie J held in the same case that the Court can award damages against a co-respondent who was ignorant that the respondent was married, but it was against sound practice to do so.
145 *Ibid.* 157.
146 *Report of the Royal Commission on Divorce and Matrimonial Causes* (Cd 6478, 1912) 126–7.
147 *Butterworth v Butterworth and Englefield* [1920] P 126, 128.
148 (15 & 16 Geo V c 49); *Rugg-Gunn v Rugg-Gunn and Archer* [1931] P 147.
149 The Morton Commission in 1956 described statutory damages as vindictive and out of touch with accepted views. However, it did not call for the abolition of statutory damages, because the Court had complete discretion in assessing the sum of damages and could keep damages within reasonable bounds. *Report of the Royal Commission on Marriage and Divorce* (1956) Cmd 9678, 120–1.
150 Law Reform (Miscellaneous Provisions) Act 1970 (UK) c 33, s 4.
151 Lord Buckmaster, 'Anomalies of Divorce' *The Times* (London, 11 October 1922) 11.

divorce law reform began in earnest immediately after World War I. The day after the Armistice, Buckmaster introduced a piecemeal reform bill in the House of Lords to make desertion or separation for five years and upwards a ground for divorce.[152] The motion for the Second Reading of the bill was introduced far too soon. The House of Lords was still occupied with wartime issues and rejected the motion.[153]

In 1920, Buckmaster introduced another bill that attempted to enact the majority report of the Gorell Commission that passed all stages of the House of Lords.[154] Although the bill had the support of Liberal Lord Chancellor Lord Birkenhead,[155] it failed to proceed to the House of Commons. A few months earlier the Liberal MP Athelstan Rendall moved a motion to introduce the bill in the House of Commons,[156] but it was defeated by 134 votes to 91.[157] Although the bill was defeated on the belief that it would damage the permanence of the marriage contract, the House of Commons resolved that there should be equal grounds to divorce between the genders.[158] In 1921, Ronald Barnes, the Third Lord Gorell, took up the cause of his late father and brother by introducing a bill to enact the agreed recommendations of the majority and minority reports of the Gorell Commission.[159] It failed to make any further progress, despite passing the House of Lords.[160]

Although the Liberal government supported these bills, the main reason they failed was due to the opposition from the Church of England and the Roman Catholic Church, which rejected any attempts to expand the grounds for divorce law.[161] On the other hand, the Archbishop of Canterbury, Randall Davidson, expressed the Church of England's support for the removal of the double standard between genders in the grounds for divorce as a matter of equality.[162] This endorsement removed a potential major hindrance to the enactment of the Matrimonial Causes Act 1923. Probert states:

> The reason for the failure of the Matrimonial Causes Bills of 1920 and 1921 was not the lack of feminist involvement but rather the fact that the Bills attempted to extend the grounds for divorce as well as equalising the position of husbands and wives.[163]

---

152 HL Deb 12 November 1918, vol 31, col 1184.
153 *Ibid.* col 1229.
154 HL Deb 22 June 1920, vol 39, col 693.
155 *Ibid.* cols 713–14.
156 HC Deb 14 April 1920, vol 127, col 1758.
157 *Ibid.* cols 1804–5.
158 *Ibid.* col 1805.
159 HL Deb 10 March 1921, vol 44, col 453.
160 HL Deb 28 April 1921, vol 45, col 102.
161 HL Deb 22 June 1920, vol 39, col 703.
162 *Ibid.* col 707.
163 Probert (n 5) 40.

Cretney also comes to the same conclusion and argues that the bills were controversial because of their challenge to Christian morality.[164] Indeed, it was not the want of feminist activism that caused the failure of these bills, but the objections to the extension of the grounds of divorce. These objections were almost always premised on Christian moral teaching. For example, the first British female MP to take her seat, Viscountess Astor, opposed Rendall's bill by appealing to the Christian faith: 'In the Christian world it is the spiritual aspect of marriage that the law attempts to protect, and it is the spiritual element which makes marriages happy.'[165] Although social attitudes on divorce had grown to be more accepting, many of those in power remained rather socially conservative on what they saw as the liberalisation of the grounds for divorce.

Interestingly, it was the Conservative government led by Prime Minister Stanley Baldwin that supported the introduction of the Matrimonial Causes Act 1923. The Act abolished the double standard and equalised the grounds of divorce between genders.[166] Thereby, it allowed married women to divorce on the sole ground of the husband's adultery without having to prove a cause of aggravated enormity. The Liberal (later Conservative) MP Major Cyril Entwistle introduced the bill in the House of Commons[167] after being lobbied by the National Union of Societies for Equal Citizenship (NUSEC).[168] In order to dispel any concern about the liberalisation of divorce, Entwistle stated at the outset, 'The sole object of this Bill is to give equality to gender in the matter of divorce, and it has no other purpose whatsoever.'[169] The DLRU was not completely satisfied with the limited scope of the Act but supported it nonetheless.[170] It overwhelmingly passed the Second Reading in the House of Commons by 257 votes to 26,[171] and the Second Reading in the House of Lords by 95 votes to 8.[172] The Act came into effect on 18 July 1923. It was the Conservative government's attempt to satisfy some of the demands of the divorce law reformers, but to keep marriage as an indissoluble contract that could only be broken through adultery.

In 1924, Buckmaster attempted to re-introduce his 1920 bill.[173] Although the bill passed its Second Reading by 88 votes to 51,[174] the Labour government,

---

164 Cretney (n 17) 219–20.
165 HC Deb 14 April 1920, vol 127, col 1792.
166 Matrimonial Causes Act 1923, s 1.
167 HC Deb 2 March 1923, vol 160, col 2355.
168 The NUSEC was a feminist organisation formed in 1919 that sought equal rights between genders. Its origins can be traced to the National Union of Women's Suffrage Societies. Harold L. Smith, *The British Women's Suffrage Campaign, 1866–1928* (2nd edn, Longman 2007) 91.
169 HC Deb 2 March 1923, vol 160, col 2355.
170 The Second Earl Russell described the bill as 'a thoroughly bad and thoroughly inadequate Bill, but that it is practically impossible for anybody to oppose it.' HL Deb 26 June 1923, vol 54, col 602.
171 HC Deb 8 June 1923, vol 164, col 2660.
172 HL Deb 26 June 1923, vol 54, col 573.
173 HL Deb 11 March 1924, vol 56, col 636.
174 *Ibid.* col 674.

which had more nominal than actual power in Parliament, did not support the bill and it made no further progress. The Labour Party won 191 out of 615 seats at the 1923 general election, which delivered a minority Labour government led by Prime Minister Ramsay MacDonald that lasted only ten months with the tacit support of the Liberal Party.[175] The bill was the last legislative attempt at major reform to the divorce law in the 1920s. The Matrimonial Causes Act 1923 effectively delayed calls for further divorce law reform. Probert argues, 'The Matrimonial Causes Act 1923 was the result of a reform process which was inspired by the contradictions, anomalies and evasions of the law.'[176] This is important in understanding the gradual repudiation of the Matrimonial Causes Act 1857. The law in practice created unexpected problems and hardships upon those seeking a divorce. The removal of the double standard was a significant departure from the underlying principles of the Matrimonial Causes Act 1857. As the decade wore on, the challenge to the divorce law intensified.

Knight bills

The Matrimonial Causes Act 1857 was characterised by two essential elements: the double standard between genders and adultery as the sole ground for divorce. The Matrimonial Causes Act 1923 introduced gender equality. The Matrimonial Causes Act 1937 went further and expanded the grounds of divorce beyond adultery. The removal of the double standard was not enough, because the sole ground of adultery still made divorce too difficult for many through the operation of the bars to divorce. After Labour won a majority in the House of Commons in 1929 for the first time, the Labour MP George Wilfred Holford Knight introduced a bill that proposed to extend the grounds of divorce to include incurable insanity for a period of at least five years, and to introduce a bar to divorce against petitioners who were found to have contributed to the respondent's insanity.[177] Knight limited his demand to include incurable insanity. He later explained that a more far-reaching bill 'making drastic and far-reaching changes in the law should be undertaken only by the Government itself.'[178] Despite the fact Knight was given leave to introduce the bill, Prime Minister Ramsay MacDonald indicated that the government was unwilling to facilitate further debate on the bill.[179] The electoral position of the nascent Labour government was so precarious that MacDonald did not want to risk losing votes by being seen as liberal on divorce.

Knight tried unsuccessfully to introduce his bill on a further two occasions. In 1931, a motion granting leave to introduce the bill was defeated by 148 votes to

---

175 Craig (n 63) 26.
176 Probert (n 5) 41.
177 HC Deb 26 February 1930, vol 235, col 2263.
178 HC Deb 30 November 1932, vol 272, col 824.
179 HC Deb 30 June 1930, vol 240, col 1602.

114.[180] Although in 1932 the bill was successfully given leave by 96 votes to 42, it did not progress further.[181] Knight grew frustrated with the lack of progress and introduced a bill in 1934 that went much further. The bill proposed to extend the grounds of divorce much more widely in line with the Gorell Commission majority report. Knight was still of the belief that the government should undertake sweeping divorce law reform.

> I desire to repeat an observation ... that in my view a review of the divorce laws of this kingdom should be undertaken by a responsible Government. Unfortunately, it is the case that no responsible Government is in sight, as far as I can see, which will undertake this task ... I have undertaken this task in the hope that the Government may be persuaded to respond to the general opinion, not only in this House but in the country, that this matter should be brought under close discussion.[182]

Once again the bill failed to make any progress. On this occasion the bill was adjourned and ran out of time for parliamentary debate.[183] There has been some suggestion that the eugenics movement influenced the demand for divorce on the ground of incurable insanity in order to prevent those deemed unfit from raising a family.[184] Although such a view was expressed by the Gorell Commission,[185] it cannot be said that it was a view held by Knight. Instead, he rejected the view of a medical practitioner who compared a spouse suffering from insanity as equivalent to a death in ending a marriage.[186] Knight was trying to induce the government into taking up the cause for comprehensive divorce law reform by initially introducing a piecemeal reform that he assumed would find consensus. After repeated failure, Knight tried to introduce comprehensive reform in an attempt to force government action. However, the political climate was such that the government was unwilling to entertain that prospect.

Hotel divorces

Despite the failure of Knight to introduce any meaningful changes to the law of divorce, there was growing enthusiasm for reform among politicians and the public. In 1934, A.P. Herbert's *Holy Deadlock* and Evelyn Waugh's *A Handful of Dust* were both published. These novels portrayed the process of divorce as one corrupted by couples colluding with each other for one of them (usually the

---

180 HC Deb 28 January 1931, vol 247, col 978.
181 HC Deb 30 November 1932, vol 272, col 828.
182 HC Deb 2 February 1934, vol 285, cols 748–9.
183 HC Deb 5 February 1934, vol 285, col 806.
184 Cretney (n 17) 225–6; Roderick Phillips, *Putting Asunder: A History of Divorce in Western Society* (Cambridge University Press 1988) 512–3.
185 *Report of the Royal Commission on Divorce and Matrimonial Causes* (Cd 6478, 1912) 100–1.
186 HC Deb 30 November 1932, vol 272, col 824.

husband) to stage an act of adultery in a 'hotel divorce.' Presenting evidence to prove adultery by inference from the circumstances alone could be difficult. For example, witness testimony of adultery could be disbelieved if it did not conform to the background knowledge of the parties.[187] This forced many couples to collude and devise a hotel divorce. Since the early operation of the Court for Divorce and Matrimonial Causes, hotel divorces were used as a way for parties to dissolve their marriages.[188] During the Gorell Commission, Sir George Lewis provided a description of hotel divorces: 'A lady goes into court in the ordinary way, and she proves that her husband has gone to a hotel, stopped with a prostitute, passed her off as his wife and in her name, and committed adultery.'[189]

Popular accounts of hotel divorces became increasingly commonplace during the Interwar period. Brighton became synonymous with hotel divorces, which were popularly referred to as a 'Brighton quickie.'[190] In fact, Brighton is the location where the hotel divorces take place in both *Holy Deadlock* and *A Handful of Dust*. The popular depictions of hotel divorces suggest they became increasingly common in the Interwar period. Stock characters in popular fiction emerged that depicted the hotel manager co-operating usually in exchange for a fee, the private detective who assisted in gathering evidence of adultery, and the chambermaid who was the classic witness.[191] It is difficult to rely on legal sources to assess the numbers of hotel divorces, because successfully executed hotel divorces evaded judicial attention. Moreover, newspaper articles may give the unhelpful impression that most couples seeking a divorce took legitimate steps during legal proceedings. In reality, newspaper articles were often self-censored or legally censored.[192] The Judicial Proceedings (Regulation of Reports) Act 1926 was passed to censor the more salacious and distasteful mention of legal proceedings by only allowing the publication of the bare facts and judgment.[193]

The shifts in public opinion on divorce also increased public antagonism towards the interventions of the King's Proctor. The case of *Bamberger v Bamberger (The King's Proctor Showing Cause)* aroused public protest towards the office of the King's Proctor.[194] The King's Proctor alleged that the petitioner, Thelma Bamberger, committed acts of adultery that barred her from being granted a divorce absolute. Therefore, the King's Proctor called for the Court to overturn her decree *nisi* pronounced on 7 December 1917, which was granted on the ground of the respondent Henry Bamberger's adultery and desertion.

---

187 *Alexander v Alexander and Amos* (1860) 2 Sw&Tr 95.
188 *Todd v Todd* (1866) LR 1 P&D 121.
189 *Royal Commission on Divorce and Matrimonial Causes* (Cd 6479, 1912) vol 1, 72.
190 Claire Langhamer, 'Adultery in Post-war England' (2006) 62(1) *History Workshop Journal* 87, 100.
191 *Ibid*. 101.
192 See Gail Savage, 'Erotic Stories and Public Decency: Newspaper Reporting of Divorce Proceedings in England' (1998) 41(2) *The Historical Journal* 511.
193 (16 & 17 Geo V c 61) s 1(b).
194 *The Times* (London, 11–13 and 18–20 March 1920).

The case was heard in the Court for six days before Sir Henry Duke, the president of the PDA Division. The president ruled in favour of the intervention of the King's Proctor and the decree *nisi* was rescinded.

The case attracted considerable attention in Parliament and subsequently led to debate into the office of the King's Proctor, particularly for the perceived waste of taxpayers' money on funding what was seen by many as a public nuisance. In this case, the King's Proctor spent £989 for the costs associated with the intervention.[195] In the House of Commons, Horatio Bottomley asked Stanley Baldwin, who was the financial secretary to the Treasury and responsible for financing the office of the King's Proctor, 'In view of the constant menace of the King's Proctor to the domestic peace of the country, will the right hon. Gentleman consider the advisability of abolishing that office altogether?'[196] Baldwin curtly replied, 'I will consider that point.'[197] However, the government made no effort to reform or abolish the office of King's Proctor. Discontentment towards the King's Proctor prevailed throughout the Interwar period.

Public criticism towards the King's Proctor heightened in the 1930s. Both Evelyn Waugh and A.P. Herbert's 1934 novels expose the intrusiveness of the King's Proctor and the absurdity of the divorce law more generally. In Waugh's *A Handful of Dust*, the protagonist Tony Last is devastated to hear that his wife Brenda is having an affair with a lout named John Beaver.[198] Brenda demands a divorce and alimony of £500 per year. Shattered, Tony agrees to Brenda's demands. Tony agrees to be divorced on the ground of adultery by staging an act of adultery in a Brighton hotel with the arrangements partially devised by his solicitor, despite never having committed adultery himself. This is an example of the infamous hotel divorces that became more common during the Interwar period.[199] He finds a night-club hostess named Milly who agrees to play the paramour. They merely give the appearance to hotel staff that they have slept with each other, but Tony in fact sleeps in a separate room. However, the scheme is hampered when Milly brings her eight-year-old daughter Winnie to the hotel. A private detective gives advice to Tony, who notes the child's involvement in the hotel may later bring the unwanted attention of the King's Proctor. Afterwards, Brenda increases her demand for alimony to £2000 per year. Tony, wishing to protect his beloved Hetton estate, refuses to continue with the divorce process and leaves for South America never to return. Waugh had personal experience of divorce and the novel may have been inspired by the events of his own life. His wife Evelyn Gardner had an extramarital affair, and soon afterwards he filed for divorce.[200] *A Handful of Dust* is not a satire or a polemic, but rather a life drama

---

195 HC Deb 29 March 1920, vol 127, col 912W.
196 HC Deb 9 August 1920, vol 133, col 32.
197 *Ibid*.
198 See Evelyn Waugh, *A Handful of Dust* (Chapman and Hall 1934).
199 Cretney (n 17) 176.
200 Martin Stannard, 'Waugh, Evelyn Arthur St John (1903–1966),' *Oxford Dictionary of National Biography* (2004) <https://doi.org/10.1093/ref:odnb/36788>.

that features a subtle critique of the existing divorce law found in the laborious description of the hotel divorce.

Herbert was a novelist, law reformer, and Member of Parliament, and is famous for satirising the state of English divorce law in his animated tragicomedy novel *Holy Deadlock*.[201] Herbert's novel has a lot of similarities with *A Handful of Dust*, but presents a more excoriating portrayal of the English divorce law. The story is about John and Mary Adam, a likeable but mismatched married English couple, hatching a scheme to get a divorce in the late 1920s. John agrees to act as the adulterer in order to protect the reputation of Mary and her paramour Martin Seal, whose job at the BBC would be in peril if the affair were exposed. John books a hotel in Brighton and arranges for an agency to provide a young woman named May Myrtle to stage an act of adultery. Mary is initially granted a divorce *nisi*, but the ruse is thwarted by the intervention of the King's Proctor, who is notified of Mary's extramarital affair with Martin. Upon the revelation, the High Court rejects the grant of divorce *nisi*.

Soon after the publication, the Scottish Unionist MP Frederick Macquisten asked both Solicitor-General Sir Donald Somervell[202] and Attorney-General Sir Thomas Inskip whether they had read *Holy Deadlock*, 'wherein His Majesty's judges and courts, and the legal code which they administer in matrimonial causes, are held up to public ridicule and contempt; and whether it is proposed to take any action in the matter?'[203] The solicitor-general declined to answer the question after claiming he was unprepared to deliver a response.[204] The attorney-general replied, 'The book in question is a work of fiction, and is not such as to require any action on my part.'[205] *Holy Deadlock* was a novel solely written to vent public ridicule of the divorce law, which had a much greater political impact than *A Handful of Dust*.

A year after *Holy Deadlock* was released, Herbert published an anthology of fictitious legal cases in *Uncommon Law*. In the fictitious case of 'Pale MR v Pale HJ and Hume (The King's Proctor Showing Cause),' Herbert again criticises the intrusiveness of the King's Proctor.

> Anonymous Letters, back-door espionage, the cross-examination of cooks, the bribery of maids and porters, the searching of hotel registers, the watching of windows, the tracking of taxi-cabs, the exploitation of malicious gossip and interested malignity—and all this done in the King's name to preserve the sanctity of the home. These are methods which serve well enough for the apprehension of the dangerous criminal … but not for the hounding of two unfortunates in love.[206]

---

201 See A.P. Herbert, *Holy Deadlock* (Methuen 1934).
202 HC Deb 4 June 1934, vol 290, col 566.
203 HC Deb 13 June 1934, vol 290, col 1690.
204 HC Deb 4 June 1934, vol 290, col 566.
205 HC Deb 13 June 1934, vol 290, col 1690.
206 A.P. Herbert, *Uncommon Law* (Methuen 1935) 449.

In his role as Member of Parliament, Herbert was one of the driving forces behind the introduction of the Matrimonial Causes Act 1937 that extended the grounds of divorce beyond adultery alone. Herbert was not alone in pushing for law reform. E.S.P. Haynes, a campaigner for divorce law reform, also argued for the abolition of the King's Proctor.[207] He states, 'The official activities of the King's Proctor are not merely degrading, un-English, and anti-social, but also expensive at a time when economy is or ought to be the order of the day.'[208] Herbert unsuccessfully attempted to abolish the divorce procedure of decree *nisi* in the 1937 Act, which would have indirectly abolished the office of the King's Proctor.[209] However, during the committee stage, the bill was amended to keep decree *nisi* as many felt it was important to preserve the sanctity of marriage.[210]

The ease of obtaining a hotel divorce was very publicly confirmed in the high-profile events surrounding Wallis Simpson, which eventually led to the abdication crisis of King Edward VIII. Simpson was married to her second husband when she met the king in 1931. The liaison later developed into an intimate relationship. On 27 October 1936, Simpson was granted a decree *nisi* in an undefended suit before the Ipswich Assizes after claiming that her husband had committed adultery with an unnamed woman in a Thames Valley hotel three months earlier.[211] However, there was suspicion of adultery between the king and Simpson, and that there was collusion in Simpson obtaining the divorce.[212] Brian Inglis has even suggested that *Holy Deadlock* was used as a procedural handbook for the hotel divorce.[213] The idea of the king marrying a twice-divorced woman was unacceptable to many of those in the establishment, and it ultimately led to the king's abdication on 11 December 1936.[214] The president of the PDA Division, Sir Boyd Merriman, made Simpson's divorce absolute on 3 May 1937 after the King's Proctor found no evidence that Simpson had committed adultery.[215] The law of divorce was attracting increasing public ridicule for the absurdity of people plotting schemes to flout the strict grounds for divorce.

---

207 See E.S.P. Haynes, 'Abolish the King's Proctor' *Spectator* (London, 24 February 1933) 7.
208 E.S.P. Haynes, 'Lord Gorell's Matrimonial Causes Bill' (May 1921) *The English Review* 459, 462–3.
209 HC Deb 20 November 1836, vol 317, cols 2088–9.
210 HL Deb 7 July 1937, vol 106, col 72.
211 'Undefended Divorce Suit' *The Times* (London, 28 October 1936) 9.
212 The Special Branch of the Metropolitan Police investigated Simpson and discovered that she had intimate relations with a secret lover. The Police did not communicate this fact with the King's Proctor. Stephen Cretney, 'The Divorce Law and the 1936 Abdication Crisis: A Supplemental Note' (2004) 120 *Law Quarterly Review* 169.
213 Brian Inglis, *Abdication* (Hodder and Stoughton 1966) 352.
214 See Stephen Cretney, 'The King and the King's Proctor: The Abdication Crisis and the Divorce Laws 1936–1937' (2000) 116 *Law Quarterly Review* 583.
215 *Simpson, W v Simpson, EA (Application by the King's Proctor for Directions)* (1937) *The Times*, 20 March 1937.

Matrimonial Causes Act 1937

On 14 November 1935, the Conservative Party won the general election with Baldwin becoming prime minister. More importantly for the divorce law reform campaign, Herbert was elected as an Independent MP for Oxford University.[216] Herbert wasted no time and presented a bill for divorce law reform three months later.[217] His bill was initially rejected, with the prime minister expressing the government's reluctance to bring it for a Second Reading.[218] Although Baldwin commanded a majority government, he was indisposed to debating what he saw as a controversial issue.[219] Herbert soon realised that he would have to compromise with the government in order for there to be any chance of the bill's success.[220] The bill was aimed at enacting the recommendations of the Gorell Commission majority report.[221]

The government was willing to allow the passage of the bill so long as it was to its satisfaction and could be practically functional, because the government would be responsible for administering the bill. The main concern of the government, as expressed by Attorney-General Sir Donald Somervell, was ensuring that the bill could reduce the amount of collusive arrangements and provide clarity on the precise details of the new grounds for divorce.[222] Moreover, it had to be introduced by Herbert as a private member's bill, since the government did not want to suffer any reputational damage associated with liberalising divorce. Despite the government's reluctance to countenance reform, there was support for change among some Conservatives. The most notable Conservative supporter was Rupert de la Bère. On 20 November 1936, de la Bère successfully moved that the bill be given a Second Reading (seconded by Herbert) that passed by 78 votes to 12.[223] De la Bère stressed that the bill was non-partisan and was motivated by his view that the 'Statute law of England fails to act along the lines traced by the Matrimonial Causes Act, 1857 ... with the result that, as many judges have asserted, the existing law is ineffective and farcical.'[224] This was a turning point as now there was support from the government, which looked favourably upon compromise.

---

216 Craig (n 63) 33.
217 HC Deb 7 February 1936, vol 308, col 505.
218 HC Deb 20 May 1936, vol 312, col 1191.
219 Dorothy Stetson, *A Woman's Issue: the Politics of Family Law Reform in England* (Greenwood Press 1982) 118.
220 A.P. Herbert, *The Ayes Have It: the Story of the Marriage Bill* (Methuen, 1937) 59; Sharon Redmayne, 'The Matrimonial Causes Act 1937: A Lesson in the Art of Compromise' (1993) 13(2) *Oxford Journal of Legal Studies* 183, 186.
221 Matrimonial causes bill 1936 (1 Ed VIII).
222 HC Deb 20 November 1936, vol 317, cols 2126–30.
223 *Ibid.* cols 2079–131.
224 *Ibid.* col 2079.

The bill passed both Houses of Parliament and received Royal Assent on 30 July 1937.[225] It came into law on 1 January 1938.[226] There were four grounds for divorce: adultery, desertion of at least three years, cruelty, and unsound mind of at least five years.[227] This was a compromise between the reformers and the government. Herbert suggested that there should be no divorce for the first five years of marriage.[228] This was not something that was ever suggested by the Gorell Commission. The aim was to demonstrate that the reformers upheld the sanctity of marriage, and to appease many of those who were opposed to the bill. Many Anglican and Roman Catholic MPs were mollified by the inclusion of this section.[229] Eventually, the House of Lords reduced the period to the first three years of marriage, which was ultimately accepted and became section 1 of the Matrimonial Causes Act 1937.[230]

Herbert made a number of other concessions, such as withdrawing a clause to allow magistrates to hear some contested divorce suits, and the proposal to abolish the King's Proctor and decree *nisi*.[231] Moreover, he acquiesced in the extension of the Court's inquisitorial powers.[232] Although some provisions remained intact with it being arguably more difficult to divorce at least for those in the first few years of marriage, the 1937 Act followed the spirit of the Gorell Commission and extended the grounds for divorce in the hopes of extricating the practical hardships found in the previous laws.

More than two decades after the Gorell Commission, substantive reform of divorce law was finally achieved. Although the political situation was propitious for the success of Herbert's bill, it alone does not account for the ultimate defenestration of the Matrimonial Causes Act 1857. Dorothy Stetson states, 'The law was forced to bend and finally break by collusion, perjury, and sham. A coalition of supporters, concerned about the tensions between the law and behaviour, united to push divorce reform over the top.'[233] The divorce law was openly mocked, especially after 1934 with the writings of Waugh and Herbert and the abdication crisis. However, Stetson's portrayal of the bill's passage is too deterministic.

Legal change was not inevitable and the unity of the supporters did not coalesce naturally. Instead as Sharon Redmayne states, 'We have seen how Herbert decided that if his measure was to have any chance of success, then certain compromises and bargains would have to be made to various quarters, most notably the

---

225 HL Deb 30 July 1937, vol 106, col 1071.
226 Matrimonial Causes Act 1937, s 14(2).
227 Matrimonial Causes Act 1937, s 2.
228 Matrimonial Causes Bill 1936, cl 1; HC Deb 20 November 1936, vol 317, cols 2084–7.
229 Cretney (n 17) 245.
230 HL Deb 7 July 1937, vol 106, cols 75–84. Lord Jessel proposed the amendment, because he considered five years too long.
231 Redmayne (n 220) 191–5.
232 *Ibid.* 196–7.
233 Stetson (n 219) 125.

162 *Reform in the early twentieth century*

Government.'[234] Herbert's political nous in harnessing popular opposition to the divorce law, and balancing that political capital with compromise, helped to ensure the government's support and the bill's successful passage. The campaign for divorce law reform can be traced to the enactment of married women's property legislation in the late nineteenth century. It spurred what proved to be an unstoppable and organised campaign for divorce law reform. Increasingly liberal attitudes on divorce and dissatisfaction with piecemeal reform ultimately led to the repeal of the 1857 Act. In the end this was enough to bring to an end the system of divorce law created under Queen Victoria.

---

234 Redmayne (n 220) 198.

7 *Quo vadis?* The road to divorce

Divorce law: A process of piecemeal reform

The introduction of the Matrimonial Causes Act 1857 amounted to more than just a procedural change, but also reflected shifts in politics, religion, and society. Legal change in family law is motivated by wider external concerns beyond abstract legal doctrines, because of its significant effect on the lives of individuals and the raising of questions of law and morality. The law of divorce faced acute changes during the transformative period of the Victorian era,[1] because of the social, political, and economic challenges that were generated from nineteenth-century industrialisation.[2] The relationship between law reform and wider social change is more obviously found in family law, which means that it is also necessary to consider external sources. Chantal Stebbings states, 'In the writing of Victorian legal history, however, the sources themselves force researchers into breaking out of this traditional approach to doctrinal legal history.'[3]

The thesis argues that the history of divorce law in Victorian England is premised on both change and continuity. This manifests itself in three thematic areas: the gradualist model of legal change, the nature of the political climate, and the compromise between Christian morality and secular values. Law reform is a complex process and the topic of divorce law in Victorian England is no different. Only through the perspective of legal history guided by relevant external sources is it possible to conclude that changes to the divorce law were part of the law reform movement, which was partly inspired by utilitarian thinkers. At the same time, neither the introduction of the 1857 Act nor the outcomes that flowed from it were inevitable. Divorce reform came with unique challenges. The 1857 Act was a controversial piece of legislation that only succeeded at all as a result of compromise.

---

1 Stephen Cretney, *Family Law in the Twentieth Century* (Oxford University Press 2003) 162.
2 Chantal Stebbings, 'Benefits and Barriers: The Making of Victorian Legal History' in Anthony Musson and Chantal Stebbings (eds), *Making Legal History: Approaches and Methodologies* (Cambridge University Press 2012) 73.
3 *Ibid*. 86.

Legal change should be understood as a gradual process, otherwise one runs the risk of coming to unhelpfully general conclusions, especially the statement that the 1857 Act was merely a procedural change. Although the 1857 Act was driven by the wider desire to abolish the Ecclesiastical Courts and improve the efficiency of the legal system, arguing that this was purely symbolic ignores the practical significance of introducing civil divorce—in particular, the introduction of a secular family justice system and the gradual decline of ecclesiastical precedents and principles. These changes gradually came to generate wider social and legal acceptance of divorce, which in turn encouraged the campaign to expand the grounds for divorce and to abolish the double standard between the genders in the early twentieth century.

The Divorce Court drew significantly on the old ecclesiastical law in interpreting statutory definitions of grounds and bars to divorce at least in the beginning. This changed over time. Individual judges exercised significant influence in interpreting statutory doctrines of divorce law. The Divorce Courts led by Cresswell Cresswell, Lord Penzance, and James Hannen relied on the familiar ecclesiastical notions to perpetuate a conservative understanding of sexual morality in the divorce law. This upheld the values of the time. In the final decades of the nineteenth century, the Divorce Court led by Charles Butt and Lord St Helier experienced a palpable but subtle shift towards interpreting the grounds of divorce more broadly and the bars to divorce more narrowly.

The Divorce Court did not remain static; more people were applying for divorce and the judges had adapted to these practical realities by applying the law with more nuance. Precedents based on the 1857 Act had developed and the Court was more confident in deviating away from some ecclesiastical principles. The extent to which individual judges drove change is shown by the way in which the few cases that were heard at appellate level tended to overrule the Divorce Court and reassert a conservative interpretation over the law of divorce. The Divorce Court under Lord Gorell saw a further step change. He began actively campaigning for divorce law reform as a matter of policy against the backdrop of a system which made it difficult to make minor changes to the substance of the law. This illustrates both the importance and the limitations of the judiciary in promoting legal change, and accentuates the part played by Parliament in leading the reform of divorce law. Although the judicial activism did not lead to immediate changes to the law, it did take on more political significance in the law reform campaign. The judiciary offered evolving interpretations that made divorce ever so slightly easier. However, it is telling that adultery remained the sole ground for divorce until 1937. Divorce continued to be granted in limited circumstances, because of the obligation to follow the 1857 Act. Only Parliament could change the divorce law in major ways.

Legal change: A process of political will

The state of the political climate was crucial for any chance of divorce law reform. Family law issues elicited strong moral concern among politicians and successive governments were usually unwilling to deal with these highly controversial issues. Moreover, family law issues were often relegated as a second-order issue to more important concerns of the day, such as military and foreign affairs. Governments were concerned with maintaining political stability and popularity. Therefore, divorce law reform seldom gained political traction unless there was a pressing need in order to promote efficiency or to address social concern. The fact that there was no organised campaign for divorce law reform delayed the political momentum. It was not until the 1850s that there was a concerted push for divorce law reform, and even then each of the proponents were motivated by their own ulterior purposes. Caroline Norton was driven by her own personal acrimonious relationship with her husband. The Law Amendment Society advocated for reform as part of its aim to fuse the common law and equity. John Stuart Mill favoured divorce reform as a means of promoting his political philosophy of liberalism. Nevertheless, their combined efforts played some role in putting divorce law on the agenda of the Whig governments. The most obvious manifestation was Lord John Russell establishing the Campbell Commission.

The majority report of the Campbell Commission motivated the Palmerston government to implement wider law reform of the Ecclesiastical Courts. As Palmerston had decisively won the 1857 election, the propitious political climate enabled him to push forward his domestic law reform agenda. The Matrimonial Causes Act 1857 was part of a package of law reforms aimed at stripping the Ecclesiastical Courts of jurisdiction over matrimonial issues, probate, and admiralty. This saw longstanding pressure for far-reaching Benthamite reform of the ecclesiastical jurisdictions finally achieve change. The most lasting legacy of the 1857 Act was the introduction of civil divorce that secularised the law of divorce and began to challenge notions of marriage as an indissoluble union. However, the 1857 Act failed to completely satisfy the demands of both reformers and conservatives. The Palmerston government offered a *via media* solution that provided an apposite compromise between the reformers who demanded the introduction of civil divorce and the conservatives who sought to limit divorce to the sole ground of adultery. Moreover, the conservatives called for the introduction of a double standard in the grounds for divorce between the genders that had never previously existed. Compromise between conservatives and reformers was a running theme throughout the operation of the Matrimonial Causes Act 1857 and the basis of subsequent piecemeal reforms.

The role of the government was indispensable in promoting divorce law reforms between the 1850s and 1930s. The Palmerston government played an important role in advocating for the introduction of civil divorce in the mid-nineteenth century, while the Baldwin government was willing to compromise with campaigners for divorce law reform in the Interwar period. The legislature introduced various laws that accompanied the operation of the 1857 Act. Throughout the second half of the nineteenth century, the various governments introduced piecemeal reform that was primarily aimed at improving the practical operation of the divorce law with the effect of gradually extending the rights of married women. However, piecemeal reform failed to address more critical issues. It did not abolish the double standard between the genders. More importantly, it failed to keep up with changing values as some of the Victorian restraints on sexual morality began to fall away. Piecemeal reform sometimes had unintended consequences that detracted from divorce law reform. For example, the Summary Jurisdiction (Married Women) Act 1895 inadvertently limited divorce for married women. A wife who was granted a judicial separation could not claim that the period after the order constituted desertion.

Double standards: A process of overcoming moral hypocrisy

The injustices of the double standard and the general strictness of the grounds for divorce led to the campaign for divorce law reform in the early twentieth century. The Gorell Commission was an important factor for the eventual abolition of the double standard and the expansion of the grounds for divorce. However, it failed to have an immediate legislative impact because of the outbreak of World War I. It would take a quarter of a century for its recommendations to come to fruition. It provides a salient example of the necessity of opportune political timing, the support of the government, and the willingness to compromise in order for significant divorce law reform to succeed. Major divorce law reform would only later be achieved, in the Interwar period, because the political climate had become conducive to legal change. After World War I, social values on divorce had become more liberal and the campaign for the reform of the Victorian divorce law had finally made a political breakthrough.

The liberalising social milieu managed to successfully persuade the Baldwin government to introduce divorce law reform. The Conservatives were seen as reasonable rather than radical proponents of legal change. Rather than rejecting change, the Baldwin government was willing to make compromises between those who advocated for change and the *status quo*. The reform of divorce law was achieved through two major pieces of legislation. The Matrimonial Causes Act 1923 abolished the double standard between genders in proving the grounds for divorce. The Matrimonial Causes Act 1937 expanded the grounds for divorce beyond adultery. This happened not as a result of a progressive agenda, but because of resistance to radical reform.

Governments in the Interwar period were risk-averse and were unwilling to promote divorce bills. The 1937 Act succeeded due to the fortuitous political and social climate, which was led by the efforts of A.P. Herbert. Just prior to 1937, the laws were publicly ridiculed in the writings of Evelyn Waugh and Herbert, and in the press, especially during the abdication crisis of Edward VIII. Unlike previous failed attempts, Herbert was willing to make compromises with the government in order to secure passage of his bill. The 1937 Act reflected the *via media* outlook of Parliament, as was the case in the 1857 Act. The 1937 Act expanded the grounds for divorce beyond adultery that satisfied the long-held ambitions of the reformers, but introduced a bar to petitioning for divorce in the first five years of marriage in order to ameliorate the concerns of conservative elements. The history of the rise and fall of the 1857 Act is one of compromise between the dominant forces of social conservatism and the ultimately prevailing campaigners for divorce law reform.

Although religious morality on divorce did not significantly change, the stance of the Church of England had adapted to the increasing acceptance of divorce. There were significant changes in sexual morality from the Victorian to the Interwar period. The 1857 Act was a product of the tripartite divorce process that reflected Elizabethan Christian values in the Victorian law. Adultery was clearly retained as the sole ground of divorce for husbands and a prerequisite ground for wives because of Christian doctrine. Prior to 1857, the Ecclesiastical Courts exercised matrimonial jurisdiction, because issues of marriage and divorce were moral questions that were to be dictated according to Christian teaching. After 1857, the Divorce Court inherited the Ecclesiastical Courts' function as the standard-bearer of Christian morality up until World War I. The dominance of the Church of England throughout the Victorian period and its conservative Christian teaching on marriage and divorce curtailed the call for changes in the divorce law for another generation.

This old style of Christian moralism began to go out of fashion by the Edwardian era, which is marked for its embrace of modernist individual rights and eudemonistic liberalism. Many influential parliamentarians in the early twentieth century were generally more conservative when it came to sensitive subjects relating to moral issues. At the same time, the Church of England had come to accept the need for divorce law reform. This was demonstrated in Archbishop of York Cosmo Gordon Lang's support for legislation enacting the consensus of the majority and minority reports of the Gorell Commission in 1914. Although by then the Church of England did not exercise the same degree of influence as it had in the Victorian period, it still remained an important stakeholder on moral issues. The end of World War I saw the continued development of modernist morality. Society had moved on and Parliament increasingly reflected the zeitgeist of the day. The cultural shift eventually could no longer be ignored by the Baldwin government. Ideas of women's rights and gender equality took hold. It was a major factor in prompting the government to introduce the 1923 Act that abolished the double standard between genders in divorce. The judiciary had done all it could to advocate for law reform given its limitation of power. The government was responsible for legislation in areas of significant moral concern. Therefore, it was incumbent on the government as it had been in the mid-nineteenth century to promote divorce law reform. The Baldwin government finally acted in 1937 and the divorce law that had persisted for 80 years prior had come to an end.

In regards to the introduction of civil divorce, the sole dissenter of the Campbell Commission, Lord Redesdale, warned, 'Once create an appetite for such licence by proposed change, and the demand to be permitted to satisfy it will become irresistible.'[4] Redesdale's prediction gradually came to be realised

---

4 *First Report of the Commissioners...Into the Law of Divorce* (1852–3) BPP vol 40, 278.

within the 80 years of the 1857 Act's operation. Legal change was initially slow in the years immediately after 1857, but the forces of change later proved to be unstoppable. The piecemeal reforms were generally *ad hoc* responses, but the Interwar reforms were as a result of many years of political pressure. As divorce became more accessible, many couples came to accept that it was a desirable remedy for the irretrievable breakdown of marriage. The divorce law came to be widely circumvented through collusion, especially in the form of hotel divorces. The law was generally behind the pace of social change. Nevertheless, religious morality and the political climate ultimately came to adapt to these shifts in social values. The legal change was brought about as a result of compromise with the effect of mitigating the more radical proposed changes to the law of divorce. The Divorce Court and Parliament generally held conservative views on marriage and divorce, but even these legal authorities gradually had to adjust to the wider societal changes on issues of morality. Warren Swain, considering the history of the law of contract over some of the same period, states, 'The process of change was complex, if not always conscious or even obvious.'[5] This equally applies to the history of English divorce law.

---

5 Warren Swain, *The Law of Contract 1670–1870* (Cambridge University Press 2015) 281.

Bibliography

Abel-Smith, Brian and Robert Stevens, *Lawyers and the Courts: A Sociological Study of the English Legal System 1750–1965* (Heinemann 1967).
Abramowicz, Sarah, 'English Child Custody Law, 1660–1839: The Origins of Judicial Intervention in Paternal Custody' (1999) 99(5) *Columbia Law Review* 1344.
Acland, Alice, *Caroline Norton* (Constable 1948).
Adshead, Samuel Adrian M., *Philosophy of Religion in Nineteenth-Century England and Beyond* (Macmillan Press 2000).
Allen, Christopher, *The Law of Evidence in Victorian England* (Cambridge University Press 1997).
Amory, Mark (ed), *The Letters of Evelyn Waugh* (Ticknor and Fields 1980).
Amussen, Susan Dwyer, 'Road to Divorce: England 1530–1987' (1991) 20(1) *History: Reviews of New Books* 12.
Anderson, Olive, 'Hansard's Hazards: An Illustration from Recent Interpretations of Married Women's Property Law and the 1857 Divorce Act' (1997) 112(449) *English Historical Review* 1202.
Andrew, Donna, '"Adultery à-la-Mode": Privilege, the Law and Attitudes to Adultery 1770–1809' (1997) 82(265) *History* 5.
Annas, Julia, 'Mill and the Subjection of Women' (1977) 52 *Philosophy* 179.
Anon, 'The English Law of Divorce' (1856) 65(128) *Westminster Review* 338.
Anon, 'Marriage, Divorce, and the Divorce Commission' (1913) 217(443) *The Edinburgh Review* 1.
Anon, *Norton v Viscount Melbourne* (William Marshall 1836).
Anon, 'November 6, 1909' (1909) 54 *Solicitors' Journal* 23.
Anon, *The Lady Mordaunt Divorce Case* (Temple Publishing Offices 1870).
Anon, *The Priest in Absolution: A Manual for Such as are Called unto the Higher Ministries in the English Church* (Joseph Masters 1866).
Ashburner, Walter, *Principles of Equity* (Butterworth and Co 1902).
Atkinson, Diane, *The Criminal Conversation of Mrs Norton* (Preface 2012).
Baigent, Elizabeth, 'Jane Elizabeth Digby (1807–1881)', *Oxford Dictionary of National Biography* (2004) <http://doi.org/10.1093/ref:odnb/40103>.
Baker, John Hamilton, 'Famous English Canon Lawyers: X Sir Robert Phillimore, QC, DCL († 1885) and the Last Practising Doctors of Law' (1997) 4(21) *Ecclesiastical Law Journal* 709.
Banks, Stephen, *A Polite Exchange of Bullets: The Duel and the English Gentleman, 1750–1850* (Boydell Press 2010).

Bibliography

Bartrip, Peter, 'A Talent to Alienate: The 2nd Earl (Frank) Russell (1865–1931)' (2012–13) 32 *Russell: The Journal of Bertrand Russell Studies* 101.

Bartrip, Peter W.J., 'Russell, John Francis Stanley [Frank], Second Earl Russell (1865–1931)', *Oxford Dictionary of National Biography* (2004) <https://doi.org /10.1093/ref:odnb/58843 >.

Beales, Derek, 'Walpole, Spencer Horatio (1806–1898)', *Oxford Dictionary of National Biography* (2004) <https://doi.org/10.1093/ref:odnb/28604>.

Bebbington, David, *The Mind of Gladstone: Religion, Homer, and Politics* (Oxford University Press 2004).

Becker, Lydia, 'The Political Disabilities of Women' (1872) 41(1) *Westminster Review* 50.

Bennett, Arnold, *Whom God Hath Joined* (David Nutt 1906).

Bentham, Jeremy, *Lord Brougham Displayed* (Robert Heward 1832).

Bernard, George W., *The King's Reformation: Henry VIII and the Remaking of the English Church* (Yale University Press 2005).

Bew, Paul, 'Parnell, Charles Stewart (1846–1891)', *Oxford Dictionary of National Biography* (2004) <https://doi.org/10.1093/ref:odnb/21384>.

Bibbings, Lois, *Binding Men: Stories About Violence and Law in Late Victorian England* (Routledge 2014).

Bird, Storm, *The Strange Life of Georgina Weldon* (Chatto and Windus 1959).

Blackstone, William, *Commentaries on the Laws of England, Volume 1* (1753).

Bland, Lucy, '"Hunnish Scenes" and a "Virgin Birth": a 1920s Case of Sexual and Bodily Ignorance' (2012) 73(1) *History Workshop Journal* 118.

Blume, Fred, 'Annotated Justinian Code' (University of Wyoming Digital Library) <http://uwdigital.uwyo.edu/islandora/object/wyu:12399>.

Boase, Frederic, *Modern English Biography, Volume I* (Cass 1965).

Boase, George Clement, 'Bouverie, Edward Pleydell (1818–1889)', *Oxford Dictionary of National Biography* (2004) <https://doi.org/10.1093/ref:odnb/3016>.

Bodichon, Barbara Leigh Smith, *A Brief Summary, in Plain Language, of the Most Important Laws Concerning Women: Together with a Few Observations Thereon* (Holyoake and Co 1856).

The Book of Common Prayer (first published 1662, Cambridge University Press 2004).

Borkowski, Andrew and Paul du Plessis, *Textbook on Roman Law* (Oxford University Press 2005).

Boulton, Jeremy, 'Lawrence Stone, *Road to Divorce: England, 1530–1987* (Oxford: Oxford University Press, 1990)' (1993) 8(1) *Continuity and Change* 140.

Bowring, John (ed), *The Works of Jeremy Bentham, Volume I* (William Tait 1859).

Bowsher, Peter, 'Incest—Should Incest between Consenting Adults be a Crime?' (2015) 3 *Criminal Law Review* 208.

Brady, Sean, *Masculinity and Male Homosexuality in Britain, 1861–1913* (Palgrave Macmillan 2005).

Braithwaite, Thomas, *The "Six Clerks in Chancery": Their Successors in Office and the "Houses" They Lived In: A Reminiscence* (Stevens and Haynes 1879).

Brand, Paul and Joshua Getzler, *Judges and Judging in the History of the Common Law and Civil Law* (Cambridge University Press 2012).

Bray, Gerald (ed), *Tudor Church Reform: The Henrician Canons of 1535 and the* Reformatio Legum Ecclesiasticarum (Boydell Press 2000).

Brontë, Charlotte, *Jane Eyre* (first published 1847, Penguin 2006).

Brooke, Christopher, *The Medieval Idea of Marriage* (The Alden Press 1989).

Brooks, David, *The Age of Upheaval: Edwardian Politics, 1899–1914* (Manchester University Press 1995).
Brundage, James, *Medieval Canon Law* (Routledge 1995).
Brundage, James, *Sex, Law and Marriage in the Middle Ages* (Variorum 1993).
Bryan, Michael, 'Early English Law Reporting' (2009) 4 *University of Melbourne Collections* 45.
Buckland, William Warwick, *A Manual of Roman Private Law* (Cambridge University Press 1925).
Buckland, William Warwick, *The Main Institutions of Roman Private Law* (Cambridge University Press 1931).
Burn, Richard and Robert Phillimore, *Ecclesiastical Law, Volume 3* (Sweet, Stevens, and Norton 1842).
Buti, Antonio, 'The Early History of the Law of Guardianship of Children: From Rome to the Tenures Abolition Act 1660' (2003) 7(1) *University of Western Sydney Law Review* 92.
Butler, Lance St John, *Thomas Hardy* (Cambridge University Press 1978).
Caine, Barbara, *English Feminism 1780–1980* (Oxford University Press 1997).
Cairns, John and Grant McLeod (eds), *The Dearest Birth Right of the People of England* (Hart Publishing 2002).
Cameron, Ewen, 'The Mid-Victorian Generation 1846–1886 by K. Theodore Hoppen' (2000) 79(207) *The Scottish Historical Review* 131.
Cane, Peter and Mark Tushnet (eds), *The Oxford Handbook of Legal Studies* (Oxford University Press 2003).
Capaldi, Nicholas, *John Stuart Mill: A Biography* (Cambridge University Press 2004).
Carbone, June, 'Feminism, Gender and the Consequences of Divorce' in Michael Freeman (ed), *Divorce: Where Next?* (Dartmouth Publishing 1996).
Chadwick, Owen, *The Victorian Church: Part I* (Adam and Charles Black 1966).
Chadwick, Owen, *The Victorian Church, Part II* (Adam and Charles Black 1970).
Chapman, John (ed), 'The English Law of Divorce' (1856) 65(128) *Westminster Review* 338.
Chase, Karen and Michael Levenson, *The Spectacle of Intimacy: A Public Life for the Victorian Family* (Princeton University Press 2000).
Chedzoy, Alan, *A Scandalous Woman: the Story of Caroline Norton* (Allison and Busby 1992).
Clewlow, Ellie, 'Browne, George Forrest (1833–1930)', *Oxford Dictionary of National Biography* (2004) <https://doi.org/10.1093/ref:odnb/32121>.
Clockie, Hugh and J. William Robinson, *Royal Commissions of Inquiry* (Octagon Books 1969).
Cobbe, Frances Power, 'Wife-Torture in England' (1878) 32 *The Contemporary Review* 55.
Cohen, Deborah, *Family Secrets: Shame and Privacy in Modern Britain* (Oxford University Press 2013).
Cohen, William, *Sex Scandal: The Private Parts of Victorian Fiction* (Duke University Press 1996).
Cole, Margaret, *Marriage Past and Present* (JM Dent 1938).
Conaghan, Joanne, '*A Brief Summary of the Most Important Laws Concerning Women*, Barbara Leigh Smith Bodichon, 1854' in Erika Rackley and Rosemary Auchmuty (eds), *Women's Legal Landmarks: Celebrating the History of Women and Law in the UK and Ireland* (Hart Publishing 2018).
Connolly, Brian, *Domestic Intimacies: Incest and the Liberal Subject in Nineteenth-Century America* (University of Pennsylvania Press 2014).

Copy of the Fifth Report Made to His Majesty by the Commissioners Appointed to Inquire into the Practice and Proceedings of the Superior Courts of Common Law (1833) BPP vol 22, 195–649.

Copy of the First Report made to His Majesty by the Commissioners Appointed to Inquire into the Law of England Respecting Real Property (1829) BPP vol 10, 263–671.

Cornish, William and Geoffrey Clark, *Law and Society in England 1750–1950* (Sweet and Maxwell 1989).

Cornish, William, J. Stuart Anderson, Ray Cocks, Michael Lobban, Patrick Polden, and Keith Smith (eds), *The Oxford History of the Laws of England: Volume XI 1820–1914: English Legal System* (Oxford University Press 2010).

Cornish, William, J. Stuart Anderson, Ray Cocks, Michael Lobban, Patrick Polden, and Keith Smith (eds), *The Oxford History of the Laws of England: Volume XII* (Oxford University Press 2010).

Cornish, William, J. Stuart Anderson, Ray Cocks, Michael Lobban, Patrick Polden, and Keith Smith (eds), *The Oxford History of the Laws of England: Volume XIII* (Oxford University Press 2010).

Cornwallis, Caroline, 'The Property of Married Women: Report of the Personal Laws Committee (of the Law Amendment Society) on the Laws Relating to the Property of Married Women' (1856) 66 *Westminster Review* 331.

Cotterell, Mary, 'Interregnum Law Reform: The Hale Commission of 1652' (1968) 83(329) *English Historical Review* 689.

Couch, Harvey, 'The Evolution of Parliamentary Divorce in England' (1978) 52 *Tulane Law Review* 513.

Craig, Frederick Walter Scott, *British Electoral Facts: 1832–1987* (Parliamentary Research Services 1989).

Craig, Randall, *The Narratives of Caroline Norton* (Palgrave Macmillan 2009).

Crawley, Charles, *The Law of Husband and Wife* (William Clowes and Sons 1892).

Cretney, Stephen, '"Disgusted, Buckingham Palace…"—The Judicial Proceedings (Regulation of Reports) Act 1926' (1997) 9(1) *Child and Family Law Quarterly* 43.

Cretney, Stephen, *Family Law in the Twentieth Century* (Oxford University Press 2003).

Cretney, Stephen, 'Haynes, Edmund Sidney Pollock (1877–1949)', *Oxford Dictionary of National Biography* (2004) <https://doi.org/10.1093/ref:odnb/38874>.

Cretney, Stephen, 'The Divorce Law and the 1936 Abdication Crisis: A Supplemental Note' (2004) 120 *Law Quarterly Review* 169.

Cretney, Stephen, 'The King and the King's Proctor: The Abdication Crisis and the Divorce Laws 1936–1937' (2000) 116 *Law Quarterly Review* 583.

Crimmins, James E., *Utilitarian Philosophy and Politics* (Continuum 2011).

Daiches, Samuel, 'Divorce in Jewish Law' (1926) 8(4) *Journal of Comparative Legislation and International Law* 215.

Daube, David and Calum Carmichael, 'The Return of the Divorcee' (Inaugural Jewish Law Fellowship Lecture) (Oxford Centre for Hebrew Studies 1993).

David, Deidre, *Intellectual Women and Victorian Patriarchy: Harriet Martineau, Elizabeth Barrett, George Eliot* (Macmillan Press 1987).

Davis, J.C., *Utopia and the Ideal Society: A Study of English Utopian Writing 1516–1700* (Cambridge University Press 1981).

Davis, William, 'Hardy and the Law: Sexual Relations and "Matrimonial Divergence"' in Rosemarie Morgan (ed), *The Ashgate Research Companion to Thomas Hardy* (Ashgate 2010).

Davis, William, *Thomas Hardy and the Law: Legal Presences in Hardy's Life and Fiction* (University of Delaware Press 2003).

von Bóné, Emese, 'The Historical Development of Grounds for Divorce in the French and Dutch Civil Codes' (2014) 20(2) *Fundamina: A Journal of Legal History* 1006.
de Montmorency, James Edward Geoffrey, 'Barnes, John Gorell, first Baron Gorell (1848–1913)', *Oxford Dictionary of National Biography* (2004) <https://doi.org/10.1093/ref:odnb/30604>.
Desai, Kumud, *Indian Law of Marriage and Divorce* (NM Tripathi Private 1978).
Devenney, James and Mel Kenny (eds), *The Transformation of European Private Law: Harmonisation, Consolidation, Codification or Chaos* (Cambridge University Press 2013).
Dicey, Albert Venn, *Lectures on the Relation Between Law and Public Opinion in England During the Nineteenth Century* (Macmillan 1905).
Dickens, Charles, *David Copperfield* (first published 1850, Penguin 1996).
Dickens, Charles, *Hard Times* (first published 1854, Penguin 1995).
Dickens, Charles, *The Pickwick Papers* (first published 1836, Oxford University Press 1986).
'Divorces in England and Wales, 2012' (Office for National Statistics 2012) <www.ons.gov.uk/ons/publications/re-reference- tables.html?edition=tcm%3A77-328994>.
di Stefano, Christine, *Configurations of Masculinity: A Feminist Perspective on Modern Political Theory* (Cornell University Press 1991).
Dobranski, Stephen (ed), *Milton in Context* (Cambridge University Press 2010).
Doe, Norman, 'Phillimore, Sir Robert Joseph, Baronet (1810–1885)', *Oxford Dictionary of National Biography* (2004) <https://doi.org/10.1093/ref:odnb/22138>.
Doggett, Maeve, *Marriage, Wife-Beating and the Law in Victorian England* (Weidenfeld & Nicholson 1992).
Dolin, Kieran, *A Critical Introduction to Law and Literature* (Cambridge University Press 2007).
Dolin, Kieran, 'A Woman's Pleading: Caroline Norton's Pamphlets on Laws for Women in Nineteenth-Century England' (1998) 10 *Australian Feminist Law Journal* 51.
Dolin, Kieran, *Fiction and the Law: Legal Discourse in Victorian and Modernist Literature* (Cambridge University Press 1999).
Dolin, Kieran, 'The Transfiguration of Caroline Norton' (2002) 30(2) *Victorian Literature and Culture* 503.
Douglas, James, 'Parliamentary Divorce, 1700–1857' (2012) 31(2) *Parliamentary History* 169.
Duxbury, Neil, *Patterns of American Jurisprudence* (Oxford University Press 1995).
Eggleston, Ben and Dale E. Miller (eds), *The Cambridge Companion to Utilitarianism* (Cambridge University Press 2014).
Elliott, John Huxtable, 'Lawrence Stone' (1999) 164 *Past & Present* 3.
Erb, Peter C. (ed), *The Correspondence of Henry Edward Manning and William Ewart Gladstone, Volume 2: 1844–1853* (Oxford University Press 2013).
Evans, Richard, *In Defence of History* (Granta Books 1997).
Fellows, Alfred, 'Changes in the Law of Husband and Wife' (1906) 22 *Law Quarterly Review* 64.
Fenn, Henry Edwin, *Thirty-Five Years in the Divorce Court* (T Werner Laurie 1910).
Ferguson, Trish, *Thomas Hardy's Legal Fictions* (Edinburgh University Press 2013).
Finlay, Henry, *To Have But Not to Hold* (The Federation Press 2005).
First Report of the Commissioners Appointed by Her Majesty to Enquire into the Law of Divorce, and More Particularly into the Mode of Obtaining Divorces a Vinculo Matrimonii (1852–3) BPP vol 40, 249–330.
Firth, Charles Harding and Robert Sangster Rait, *Acts and Ordinances of the Interregnum* (Wyman and Sons 1911).

Fogel, Robert William and G.R. Elton (eds), *Which Road to the Past? Two Views of History* (Yale University Press 1983).
Frew, Charlotte, 'The Marriage to a Deceased Wife's Sister Narrative: A Comparison of Novels' (2012) 24(2) *Law and Literature* 265.
Furneaux, Rupert, *Tried By Their Peers* (Cassell 1959).
Garratt, Geoffrey Theodore, *Lord Brougham* (Macmillan 1935).
Gash, Norman, 'Jenkinson, Robert Banks, Second Earl of Liverpool (1770–1828)', *Oxford Dictionary of National Biography* (2004) <https://doi.org/10.1093/ref:odnb/14740>.
Geis, Gilbert, 'Lord Hale, Witches, and Rape' (1978) 5(1) *British Journal of Law and Society* 26.
Getzler, Joshua, 'Cresswell, Sir Cresswell (1793–1863)', *Oxford Dictionary of National Biography* (2004) <https://doi.org/10.1093/ref:odnb/6673>.
Gilliland, Jean, 'Opdebeck [Née Douglas-Hamilton], Lady Susan Harriet Catherine [Other Married Name Susan Harriet Catherine Pelham-Clinton, Countess of Lincoln]', *Oxford Dictionary of National Biography* (2004) <https://doi.org/10.1093/ref:odnb/39436>.
Gillis, John, *For Better, For Worse: British Marriages 1600 to the Present Day* (Oxford University Press 1985).
Gilmore, Stephen, Jonathan Herring, and Rebecca Probert (eds), *Landmark Cases in Family Law* (Hart Publishing 2011).
Glassman, Peter, *J.S. Mill: The Evolution of a Genius* (University of Florida Press 1985).
Goldstein, Leslie, 'Mill, Marx, and Women's Liberation' (1980) 18(3) *Journal of the History of Philosophy* 319.
Goldsworthy, John, *In Chancery* (William Heinemann 1920).
Grosskurth, Phylliss, *Byron: The Flawed Angel* (Hodder and Stoughton 1997).
Grotius, Hugo, *The Jurisprudence of Holland* (R.W. Lee trans, Oxford University Press 1926).
Grubbs, Judith Evans, *Women and the Law in the Roman Empire* (Routledge 2002).
Guthrie, Charles, 'The History of Divorce in Scotland' (1910) 8(29) *The Scottish Historical Review* 39.
Hardcastle, Mary (ed), *Life of John, Lord Campbell, Lord High Chancellor of Great Britain, Volume 1* (John Murray 1881).
Hardcastle, Mary (ed), *Life of John, Lord Campbell, Lord High Chancellor of Great Britain, Volume 2* (John Murray 1881).
Hale, Matthew, *The History of the PLEAS of the Crown, Volume 1* (Nutt 1736).
Hall, Catherine, 'Lawrence Stone's New Book, *Road to Divorce: England, 1530–1987* (Oxford: Oxford University Press, 1990)' (1992) 34(4) *Comparative Studies in Society and History* 782.
Hall, Lesley (ed), *Outspoken Women: An Anthology of Women's Writing on Sex, 1870–1960* (Routledge 2005).
Hall, Lesley, *Sex, Gender and Social Change in Britain Since 1880* (Macmillan Press 2000).
Halsbury, Lord (ed), *The Laws of England: Volume XVI* (Butterworth 1911).
Hamilton, Carolyn, *Family, Law and Religion* (Sweet and Maxwell 1995).
Hamilton, Elizabeth, *The Warwickshire Scandal* (Michael Russell 1999).
Hamilton, John Andrew, 'Wood, William Page, Baron Hatherley (1801–1881)', *Oxford Dictionary of National Biography* (2004) <https://doi.org/10.1093/ref:odnb/29901>.
Hamilton, Susan, '"A Whole Series of Frightful Cases": Domestic Violence, the Periodical Press and Victorian Feminist Writing' (2005) 13 *TOPIA* 89.
Hardy, Thomas, *Jude the Obscure* (first published 1895, Penguin 2019).

Hardy, Thomas, *Mayor of Casterbridge* (first published 1886, Penguin 2003).
Harvey, Geoffrey, 'Reading "The Forsyte Saga"' (1996) 26 *The Yearbook of English Studies* 127.
Hay, J.Roy, *The Origins of the Liberal Welfare Reforms 1906–1914* (Macmillan 1975).
Haynes, Edmund Sidney Pollock, *Divorce Problems of Today* (W Heffer and Sons 1912).
Haynes, Edmund Sidney Pollock, 'Lord Gorell's Matrimonial Causes Bill' (May 1921) *The English Review* 459.
Haynes, Edmund Sidney Pollock, *The Lawyer: A Conversation Piece* (Eyre and Spottiswoode 1951).
Hedley, Stephen, 'Keeping Contract in its Place—Balfour v Balfour and the Enforceability of Informal Agreements' (1985) 5(3) *Oxford Journal of Legal Studies* 391.
Hefling, Charles and Cynthia Shattuck (eds), *The Oxford Guide to The Book of Common Prayer: A Worldwide Survey* (Oxford University Press 2006).
Herbert, A.P., *Holy Deadlock* (Methuen 1934).
Herbert, A.P., *The Ayes Have It: the Story of the Marriage Bill* (Methuen 1935).
Herbert, A.P., *Uncommon Law* (Methuen 1937).
Helmholz, Richard H., *Roman Canon Law in Reformation* Law (Cambridge University Press 1990).
Helmholz, Richard H., 'Writs of Prohibition and Ecclesiastical Sanctions in the English Courts Christian' (1976) 60 *Minneapolis Law Review* 1011.
Herstein, Sheila, *A Mid-Victorian Feminist Barbara Leigh Smith Bodichon* (Yale University Press 1985).
Herstein, Sheila, 'The Langham Place Circle and Feminist Periodicals of the 1860s' (1993)26(1) *Victorian Periodicals Review* 24.
Heuston, Robert Francis Vere, *Lives of the Lord Chancellor 1885–1940* (Oxford University Press 1964).
Heydt, Colin, *Rethinking Mill's Ethics* (Continuum 2006).
Hibbert, Christopher, 'George IV (1762–1830)', *Oxford Dictionary of National Biography* (2004) <https://doi.org/10.1093/ref:odnb/10541>.
Hilton, Boyd, *A Mad, Bad, and Dangerous People?* (Oxford University Press 2006).
Himmelfarb, Gertrude, *On Liberty and Liberalism: The Case of John Stuart Mill* (Alfred A. Knopf 1974).
Hirschfeld, Julius, 'The Law of Divorce in England and Germany' (1897) 13 *Law Quarterly Review* 395.
Hoge, James and Clarke Olney (eds), *The Letters of Caroline Norton* (Ohio State University Press 1974).
Holcombe, Lee, *Wives and Property: Reform of the Married Women's Property Law in Nineteenth-Century England* (University of Toronto Press 1983).
Holmes, Ann Sumner, ' "Don't Frighten the Horses": the Russell Divorce Case' in George Robb and Nancy Erber (eds), *Disorder in the Court: Trials and Sexual Conflict at the Turn of the Century* (New York University Press 1999).
Holmes, Ann Sumner, *The Church of England and Divorce in the Twentieth Century: Legalism and Grace* (Routledge 2017).
Holmes, Ann Sumner, 'The Double Standard in the English Divorce Laws, 1857–1923' (1995) 20(2) *Law and Social Inquiry* 601.
Hoppen, K. Theodore, *The Mid-Victorian Generation 1846–1886* (Oxford University Press 2003).
Horstman, Allen, *Victorian Divorce* (St Martin's Press 1985).
Horwitz, Morton, *The Transformation of American Law, 1780–1860* (Harvard University Press 1977).

Horwitz, Morton, *The Transformation of American Law, 1870–1960: The Crisis of Legal Orthodoxy* (Oxford University Press 1992).

Holton, Sandra Stanley, 'Elmy, Elizabeth Clarke Wolstenholme (1833–1918)', *Oxford Dictionary of National Biography* (2004) <https://doi.org/10.1093/ref:odnb/38638>.

House of Lords, *The Sessional Papers, Volume 44* (1850).

Howard, Scott and Sara van den Berg (eds), *The Divorce Tracts of John Milton* (Duquesne University Press 2010).

Huddleston, Joan, *Caroline Norton's Defence: English Laws for Women in the Nineteenth Century* (Academy Chicago 1982).

Hurst, Willard, '*The Transformation of American Law, 1780–1860* by Morton J. Horwitz' (1977) 21(2) *The American Journal of Legal History* 175.

Inglis, Brian, *Abdication* (Hodder and Stoughton 1966).

Ingram, Martin, *Church Courts, Sex and Marriage in England 1570–1640* (Cambridge University Press 1987).

Isba, Anne, *Gladstone and Women* (Hambledon Continuum 2006).

Israel, Kali, *Names and Stories: Emilia Dilke and Victorian Culture* (Oxford University Press 1999).

Jackson, Joseph, *The Formation and Annulment of Marriage* (Butterworths 1969).

James, Viscount of Stair, *The Institutions of the Law of Scotland: Deduced from its Originals, and Collated with the Civil, Canon, and Feudal Laws, and with the Customs of Neighbouring Nations* (University Presses of Edinburgh and Glasgow 1981).

James, Susan, 'Parr, William, Marquess of Northampton (1513–1571)', *Oxford Dictionary of National Biography* (2004) <https://doi.org/10.1093/ref:odnb/21405>.

Jenkins, Roy, *Sir Charles Dilke: A Victorian Tragedy* (Collins 1958).

Jenkins, Roy, *Gladstone* (Random House 1997).

Johnson, Paul E., 'Looking Back at Social History' (2011) 39(2) *Reviews in American History* 379.

Jones, Gareth and Vivienne Jones, 'Campbell, John, First Baron Campbell of St Andrews (1779–1861)', *Oxford Dictionary of National Biography* (2004) <https://doi.org/10.1093/ref:odnb/4521>.

Judicature Commission: First Report of the Commissioners (1868–9) BPP vol 25.

Kamm, Josephine, *John Stuart Mill in Love* (Gordon and Cremonesi 1977).

Kelman, Mark, *A Guide to Critical Legal Studies* (Harvard University Press 1987).

Khetarpal, Suraj Parkash, 'The Modern Concept of Cruelty (A Comparative Study)' (1964) 6(2) *Malaya Law Review* 303.

Kinzer, Bruce, Ann Robson and John Robson, *A Moralist in and Out of Parliament: John Stuart Mill at Westminster, 1865–1868* (University of Toronto Press 1992).

Lacey, Candida Ann (ed), *Barbara Leigh Smith Bodichon and the Langham Place Group* (Routledge and Kegan Paul 1987).

The Lambeth Conference: Resolutions Archive from 1908 (Anglican Communion Office 2005).

Laqueur, Thomas, 'The Queen Caroline Affair: Politics as Art in the Reign of George IV' (1982) 54(3) *Journal of Modern History* 417.

Laslett, Peter, Karla Oosterveen and Richard M. Smith (eds), *Bastardy and its Comparative History* (Harvard University Press 1980).

Lathbury, Daniel Conner (ed), *Correspondence on Church and Religion of William Ewart Gladstone, Volume 2* (The Macmillan Company 1910).

Law Amendment Society, 'Divorce' (1845) 1(2) *Law Review* 353.

Law Amendment Society, 'Fusion of Law and Equity' (1852) 16(1) *Law Review* 184.
Law Commission, *Family Law The Ground for Divorce*, No 192 (1990).
Lee, Bong Ho, *Divorce Law Reform in England* (Peter Owen 1974).
Leneman, Leah, *Alienated Affections: The Scottish Experience of Divorce and Separation, 1684–1830* (Edinburgh University Press 1998).
Lewis, Andrew and David Ibbetson (eds), *The Roman Law Tradition* (Cambridge University Press 1994).
Lewis, Andrew and Michael Lobban (eds), *Law and History* (Oxford University Press 2004).
Lewis, George, 'Marriage and Divorce' (May 1885) 37(221) *Fortnightly Review* 640.
Lindley, Dwight and Francis Mineka (eds), *The Later Letters of John Stuart Mill, Volume XIV* (Routledge and Kegan Paul 1972).
Lobban, Michael, 'Henry Brougham and Law Reform' (2000) 115 *The English Historical Review* 1184.
Lobban, Michael, 'Preparing for Fusion: Reforming the Nineteenth Century Court of Chancery: Part I' (2004) 22(2) *Law and History Review* 389.
Lobban, Michael, 'Preparing for Fusion: Reforming the Nineteenth Century Court of Chancery: Part II' (2004) 22(3) *Law and History Review* 565.
Loewenstein, Mark, 'Jewish Divorce and the Secular Law' (1990) 39(1) *Judaism* 7.
MacFarlane, Alan, *Marriage and Love in England 1300–1840* (Backwell 1986).
MacMillan, Catharine, *Mistakes in Contract Law* (Hart Publishing 2010).
Macqueen, John Fraser, *A Practical Treatise on the Appellate Jurisdiction of the House of Lords and Privy Council Together with the Practice on Parliamentary Divorce* (A. Maxwell and Son 1842).
Macqueen, John Fraser, *A Practical Treatise on Divorce and Matrimonial Jurisdiction under the Act of 1857 and New Orders* (W. Maxwell 1858).
Macqueen, John Fraser, *A Practical Treatise on the Law of Marriage, Divorce, and Legitimacy: As Administered in the Divorce Court and in the House of Lords* (W. Maxwell 1860).
Macqueen, John Fraser, *The Rights and Liabilities of Husband and Wife* (T. and J.W. Johnson 1848).
Maddox, Peter, 'The Background of, and Contemporary Reaction to, the Matrimonial Causes Act, 1857' (1987) 18 *Cambrian Law Review* 62.
Manchester, A.H., 'The Principles and Rules of Ecclesiastical Law and Matrimonial Relief' (1968) 6(1) *Sydney Law Review* 25.
Manson, Edward, *Builders of Our Law During the Reign of Queen Victoria* (2nd edn, Horace Cox 1904).
Marshall, Rosalind, 'Bowes, Mary Eleanor, Countess of Strathmore and Kinghorne (1749–1800)', *Oxford Dictionary of National Biography* (2004) <https://doi.org/10.1093/ref:odnb/3056>.
Martin, John, 'Weldon, Georgina (1837–1914)', *Oxford Dictionary of National Biography*, 2004 <https://doi.org/10.1093/ref:odnb/53148>.
Martineau, Harriet, *Harriet Martineau's Autobiography, Volume 1* (first published 1877, Cambridge University Press 2010).
Marwick, Arthur, *The Deluge* (Bodley Head 1965).
Mason, Michael, *The Making of Victorian Sexuality* (Oxford University Press 1994).
Matthew, Henry Colin Gray, *The Gladstone Diaries, Volume V* (Oxford University Press 1978).
McCalmon, Ian, 'Unrespectable Radicalism: Infidels and Pornography in Early Nineteenth-Century London' (1984) 104 *Past and Present* 74.

McCarthy, Conor (ed), *Love, Sex and Marriage* (Routledge 2004).

McClain, Charles, 'Legal Change and Class Interests: A Review Essay on The Transformation of American Law' (1980) 68(2) *California Law Review* 382.

McGregor, Oliver Ross, *Divorce in England* (Heinemann 1957).

McLaren, Dorothy, 'The Marriage Act of 1653: Its Influence on the Parish Registers' (1974) 28(2) *Population Studies* 319.

Meacham, Standish, *Lord Bishop: The Life of Samuel Wilberforce* (Harvard University Press 1970).

Mendus, Susan, 'John Stuart Mill and Harriet Taylor on Women and Marriage' (1994) 6(2) *Utilitas* 287.

Menefee, Samuel, *Wives for Sale* (Basil Blackwell Publisher 1981).

Metzger, Ernest (ed), *A Companion to Justinian's Institutes* (Cornell University Press 1998).

Milsom, Stroud Francis Charles, *A Natural History of the Common Law* (Columbia University Press 2003).

Milsom, Stroud Francis Charles, *Historical Foundations of the Common Law* (2nd edn, Butterworths 1981).

Milsom, Stroud Francis Charles, *The Legal Framework of English Feudalism* (Cambridge University Press 1976).

Mineka, Francis and Dwight Lindley (eds), *The Later Letters of John Stuart Mill 1849–1873 Part I* (University of Toronto Press 1972) vol 14.

Mitchell, Charles and Paul Mitchell (eds), *Landmark Cases in the Law of Contract* (Hart Publishing 2008).

Mitchell, Leslie George, *Lord Melbourne 1779–1848* (Oxford University Press 1997).

Mitchell, Sally, *Frances Power Cobbe: Victorian Feminist, Journalist, Reformer* (University of Virginia Press 2004).

Minutes of Evidence Taken Before the Royal Commission on Divorce and Matrimonial Causes, Volume 1 (1912) Cd 6479.

Minutes of Evidence Taken Before the Royal Commission on Divorce and Matrimonial Causes, Volume 2 (1912) Cd 6480.

Minutes of Evidence Taken Before the Royal Commission on Divorce and Matrimonial Causes, Volume 3 (1912) Cd 6481.

Monk, Ray, *Bertrand Russell: The Spirit of Solitude* (Jonathan Cape 1996).

Monypenny, William Flavelle and George Earle Buckle (eds), *The Life of Benjamin Disraeli, Earl of Beaconsfield, Volume 6* (The Macmillan Company 1920).

Moore, Doris Langley, *Ada: Countess of Lovelace* (Camelot Press 1977).

Moore, George, *Esther Waters* (first published 1894, Oxford University Press 2012).

Moorehead, Caroline, *Bertrand Russell* (Sinclair-Stevenson 1992).

Moyse, Cordelia Ann, 'Reform of Marriage and Divorce Law in England and Wales 1909–1937' (DPhil thesis, University of Cambridge 1996).

Munby, James, 'Marriage from the 18th to 21st Century' (The Incorporated Council of Law Reporting Annual Lecture for 2013, the Law Society of England and Wales) (London, 25 April 2013).

Munsell, Darrell, 'Clinton, Henry Pelham Fiennes Pelham-, Fifth Duke of Newcastle under Lyme,' *Oxford Dictionary of National Biography* (2004) <https://doi.org/10.1093/ref:odnb/5686>.

Murdoch, Lydia, *Daily Life of Victorian Women* (Greenwood 2014).

Murray, Jacqueline, *Love, Marriage and Family in the Middle Ages* (University of Toronto Press 2010).

Musson, Anthony and Chantal Stebbings (eds), *Making Legal History: Approaches and Methodologies* (Cambridge University Press 2012).

Nardo, Anna, *George Eliot's Dialogue with John Milton* (University of Missouri Press 2003).

Newcombe, David Gordon, *Henry VIII and the English Reformation* (Routledge 1995).

Norman, Edward Robert, *Church and Society in England: 1770–1970* (Oxford University Press 1976).

Norton, Caroline, *English Laws for Women in the Nineteenth Century* (J. Wertheimer and Co. 1854).

Norton, Caroline, *A Letter to the Queen on Lord Chancellor Cranworth's Marriage and Divorce Bill* (Longman, Brown, Green, and Longmans 1855).

Norton, Caroline, *A Letter to the Right Reverend the Lord Bishop of Exeter on the Custody of Infants* (Edward Churton 1839).

Norton, Caroline, *A Plain Letter to the Lord Chancellor on the Infant Custody Bill James* (Ridgway 1839).

Norton, Caroline, *The Separation of Mother and Child by the Law of Custody of Infants, Considered* (Roake and Varty 1838).

Nourse, G.B., 'Law Reform under the Commonwealth and Protectorate' (1959) 75 *Law Quarterly Review* 512.

Ogilvie, Robert Maxwell, *Latin and Greek: A History of the Influence of the Classics on English Life from 1600 to 1918* (Routledge and Kegan Paul 1964).

Orme, Eliza, 'Hunter, William Alexander (1844–1898)', *Oxford Dictionary of National Biography* (2004) <https://doi.org/10.1093/ref:odnb/14236>.

Outhwaite, Richard Brian, *Clandestine Marriage in England 1500–1850* (Hambledon Press 1995).

Outhwaite, Richard Brian, *The Rise and Fall of the English Ecclesiastical Courts 1500–1860* (Cambridge University Press 2006).

Parker, Stephen, *Informal Marriage, Cohabitation and the Law 1750–1989* (Macmillan 1990).

Parry, Jonathan Philip, *Democracy and Religion: Gladstone and the Liberal Party 1867–1875* (Cambridge University Press 1986).

Parry, Jonathan Philip, *The Rise and Fall of Liberal Government in Victorian Britain* (Yale University Press 1993).

Paton, George Campbell Henderson (ed), *An Introduction to Scottish Legal History* (Stair Society 1958).

Paz, Denis G., *Popular Anti-Catholicism in Mid-Victorian England* (Stanford University Press 1992).

Pedersen, Frederik, *Marriage Disputes in Medieval England* (Hambledon Press 2000).

Peel, Edwin and James Goudkamp, *Winfield and Jolowicz on Tort* (19th edn, Thomson Reuters 2014).

Perkin, Joan, *Victorian Women* (John Murray 1993).

Perkin, Joan, *Women and Marriage in Nineteenth-Century England* (Routledge 1989).

Perkins, Jane Gray, *The Life of the Honourable Mrs. Norton* (Henry Holt and Company 1909).

Perkins, Willis, 'The English Judicature Act of 1873' (1914) 12(4) *Michigan Law Review* 277.

Phegley, Jennifer, *Courtship and Marriage in Victorian England* (ABC-CLIO 2012).

Phillips, Roderick, *Putting Asunder: A History of Divorce in Western Society* (Cambridge University Press 1988).

Phillips, Roderick, *Untying the Knot: A Short History of Divorce* (Cambridge University Press 1991).

Polden, Patrick, *A History of the County Court 1846–1971* (Cambridge University Press 1999).

Polden, Patrick, 'Hannen, James, Baron Hannen (1821–1894)', *Oxford Dictionary of National Biography* (2004) <https://doi.org/10.1093/ref:odnb/12216>.

Polden, Patrick, 'Mingling the Waters: Personalities, Politics and the Making of the Supreme Court of Judicature' (2002) 61(3) *Cambridge Law Journal* 575.

Poovey, Mary, *Uneven Developments: The Ideological Work of Gender in Mid-Victorian England* (Virago Press 1988).

Porter, Roy, Helen Nicholson, and Bridget Bennett (eds), *Women, Madness, and Spiritualism: Georgina Weldon and Louisa Lowe, Volume 1* (Routledge 2003).

Prichard, Michael J. and David Eryl Corbet Yale (eds), *Hale and Fleetwood on Admiralty Jurisdiction* (Selden Society 1993).

Probert, Rebecca, 'Hyde v Hyde: Defining or Defending Marriage?' (2007) 19 *Child and Family Law Quarterly* 322.

Probert, Rebecca, *Marriage Law and Practice in the Long Eighteenth Century* (Cambridge University Press 2009).

Probert, Rebecca, '*R v Hall* and the Changing Perceptions of the Crime of Bigamy' (2019) 39 *Legal Studies* 1.

Probert, Rebecca, *The Changing Legal Regulation of Cohabitation: From Fornicators to Family, 1600–2010* (Cambridge University Press 2012).

Probert, Rebecca, 'The Controversy of Equality and the Matrimonial Causes Act 1923' (1999) 11 *Child and Family Law Quarterly* 33.

Probert, Rebecca, 'The Double Standard of Morality in the Divorce and Matrimonial Causes Act 1857' (1999) 28 *Anglo-American Law Review* 73.

Prochaska, Franklyn Kimmel, *Women and Philanthropy in Nineteenth-Century England* (Oxford University Press 1980).

Purvis, June, *Christabel Pankhurst: A Biography* (Routledge 2018).

Qureshi, Mohammed Ahmed, *Marriage and Matrimonial Remedies: A Uniform Civil Code for India* (Concept Publishing Company 1977).

Radzinowicz, Leon, *A History of English Criminal Law and its Administration from 1750, Volume I* (Stevens and Sons 1948).

Rayden, William, *Practice and Law in the Divorce Division of the High Court of Justice and On Appeal Therefrom* (Butterworth 1910).

Rawson, Beryl (ed), *Marriage Divorce and Children in Ancient Rome* (Oxford University Press 1991).

Read, Donald, *The Age of Urban Democracy: England 1868–1914* (Routledge 2014).

Redesdale, Lord and Cardinal Manning, *The Infallible Church and Communion under One Kind* (Lane and Son 1875).

Redesdale, Lord, *The Law of Scripture against Divorce* (Rivingtons 1856).

Redmayne, Sharon, 'The Matrimonial Causes Act 1937: A Lesson in the Art of Compromise' (1993) 13(2) *Oxford Journal of Legal Studies* 183.

Reeves, Richard, *John Stuart Mill: Victorian Firebrand* (Atlantic Books 2007).

Report of the Royal Commission on Divorce and Matrimonial Causes (1912) Cd 6478.

Rex, Richard, *Henry VIII and the English Reformation* (Macmillan 1993).

Reynolds, Philip L., *How Marriage Became One of the Sacraments: The Sacramental Theology of Marriage from Its Medieval Origins to the Council of Trent* (Cambridge University Press 2016).

Rheinstein, Max, *Marriage Stability, Divorce and the Law* (University of Chicago Press 1972).

Riga, Peter, 'Divorce in the Justinian Code: Harbinger of Things to Come?' (1986-7) 8 *Whittier Law Review* 917.

Rigg, James Macmullen, 'Butt, Sir Charles Parker (1830-1892)', *Oxford Dictionary of National Biography*, Oxford University Press (2004) <https://doi.org/10.1093/ref:odnb/4220>.

Rigg, J.M., 'Wilde, James Plaisted, Baron Penzance (1816-1899)', *Oxford Dictionary of National Biography* (2004) < https://doi.org/10.1093/ref:odnb/29397>.

Robb, George and Nancy Erber (eds), *Disorder in the Court: Trials and Sexual Conflict at the Turn of the Century* (New York University Press 1999).

Robson, Ann, 'No Laughing Matter: John Stuart Mill's Establishment of Women's Suffrage as a Parliamentary Question' (1990) 2(1) *Utilitas* 88.

Robson, John (ed), *Essays on Equality, Law, and Education, Collected Works*, vol 21 (University of Toronto Press 1984).

Robson, John (ed), *Essays on Politics and Society*, vol 18 (University of Toronto Press 1977).

Rosen, Lionel, 'Cruelty in Matrimonial Causes' (1949) 12(3) *The Modern Law Review* 324.

Rosman, Doreen, *The Evolution of the English Churches, 1500-2000* (Cambridge University Press 2003).

Rowntree, Griselda and Norman Carrier, 'The Resort to Divorce in England and Wales, 1858-1957' (1958) 11(3) *Population Studies* 188.

Royal Commission on Loss of Life at Sea: Final Report (1887) BPP vol 63, 5227.

Rubin, Gerry and David Sugarman (eds), *Law, Economy and Society, 1750-1914: Essays in the History of English Law* (Professional Books 1984).

Russell, Bertrand, *Marriage and Morals* (George Allen & Unwin 1929).

Russell, Bertrand, *The Autobiography of Bertrand Russell: 1872-1914* (George Allen & Unwin 1967).

Russell, Earl, *Divorce* (Heinemann 1912).

Russell, Earl, *My Life and Adventures* (Cassell 1923).

Russell, Penelope, 'Matrimonial Causes Act 1857' in Erika Rackley and Rosemary Auchmuty (eds), *Women's Legal Landmarks: Celebrating the History of Women and Law in the UK and Ireland* (Hart Publishing 2018).

Sandars, Thomas Collett, *The Institutes of Justinian* (Longmans, Green and Co 1883).

Sanders, Lloyd Charles, 'Mitford, John Thomas Freeman, First Earl of Redesdale (1805-1886)', *Oxford Dictionary of National Biography* (2004) <https://doi.org/10.1093/ref:odnb/18858>.

Sarat, Austin and Jonathan Simon (eds), *Cultural Analysis, Cultural Studies, and the Law: Moving Beyond Legal Realism* (Duke University Press 2003).

Savage, Gail, 'Divorce and the Law in England and France Prior to the First World War' (1988) 21(3) *Journal of Social History* 499.

Savage, Gail, '"…Equality from the Masculine Point of View…": The 2nd Earl Russell and Divorce Law Reform in England' (1996) 16 *Russell: The Journal of Bertrand Russell Studies* 67.

Savage, Gail, 'Erotic Stories and Public Decency: Newspaper Reporting of Divorce Proceedings in England' (1998) 41(2) *The Historical Journal* 511.

Savage, Gail, 'More than One Mrs Mir Anwaruddin: Islamic Divorce and Christian Marriage in Early Twentieth- Century London' (2008) 47(2) *Journal of British Studies* 348.

Savage, Gail, 'The Divorce Court and the Queen's/ King's Proctor: Legal Patriarchy and the Sanctity of Marriage in England, 1861-1937' (1989) 24(1) *Historical Papers* 210.

Savage, Gail, '"…The Instrument of an Animal Function": Marital Rape and Sexual Cruelty in the Divorce Court, 1858-1908' in Lucy Delap, Ben Griffin, and Abigail Wills (eds), *The Politics of Domestic Authority in Britain since 1800* (Palgrave Macmillan 2009).

Savage, Gail, '"The Magistrates are Men": Working-Class Marital Conflict and Appeals from the Magistrates' Court to the Divorce Court after 1895' in George Robb and Nancy Erber (eds), Disorder in the Court: *Trials and Sexual Conflict at the Turn of the Century* (New York University Press 1999).

Savage, Gail, 'The Operation of the 1857 Divorce Act, 1860–1910 a Research Note' (1983) 16(4) *Journal of Social History* 103.

Savage, Gail, 'They Would if They Could: Class, Gender, and Popular Representation of English Divorce Litigation, 1858–1908' (2011) 36(2) *Journal of Family History* 173.

Savage, Gail, '"What Will Most Tend towards Morality": Sir Cresswell Cresswell and the Divorce Court, 1858–1863' in James Gregory, Daniel J.R. Grey, and Annika Bautz (eds), *Judgment in the Victorian Age* (Routledge 2019).

Savage, Gail, '"The Wilful Communication of a Loathsome Disease" : Marital Conflict and Veneral Disease in Victorian England' (1990) 34(1) *Victorian Studies* 35.

Scarisbrick, J.J., *Henry VIII* (Eyre Methuen 1968).

Schellekens, Jona, 'Courtship, the Clandestine Marriage Act, and Illegitimate Fertility in England' (1995) 25(3) *The Journal of Interdisciplinary History* 433.

Schneider, Wendie Ellen, 'Secrets and Lies: The Queen's Proctor and Judicial Investigation of Party Controlled Narratives' (2002) 27(3) *Law & Social Inquiry* 449.

Schofield, Philip and Jonathan Harris (eds), *"Legislator of the World": Writings on Codification, Law, and Education* (Oxford University Press 1998).

Schofield, Philip, *Utility and Democracy: The Political Thought of Jeremy Bentham* (Oxford University Press 2006).

Scotland, Nigel, *John Bird Sumner: Evangelical Archbishop* (Gracewing 1995)

Scotland, Nigel, 'John Bird Sumner in Parliament' (1990) 7(2) *Anvil* 141.

Scottish Law Commission, *Divorce: The Grounds Considered*, Cmnd 3256 (1967).

Searle, Geoffrey, *A New England?: Peace and War 1886–1918* (Oxford University Press 2004).

Shanley, Mary Lyndon, *Feminism, Marriage, and the Law in Victorian England, 1850–1895* (Princeton University Press 1989).

Shanley, Mary Lyndon, 'Marital Slavery and Friendship: John Stuart Mill's The Subjection of Women' (1981) 9(2) *Political Theory* 229.

Shanley, Mary Lyndon, '"One Must Ride Behind:" Married Women's Rights and the Divorce Act of 1857' (1982) 25(3) *Victorian Studies* 355.

Shannon, Richard, *Gladstone, Volume 1* (Hamish Hamilton 1982).

Shannon, R.W., 'The Countess of Strathmore versus Bowes' (1923) 1(5) *Canadian Bar Review* 425.

Shapiro, Barbara, 'Law Reform in Seventeenth Century England' (1975) 19(4) *American Journal of Legal History* 288.

Shapiro, Fred and Jane Garry, *Trial and Error: An Oxford Anthology of Legal Stories* (Oxford University Press 1998).

Shelford, Leonard, *A Practical Treatise of the Law of Marriage and Divorce* (Sweet, Stevens, Norton 1841).

Shiman, Lillian Lewis, *Women and Leadership in Nineteenth-Century England* (St Martin's Press 1992).

Skorupski, John (ed), *The Cambridge Companion to Mill* (Cambridge University Press 1998).

Smart, Carol, *Feminism and the Power of Law* (Routledge 1989).

Smith, Ernest Anthony, 'Caroline (1768–1821)', *Oxford Dictionary of National Biography* (2004) <https://doi.org/10.1093/ref:odnb/4722>.

Smith, Harold L., *The British Women's Suffrage Campaign, 1866–1928* (2nd edn, Longman 2007).
Smith, Keith John Michael and John P.S. McLaren, 'History's Living Legacy: An Outline of Modern Historiography of the Common Law' (2001) 21 *Legal Studies* 251.
Snell, Keith David Malcolm, *Annals of the Labouring Poor: Social Change and Agrarian England, 1660– 1900* (Cambridge University Press 1985).
Sokol, Mary, *Bentham, Law and Marriage: A Utilitarian Code of Law in Historical Contexts* (Continuum International Publishing Group 2011).
Sokol, Mary, 'Blackstone and Bentham on the Law of Marriage' in Wilfrid Prest (ed), *Blackstone and His Commentaries: Biography, Law, History* (Hart Publishing 2009).
Sokol, Mary, 'Jeremy Bentham on Love and Marriage: A Utilitarian Proposal on Short-Term Marriage' (2009) 30(1) *Journal of Legal History* 1.
Spalding, James, 'The *Reformatio Legum Ecclesiasticarum* of 1552 and the Furthering of Discipline in England' (1970) 39(2) *Church History* 162.
Spalding, James, *The Reformation of the Ecclesiastical Laws of England 1552* (Sixteenth Century Journal Publishers 1992).
The Special and General Reports made to His Majesty by the Commissioners Appointed to Inquire into the Practice and Jurisdiction of the Ecclesiastical Courts in England and Wales (1831–2) BPP vol 24, 1–78.
Squibb, George Drewry, *Doctors' Commons: A History of the College of Advocates and Doctors of Law* (Oxford University Press 1977).
Squibb, George Drewry, *The High Court of Chivalry: A Study of the Civil Law in England* (Oxford University Press 1959)
St Helier, Lady Mary, *Memories of Fifty Years* (Edward Arnold 1909).
Stannard, Martin, 'Waugh, Evelyn Arthur St John (1903–1966)', *Oxford Dictionary of National Biography* (2004) <https://doi.org/10.1093/ref:odnb/36788>.
Staves, Susan, *Married Women's Separate Property in England, 1660–1833* (Harvard University Press 1990).
Stead, William Thomas, 'The Maiden Tribute of Modern Babylon' in Antony E. Simpson (ed), *The Maiden Tribute of Modern Babylon: The Report of the Secret Commission* (True Bill Press 2007) 51–206.
Stebbings, Chantal, *Legal Foundations of Tribunals in Nineteenth Century England* (Cambridge University Press 2006).
Stebbings, Chantal, *The Private Trustee in Victorian England* (Cambridge University Press 2002).
Steele, David, 'Law, Edward, First Earl of Ellenborough (1790–1871)', *Oxford Dictionary of National Biography* (2004) <https://doi.org/10.1093/ref:odnb/16143>.
Stein, Peter, *Roman Law in European History* (Cambridge University Press 1999).
Stephen, Herbert, 'Jeune, Francis Henry, Baron St Helier (1843–1905)', *Oxford Dictionary of National Biography* (2004) <https://doi.org/10.1093/ref:odnb/34188>.
Stephens, William Richard Wood (ed), *A Memoir of the Right Hon. William Page Wood, Baron Hatherley, Volume 2* (Richard Bentley & Son 1883).
Stetson, Dorothy, *A Woman's Issue: the Politics of Family Law Reform in England* (Greenwood Press 1982).
Stretton, Tim and Krista Kesselring (eds), *Married Women and the Law: Coverture in England and the Common Law World* (McGill Queen's University Press 2013).
Stone, Lawrence, *Broken Lives: Separation and Divorce in England 1660–1857* (Oxford University Press 1993).
Stone, Lawrence, *Road to Divorce: England 1530–1987* (Oxford University Press 1990).

184 Bibliography

Stone, Lawrence, *Uncertain Unions and Broken Lives: Marriage and Divorce in England, 1660–1857* (Oxford University Press 1995).

Stopes, Marie, *Married Love* (first published 1918, Oxford University Press 2004).

Summerscale, Emma, *Mrs Robinson's Disgrace: The Private Diary of a Victorian Lady* (Bloomsbury 2012).

Surtees, Virginia, *A Beckford Inheritance: The Lady Lincoln Scandal* (Michael Russell 1977).

Sutherland, John, *The Longman Companion to Victorian Divorce* (Routledge 2009).

Swain, Warren, '"A Little of the Way Place": the Civilians in England' (2013) 1 *Pandora's Box* 27.

Swain, Warren, *The Law of Contract 1670–1870* (Cambridge University Press 2015).

Tait, Allison Anna, 'The Beginning of the End of Coverture: A Reappraisal of the Married Woman's Separate Estate' (2014) 26(2) *Yale Journal of Law and Feminism* 166.

Taylor, Alan John Percivale, *Essays in English History* (Pelican 1976).

Tenth Annual Report of the Registrar-General of Births, Deaths and Marriages in England (Longman, Brown, Green, and Longmans 1852).

Thomas, Joseph Anthony Charles, *Textbook of Roman Law* (North-Holland Publishing Company 1976).

Thomas, Joseph Anthony Charles, *The Institutes of Justinian* (North-Holland Publishing Company 1975).

Thompson, Francis Michael Longstreth, *English Landed Society in the Nineteenth Century* (Routledge and Keegan Paul 1971).

Treggiari, Susan, *Roman Marriage* (Oxford University Press 1991).

Treherne, Philip, *A Plaintiff in Person: The Life of Mrs Weldon* (William Heinemann 1923).

Trevor-Roper, Hugh, 'The Elizabethan Aristocracy: An Anatomy Anatomized' (1951) 3(3) *The Economic History Review* 279.

Urbinati, Nadia and Alex Zakaras (eds), *J.S. Mill's Political Thought: A Bicentennial Reassessment* (Cambridge University Press 2007).

van Wingerden, Sophia, *The Women's Suffrage Movement in Britain, 1866–1928* (Palgrave Macmillan 1999).

Veall, Donald, *The Popular Movement for Law Reform, 1640 to 1660* (Oxford University Press 1970).

Vieira, Ryan, *Time and Politics: Parliament and the Culture of Modernity in Britain and the British World* (Oxford University Press 2015).

Vincent, John Russell (ed), *Disraeli, Derby and the Conservative Party: Journals and Memoirs of Edward Henry, Lord Stanley, 1849–1869* (Harvester Press 1978).

Virdi, P.K., *The Grounds for Divorce in Hindu and English Law: A Study in Comparative Law* (Motilal Banarsidass 1972).

Waddams, Stephen, 'Damages for Wrongful Death: Has Lord Campbell's Act Outlived Its Usefulness' (1984) 47 *The Modern Law Review* 437.

Waddams, Stephen, 'English Matrimonial Law on the Eve of Reform (1828–57)' (2000) 21(2) *Journal of Legal History* 59.

Waddams, Stephen, 'Equity in English Contract Law: the Impact of the Judicature Act (1873–75)' (2012) 33(2) *Journal of Legal History* 185.

Waddams, Stephen, *Law, Politics and the Church of England: The Career of Stephen Lushington* (Cambridge University Press 1992).

Waddams, Stephen, 'Lushington, Stephen (1782–1873),' *Oxford Dictionary of National Biography* (2004) <https://doi.org/10.1093/ref:odnb/17213>.

Wadlow, Christopher, 'The Incredible Affair of the Secret Santa' (2012) 7(12) *Journal of Intellectual Property Law and Practice* 1.

Wagner, John, *Voices of Victorian England: Contemporary Accounts of Daily Life* (Greenwood 2014).

Walkowitz, Judith, *Prostitution and Victorian Society: Women, Class and the State* (Cambridge University Press 1980).
Ward, Ian, *Law and Literature: Possibilities and Perspectives* (Cambridge University Press 1995).
Ward, Ian, *Sex, Crime and Literature in Victorian England* (Hart Publishing 2014).
Watson, Alan, Theodor Mommsen, and Paul Krueger (eds), *The Digest of Justinian, Volume 1* (University of Pennsylvania Press 1985).
Watson, Alan, Theodor Mommsen, and Paul Krueger (eds), *The Digest of Justinian, Volume 2* (University of Pennsylvania Press 1985).
Watson, Alan, Theodor Mommsen, and Paul Krueger (eds), *The Digest of Justinian, Volume 3* (University of Pennsylvania Press 1985).
Watson, Alan, Theodor Mommsen, and Paul Krueger (eds), *The Digest of Justinian, Volume 4* (University of Pennsylvania Press 1985).
Watson, Ian, 'Mollie, Countess Russell' (2003) 23 *Russell: The Journal of Bertrand Russell Studies* 65.
Watt, George, *The Fallen Woman in the Nineteenth-Century English Novel* (Croom Helm 1984).
Waugh, Evelyn, *A Handful of Dust* (Chapman and Hall 1934).
Weil, Rachel, *Political Passions: Gender, the Family and Political Argument in England 1680–1714* (Manchester University Press 1999).
White, G. Edward, 'From Realism to Critical Legal Studies: A Truncated Intellectual History' (1986) 40 *Southwestern Law Journal* 819.
Wilberforce, Reginald (ed), *Life of Samuel Wilberforce, with Selections from his Diary and Correspondence* (John Murray 1881).
Wilken, Sean and Karim Ghaly, *The Law of Waiver, Variation and Estoppel* (Oxford University Press 2012).
Williams, Melanie, *Secrets and Laws: Collected Essays in Law, Lives, and Literature* (UCL Press 2005).
Williams, Melanie, 'The Law of Marriage in *Jude the Obscure*' (1996) 5 *Nottingham Law Journal* 168.
Witte, John, *From Sacrament to Contract: Marriage, Religion, and Law in the Western Tradition* (2nd edn, Westminster John Knox Press 2012).
Wolf, Naomi, *Outrages: Sex, Censorship and the Criminalisation of Love* (Virago 2019).
Wolfram, Sybil, 'Divorce in England 1700–1857' (1985) 5(2) *Oxford Journal of Legal Studies* 155.
Wolfram, Sybil, *In-Laws and Outlaws; Kinship and Marriage in England* (St Martin's Press 1987).
Woodhouse, Margaret K., 'The Marriage and Divorce Bill of 1857' (1959) 3(3) *American Journal of Legal History* 260.
Woodward, Llewellyn, *The Age of Reform 1815–1870* (Oxford University Press 1938).
Worthington, Sarah, *Equity* (2nd edn, Oxford University Press 2006).
Wright, Danaya, 'Untying the Knot: An Analysis of the English Divorce and Matrimonial Causes Court Records, 1858–1866' (2004) 38 *University of Richmond Law Review* 903.
Wright, Maureen, *Elizabeth Wolstenholme Elmy and the Victorian Feminist Movement: The Biography of an Insurgent Woman* (Manchester University Press 2011).
Wroath, John, *Until They are Seven: The Origins of Women's Legal Rights* (Waterside Press 1998).
Zaher, Claudia, 'When a Woman's Marital Status Determined Her Legal Status: A Research Guide on the Common Law Doctrine of Coverture' (2002) 94(3) *Law Library Journal* 459.

Index

Abdy, W. 56
'Act for the Illegitimisation of the Children of the Lady Anne Roos, An' 20
Act of Supremacy, 1534 15
'Act touching Marriages and the registration thereof; and also touching Births and Burials, An' 18
Addison, E. 24, 80–81
Addison, J. 24, 80–81
Addison/Campbell Divorce Act 1801 24
adultery 24, 68; Campbell Commission on 51, 52–53; in case of Caroline Norton 39–40; in case of Earl of Ellenborough divorce 33–35; defined in the case of Lord and Lady Byron 26; double standard on 60–61, 79–80; granting divorce in spite of petitioner's 130–132; incestuous 24, 79–82; innocent 131; under the Matrimonial Causes Act 1857 75–79; petitioner's, as bar to divorce 106–107; Scots law of divorce on 30; statutory damages recovery in cases of 65–66
affinity, marriages of 80–81
Alexander v Alexander and Amos 76
alimony 51, 66
Anson, W. R. 145
Asquith, H. H. 143, 147

Badcock v Badcock and Chamberlain 97
Baldwin, S. 153
Balfour, F. 144
Barnes, H. G. 147
Barnes, J. G. 138–141, 142
Barnes, R. 152

bars to divorce under the Matrimonial Causes Act 1857 97–109; collusion 97–100; condonation 103–106, 131; connivance 100–103; petitioner's adultery 106–107; recrimination and unreasonable delay 107–109
Beaumont, Baron 47, 48
Belcher v Belcher 53
Bell v Bell and Marquis of Anglesey 95, 96
Bennett, A. 140
Bentham, J. 30–31, 63
Bergami, B. 28
bestiality 86–87
Bethel, R. 65–66, 111
bigamy 23, 44; under the Matrimonial Causes Act 1857 82–84
Bigham, J. 146
Birkenhead, Lord 152
Blackstone, W. 9, 19, 88
Bodichon, B. L. S. 39, 45–46
Book of Common Prayer 15–16, 21, 22, 80, 144
Bosworthick v Bosworthick 85
Boulting v Boulting 102
Bouverie, E. 47, 48–49
Bowyer, G. 69
Boyce, S. 26
Brontë, C. 23
Brooks, D. 136
Brook v Brook 112
Brougham, H. 36, 38, 45, 49, 57, 74, 112, 118; call for reform of divorce laws 32–33; on initial aims of Matrimonial Law bill 60; on *Mrs Turton's Case* 81; trial of Queen Caroline and 28–29
Browne, G. F. 142
Brydges v Brydges and Wood 95

Buckmaster, Lord 151–152, 153
Butler v Butler and Burnham 99, 117
Butt, C. 109, 120–122, 126–127, 164
Byrne, E. 129–130
Byron, Lord and Lady 25–28

Caine, B. 42
Cairns, Lord 118
Calvin, J. 14
Campbell, J. 39–41, 62–63, 74
Campbell Commission of 1853 9, 27, 29, 35, 39, 47–51, 64, 165; majority report of 51–58, 107; minority report of 58–60
Caroline, Queen 28–30
Catherine of Aragon 80
Charles I, King 17
Chase, K. 43
Chelmsford, Lord 102–103
children: born out of wedlock 77–78; custody laws regarding 41, 53–54, 130
Christian teachings on marriage 13, 138, 144, 145–146, 153
Church of England 38; 20th-century reforms to divorce law and 138, 142–143, 145–146, 152, 167; informal marriages and 21–22; Protestant Reformation and 14–17; reform of the Ecclesiastical Courts and 31–32; stance on the Matrimonial Causes Act 1857 64–65, 71; support for expansion of grounds for divorce 138
Churchward v Churchward and Holliday 100, 132–133
civil marriage, introduction to 18
Clarke v Clarke and Clarke 107
Cobbe, F. P. 123
Coffey v Coffey 85
Cole, Lord 116–117
collusion 97–100
Commentaries on the Laws of England 9
common law 6–7, 114
condonation 103–106, 131
connivance 100–103
Constantinidi v Constantinidi and Lance 132
constructive cruelty 90–91
Contagious Diseases Acts 89
contract marriage 22–23
Cooke, M. 84

Cornish, W. 7, 47
cost of divorce 54–55
Council of Florence 14
Council of Trent 14, 21
Countess of Strathmore v Bowes, The 26
Court for Divorce and Matrimonial Causes 1
coverture, doctrine of 45
Cramp v Cramp and Freeman 105
Cranmer, T. 15
Cranworth, Lord 60, 61, 62, 63, 68, 70
Crawford, D. 76–77, 127
Crawford, V. 76–77
Crawford v Crawford and Dilke 76
Cresswell, C. 164; Divorce Courts and 111–112; legacy of 115; Queen's Proctor and 114
Cretney, S. 2, 7–8, 57, 63, 97, 100, 112; on divorce law reforms 135, 153
Crewe v Crewe 98
cruelty 26–27, 68; Campbell Commission on 51; under the Matrimonial Causes Act 1857 87–91

Darwin, C. 61
David Copperfield 33
Davidson, R. 143, 152
De Bock, G. 35
Deceased Wife's Sister's Marriage Act 1907 81
de la Bère, R. 160
desertion 53; under the Matrimonial Causes Act 1857 91–94
Dibdin, L. T. 145
Dickens, C. 9, 33, 40, 54–55
Digby, J. E. *see* Earl of Ellenborough
Dilke, C. 76–77, 127
Disraeli, B. 47
divorce courts: under Butt 126–127; creation of Probate, Divorce and Admiralty Division 117–120; under Cresswell 111–115; establishment of 110–112; under Gorell 138–141; granting divorce in spite of petitioner's adultery 130–132; under Hannen 121–123; introduction of the Queen's Proctor and 112–115; under Jeune 127–129; legacy of Lord St Helier in 132–133; Married Women Act 1895 and 129–130; Matrimonial Causes Act 1878 and 123–124; Matrimonial Causes Act 1884 and 124–125; piecemeal

reforms to 163–164; reform of the Queen's Proctor and 120–121; under Wilde 115–117
divorce law: on adultery 24, 26, 60–61, 68; on bigamy 23, 44; Campbell Commission on (*see* Campbell Commission of 1853); in case of Caroline Norton and trial of Lord Melbourne 39–44; in case of Earl of Ellenborough 33–35; in case of Lord and Lady Byron 25–28; Christian teachings and 18–19, 58–59; common law and 6–7; on cruelty 26–27, 68; divorces initiated by women and 24; double standards in 60–61, 79–80, 166–168; feminist histories on 5–6, 7; foreign divorces and 56–57; historical sources on 8–10; hotel divorces 155–159; Hunter bill and 134–135; increases in formal divorce and 23; influence of English Reformation on 13–17; informal divorce 20–24, 25–28; legal historiography of 3–8; Matrimonial Causes Act 1857 and 1–3; reflections on reform of 72–74; reform of Ecclesiastical Courts and 30–33; reforms to (*see* reforms); regarding incestuous adultery 24; remarriage and 22–23, 56; Russell bills and 135–138; 17th century 17–20; in trial of Queen Caroline 28–30; tripartite system of 20–24, 34; *see also* Matrimonial Causes Act 1857
Divorce Law Reform Association 137–138
Divorce Law Reform Union (DLRU) 138, 153
Divorce Reform Act 1969 151
Doctrine and Discipline of Divorce, The 18
Dodd v Dodd 139, 140–141, 142, 145
Dolin, K. 9, 44
double standards 60–61, 79–80, 166–168
Drew v Drew 92
Drummond v Drummond 113
Duk of Norfolk 20–21
Durham v Durham 122
durnkenness 90
Duxbury, N. 5
Dyke, F. H. 120

Earl of Ellenborough 33–35
Ecclesiastical Courts 1, 2, 4, 5, 9, 19, 167; Campbell Commission and 55; case of Earl of Ellenborough 33–35; case of Lord and Lady Byron and 25–28; reform of 30–33; Royal Commission inquiry into 36–37; trial of Queen Caroline and 28–30
Edward VI, King 17
Edward VIII, King 166
Elizabeth I, Queen 17
Elmy, E. W. 134
Elton, G. R. 3
English Civil War 17, 31
English Laws for Women in the Nineteenth Century 43
English Reformation and divorce law 13–17
English Women's Journal 46
Entwistle, C. 153
Esther Waters 127–128
Evans, R. 3, 114
Evans v Evans 27, 87–88
Evans v Evans and Platts 95

Fairfax, W. G. R. 146
Fellows, A. 133
feminism: Barbara Leigh Smith Bodichon and 45–46; Caroline Norton and 42–43; and feminist histories on divorce law 5–6, 7; liberal 46; militant 136
First Report of the Commissioners Appointed by Her Majesty to Enquire into the Law of Divorce, and More Particularly into the Mode of Obtaining Divorces a Vinculo Matrimonii, The 47
fleet marriages 21
Follett, W. 39–40
foreign divorces 56–57
formal divorce 23–24
Forsyte Saga, The 149

Galsworthy, J. 149
Geils v Geils 86
George IV, King 28–30
Germain, J. 20–21
Gipps v Gipps and Hume 102
Gladstone, W. 3, 47, 49, 62, 64, 70, 76, 121
Gleen v Gleen 77
Glorious Revolution of 1688 21

Gorell, Lord 109, 128, 132, 164;
    divorce courts under 138–141;
    second Gorell bills and 141–143,
    147–148
Gorell Commission 9, 84, 121, 137,
    143–147, 152, 155
Gott, S. 18
Grey, G. 47, 70
grounds for divorce under the
    Matrimonial Causes Act 1857
    75–97; adultery 75–79; bigamy
    82–84; cruelty 87–91; desertion
    91–94; incest 79–82; rape 84–85;
    statutory damages 94–97; unnatural
    offences 86–87

Hale, M. 85
Hale Commission of 1652 17–18,
    19
Hales, M. 9
Hall v Hall and Kay 105, 132
Halsbury, Lord 137
Halsbury's Laws of England 9
Hamilton, S. 49
Hannen, J. 117–118, 120, 121–123,
    125, 127, 164
Hard Times 54–55
Hardy, T. 23, 127
Harrington, J. 18
Hatherley, Lord 119
Hay, J. R. 141
Haynes, E. S. P. 138
Helmholz, R. H. 16
Henry VIII, King 15, 16, 80
Herbert, A. P. 9, 98, 119,
    161–162, 166
Herschell, F. 125
Hill, C. 4
historical sources on divorce law
    8–10
*History of the Pleas of the Crown,
    The* 9
Hobsbawm, E. 4
Hodgson v Hodgson and Turner 139
Holcombe, L. 5
Holmes, A. S. 130, 148–149
Holy Deadlock 119
Hope v Hope 114
Horstman, A. 8, 63, 73
hotel divorces 155–159
Howitt, M. 46
Hume, J. 35
Hunter, W. A. 134

Hunter bill 134–135
Hyde v Hyde and Woodmansee 16, 116

incest 24, 79–82
In Chancery 149–150
Infant Custody Act 1839 41
informal divorce 20–24; case of Lord
    and Lady Byron and 25–28
innocent adultery 131
Innocent III, Pope 13
Iredale v Ford and Bramworth 114
Israel, K. 77

Jane Eyre 23
Jeapes v Jeapes 128–129
Jenner, H. 53
Jeune, F. 127–129, 132–133
Jude the Obsure 127
Judicature Commission 118–119
Juries Act 1918 151

Keats v Keats and Montezuma 104, 105,
    114–115
Knight, G. W. 154–155
Knight bills 154–155

Lambeth Conference of 1908 141–142
Lambeth Conference of 1920 149
Lane, E. 79
Lang, C. G. 144, 167
Langrick v Langrick and Funnell 150
Lautour v Her Majesty's Proctor 106
Law Amendment Society 4, 39, 45–46,
    118, 165
*Law of Scripture against Divorce,
    The* 60
Law Review 45
Learmouth v Learmouth and Austin 97
Letter to the Queen, A 61
Levenson, M. 43
Lewis, G. 146
liberal feminism 46
Lister v Lister 126
Liverpool, Lord 28–29
Lobban, M. 118
Lolley, W. 56–57
Lord St John v Lady St John 53
Lord v Lord and Lambert 139
Loreburn, Lord 142–143
Lucius III, Pope 13
Lushington, S. 27, 29, 34, 35, 47,
    48, 111
Luther, M. 14

Lyndhurst, Lord 33–34, 56, 61, 62, 65, 69, 81

MacDonald, R. 154
MacQueen, J. F. 9, 82, 112
Maiden Tribute of Modern Babylon, The 4
Manners, J. 69
Manning, H. E. 64
Marquees of Lansdowne 61
Marriage Act 1753 21, 22, 38
Marriage Act 1836 38, 58–59
marriage(s): of affinity 80–81; Christian teachings on 13, 138, 144, 145–146, 153; civil 18; contract 22–23; ecclesiastical 18–19; fleet 21; Mosaic teaching on divorce and 18–19, 59; private separation deeds and 19; second 22–23, 56, 70–71
Married Love 149
Married Women Act 1895 129–130, 139, 140, 166
Married Women's Property Act 1882 67, 134
Married Women's Property Committee 42
Martineau, H. 42
Marwick, A. 149
Mary I, Queen 17
Matrimonial Causes Act 1857 1, 8, 10–11, 20, 33; Barbara Leigh Smith Bodichon and Law Amendment Society and 39, 45–46; bars to divorce under 97–109; Campbell Commission and (*see* Campbell Commission of 1853); Caroline Norton and the trial of Lord Melbourne and 39–44; Church of England stance on 64–65, 71; compromise between English divorce law and Christian morality in 13; cultural change and 2–3; divorce courts established by 110–112; double standard in 68–70; grounds for divorce under 75–97; initial failed attempts to pass 60–63; legal historiography of 4–8; Mr. Justice Maule and 39, 44–45; as part of larger package of reforms 165; passage of 63–72; Queen's Proctor and 112–115; reflections on reform of divorce law through 72–74; reforms to (*see* reforms); state of affairs in early Victorian England prior to 38–39;

women's rights and 1–2; *see also* divorce law
Matrimonial Causes Act 1878 123–124
Matrimonial Causes Act 1884 124–125
Matrimonial Causes Act 1923 151–154
Matrimonial Causes Act 1937 137, 160–162, 166
Maule, J. 39, 44–45
Mayor of Casterbridge, The 23
M'Carthy v DeCaix 57
Melbourne, Lord 39–44
Mette v Mette 111
Meyern v Meyern and Myers 95
Mill, J. S. 39, 45–46, 165
Milnes, R. M. 45, 67
Milsom, S. F. C. 6–7
Milton, J. 18, 19
Mitchell, L. G. 39
Mogg v Mogg 86
Moncreiffe, T. 116
Moore, G. 127–128
Moore, L. 48
Moral Reform Union 135
Mordaunt, C. 116–117
Mordaunt, H. 116–117
Mordaunt, M. 20–21
Mordaunt v Mordaunt, Cole and Johnstone 116–117
Morning Chronicle 40
Mothers' Union 138
Mozley Stark v Mozley Stark 95
Mrs. Turton's Case 81

National Union of Societies for Equal Citizenship (NUSEC) 153
Newcomes, The 43
Northover v Northover 132
Norton, C. 9, 39–44, 70, 165
Norton, G. 39–44
Norton v Viscount Melbourne 39–44

Otway v Otway and Hoffer 126
Outhwaite, R. B. 22
Oxford History of the Laws of England: Volume XIII 7

Palmer, F. 146
Palmer, R. 118
Palmerston, Lord 71, 165
Pankhurst, C. 89
Parker, M. 80
Parkes, B. 46
Parr, W. 34

Past and Present 4
Peel, R. 36
Pelham-Clinton, H. L. H. P. F. 49
Penzance, Lord 117, 123, 164
Perkin, J. 5, 29
Perry, E. 67
petitioner's adultery 106–107, 130–132
Phillimore, J. 23, 35, 36, 121–122, 126
Phillpotts, H. 41
Pickwick Papers, The 40
Pierrepoint, A. 20
Polden, P. 145
Poovey, M. 42
post-war English society 148–150
Powis, Lord 34
Practical Treatise of the Law of Marriage and Divorce, A 54
private separation deeds 19
Privy Council Appeals Act 1832 36
Probate, Divorce and Admiralty Division 117–120; *see also* divorce courts
Probert, R. 8, 20, 22, 135
property rights of women 46, 66–67, 134
prostitutes, female 89
Protestant Reformation 14–17
Public Worship Regulation Act 1874 117
Pulleyn, C. 43–44

Queen's Proctor: introduction of 112–115; reform of 120–121

rape 84–85, 132
Rayden, W. 9
recrimination 107–109
Redesdale, Lord 47, 50, 58–60, 61, 167–168
Redmayne, S. 161–162
Reeves v Reeves 52
reforms: decline of statutory damages and 150–151; first Russell bills 135–138; Gorell Commission and 143–147; Gorell court and calls for 138–141; hotel divorces 155–159; Hunter bill 134–135; Knight bills 154–155; Matrimonial Causes Act 1923 151–152, 154; Matrimonial Causes Act 1937 160–162; to overcome moral hypocrisy and double standards 166–168; piecemeal 163–164; post-war English society and 148–150; as process of political

will 164–166; second Lord Gorell bill and 147–148; second Russell and Gorell bills 141–143
remarriage 22–23, 56, 70–71
Rendall, A. 152
Rex, R. 15
Road to Divorce 4
Robinson, H. 79
Robinson, I. 79
Robinson v Robinson and Lane 79
Roman Catholic Church 13–14, 20, 21
Roos Case 20
Rose v Rose 104
Royal Commission inquiry into the Ecclesiastical Courts 36–37
Russell, C. 77–78
Russell, Earl 83–84
Russell, J. 47, 136–138, 165
Russell, J. H. 77–78
Russell bills: first 135–138; second 141–143
Russell v Russell 77, 83–84, 87, 91, 129
R v Hall 45
R v Lolley 56–57

Saunders v Saunders 27
Savage, G. 112, 121
Schneider, W. E. 120
Schofield, P. 31
Schwarzenbergh, Prince 33
Scots law of divorce 30
Scott, M. E. 83
Scott, W. 27
Scottish Reformation 15
Scott v Sebright 126
Second Council of Lyon 14
second marriages 22–23, 56, 70–71
separation: deeds, private 19; judicial 68
sexually transmitted diseases 89–90
Shand, Lord 87
Shanley, M. L. 5, 7, 42, 57
Shelford, L. 54
Sheridan, R. B. 43
Smith v Smith and Reed 139
Society for Promoting Reforms in Marriage and Divorce Laws in England 137–138
sodomy 86–87
Solicitor's Journal 144
Somerhill, Lord 61
Somervell, D. 160
Sopwith v Sopwith 114
Spectator, The 114–115

Squibb, G. D. 31
statutory damages 65–66; decline of 150–151; under the Matrimonial Causes Act 1857 94–97
Stead, W. T. 4
Stebbings, C. 163
Steele, M. 33
Stephenson, A. K. 120–121
Stetson, D. 5, 161
St Helier, Lord 109, 121, 164; legacy of 132–133
St Leonards, Lord 61, 66–67
Stone, L. 3, 4, 8, 22, 34, 67
Stopes, M. 149
Stowell, Lord 87–88, 98, 114
Sugden, E. 36
Summary Jurisdiction Act 1895 129–130, 139, 140, 166
Summerscale, E. 79
Sumner, J. B. 65

Tarry v Browne 18
Teagle v Teagle and Nottingham 97
Tennant, M. E. 144
Thackeray, W. 9, 43
Thompson, E. P. 4
Thompson v Thompson 85
Times, The 114, 117–118, 122, 126, 151
Tindal, N. C. 39
Todd v Todd 99
Tollemache v Tollemache 112
Tomkins v Tomkins 114
trade unionism 136
Treggiari, S. 51
Trial of Earl Russell 83
tripartite divorce system 20–24, 34

unnatural offences 86–87
unreasonable delay 107–109

venereal disease 89–90
Vicars, J. 81
Vicars, M. A. 81
Vicars, N. 81
Vicars v Vicars 81
Victoria, Queen 38, 162
Victorian Divorce 8

Waddams, S. 7–8
Wales v Wales and Cullen 76
Walpole, S. 47, 49
Ward v Ward 114
Warrender v Warrender 56
Waugh, E. 9, 166
Webster, R. 135
Weldon, G. 125
Weldon, W. H. 124–125
Weldon v Weldon 124–125
Westbury, Lord 102
Whom God Hath Joined 140
Wife-Torture in England 123
Wilberforce, S. 47, 61–62
Wilde, J. P. 16, 114–116
Wilkinson v Kitzinger 116
Williams, W. C. 143
Winstanley, G. 18
Winterbotham, W. H. 143
Wolfram, S. 3–4, 54, 73, 74
Wolverhampton, Lord President Viscount 142–143
Women's Emancipation Union 134–135
Women's Liberal Federation 134
women's rights 1–2, 5–6, 7, 24; Caroline Norton and 42–43; case of Lord and Lady Byron and 25–28; double standard on adultery and 60–61; Hunter bill and 134–135; Married Women Act 1895 and 129–130, 139, 140, 166; property ownership and 46, 66–67, 134; trial of Queen Caroline and 29–30
Wood, W. P. 47, 49–50
Woodhouse, M. 7–8, 73
Wyndford, Lord 61
Wynne v Wynne 92

Zwingli, H. 14